Strategies for Empirical Research in Writing

Mary Sue MacNealy
The University of Memphis

Longman

New York   San Francisco   Boston
London   Toronto   Sydney   Tokyo   Singapore   Madrid
Mexico City   Munich   Paris   Cape Town   Hong Kong   Montreal

This book is dedicated to the many caring and inspiring teachers who taught me, and to the many eager and enthusiastic students I have been privileged to teach.

Vice President: Eben W. Ludlow
Series Editorial Assistant: Linda M. D'Angelo
Executive Marketing Manager: Lisa Kimball
Composition and Prepress Buyer: Linda Cox
Manufacturing Buyer: Suzanne Lareau
Cover Administrator: Jenny Hart
Production Editor: Christopher H. Rawlings
Editorial-Production Service: Omegatype Typography, Inc.
Electronic Composition: Omegatype Typography, Inc.

ADDISON WESLEY LONGMAN
1185 Avenue of the Americas
New York, NY 10036

Internet: www.abacon.com
American Online: Keyword: College Online

Library of Congress Cataloging-in-Publication Data

MacNealy, Mary Sue.
    Strategies for empirical research in writing / Mary Sue MacNealy.
      p. cm.
    Includes bibliographical references and index.
    ISBN 0-205-27253-3
    1. English language—Rhetoric—Study and teaching—Research—
Methodology. 2. Report writing—Study and teaching—Research—
Methodology. 3. English teachers—Training of—Research—
Methodology. I. Title.
PE1404.M34   1999
808'.042'072—dc21   98-4890
                                     CIP

Printed in the United States of America
10 9 8 7 6 5 4 3 2 1   03 02 01 00 99 98

Contents

Preface

WHY A BOOK ON STRATEGIES FOR EMPIRICAL RESEARCH IN WRITING?

As you open this book, you may rightly suspect that past experience in writing research papers for freshman composition and other college courses is insufficient background for the work you now do, whether you have a job in your chosen career or whether you are a student writing a paper, thesis, or dissertation in your major area of study. Even the traditional library-based thesis, so common in English departments, requires strategies not taught in undergraduate composition courses. In addition, many people who have embarked on careers in writing now find that they are expected to know about or participate in empirical research projects even though they have had no prior training in this type of research. Many students have found that, although the growing disciplines of composition studies and professional communications rely on and tend to expect major papers, theses, and dissertations based on empirical research, books on research methods in composition or business and technical writing are rare. In addition, books on research methods often assume that students have quite a lot of background information—especially in statistics.

In contrast, this book is intended for novices: those with *no* background in empirical research and even those who are afraid of math or anything which sounds remotely scientific. You should find the information here relatively easy to understand because it originated in handouts I prepared for my own students, some of whom were intimidated by the very words, "empirical research." The enthusiastic response and helpful feedback from these students caused those handouts to grow into the book you now hold.

WHAT'S IN THIS BOOK?

This book is primarily intended as an introduction to strategies for conducting and reporting empirical research in writing. Chapters 1 and 3 present an overview and some basic concepts of good empirical research. Chapter 2 covers some strategies which can help you if you are planning to write a library-based paper, thesis, or dissertation. Generally speaking, the rest of the chapters cover specific types of empirical research. These types are arranged along a continuum from highly *quantitative* methods such as experiments and meta analysis (chapters 4, 5, and 6), through *quantitative descriptive* methods such as discourse analysis and surveys (chapters 7 and 8), to primarily *qualitative* methods such as focus groups, case studies, and ethnographies (chapters 9, 10, and 11). The final chapter in the book discusses two specialized qualitative methods—feminist research and teacher research. Some of the chapters in the book (e.g., chapters 1 though 4 and chapters 9 through 11) are independent enough that you can read them in any order you wish, or that your teacher assigns. You could easily read chapters 10 through 12 without reading any of the other chapters in the book, although I would suggest that you read them in that order. I also think you would find it helpful to read chapters 4 through 8 in sequential order.

Although I describe strategies that are particularly useful in carrying out each type of empirical research, you should be aware that there are no guaranteed, step-by-step recipes that a beginning researcher can use. However, this book does contain many examples of research projects that could serve as models. (I should warn you now, I suppose, that some of these examples are imaginary and downright goofy, but most examples are real projects, reported in composition and technical writing literature.) Some of the examples can also serve as basic models which can be adapted to other research questions, and the basic concepts and strategies described in the various chapters should help you make such adaptations effective.

This book also introduces some statistical procedures that are particularly suitable for the various types of research, although it does not cover these procedures in great detail—an entire book would be needed to do that well. As you begin to think about possible statistical procedures to use in analyzing your data, you should consult one of the many books on statistics, especially those written for students in the social sciences. You will find recommended reading materials at the end of each chapter in this book. Also, most college and university campuses have experts in statistics who are willing to help a novice.

HOW CAN THIS BOOK HELP YOU BECOME A BETTER CONSUMER AND PRODUCER OF RESEARCH?

As our society demands greater specialization, to be good at your job you will have to be a good consumer of research. What you learn in any writing program is only a foundation for the future. You needn't look far outside the composition and professional communication fields for an example of the importance of keeping up with the latest research findings. Can you imagine choosing as your family physician someone who graduated from medical school 20 or even 10 years ago who knows nothing about the diagnostic techniques and medicines discovered since his or her graduation? Likewise, the business or professional writer or teacher of writing who doesn't keep up with the literature as the field continues to develop is going to be only marginally effective on the job. But how can you be a wise consumer of what you read? Becoming familiar with the research strategies presented in this book will help you to evaluate research findings, theories, and claims—to choose those worth adopting and those to disregard. In fact, a student in the last research course I taught told me that the course had changed the way she looks at all new products and consumer advice—everything from claims about cosmetics to advice on good nutrition. She said, almost regretfully, that her days as a naive consumer are over.

Moreover, I hope that many of you who read this book will become producers as well as consumers of research in writing. If you are interested in doing research in writing, this book will be only an introduction—a taste, as it were, of adventures to come.

Finally, if you find yourself in, or headed for, a career in which carrying out empirical research is part of the job description, no doubt you will want to go on to courses in statistics and advanced research methodology beyond the scope of this book since it is intended for the novice researcher. Whatever the case, I hope this book serves you well and that you will find its ideas challenging, its advice helpful, and its informal style encouraging.

ACKNOWLEDGMENTS

There is no way to acknowledge by name the countless people who have helped me as I learned to do empirical research and as I wrote this book. I especially wish I could thank by name every student who read parts of this book and gave me helpful suggestions, but that too is impossible. However, I would be remiss if I did not acknowledge two special colleagues, Reta Douglas and Bruce Speck, who patiently read multiple drafts and unstintingly gave me kind advice and support. Another person who generously gave support and encouragement is my editor at Allyn and Bacon, Eben Ludlow. I am also extremely grateful to the following reviewers, whose suggestions were invaluable in helping me see the text through a reader's eyes: Alexander Friedlander of Drexel University, John R. Hayes of Carnegie Mellon University, Meg Morgan of the University of North Carolina at Charlotte, and David L. Wallace of Iowa State University.

Finally, I want to thank The University of Memphis for giving me a one-semester professional development leave to finish writing this book.

Empirical Research in the Humanities

WHY DO RESEARCH IN WRITING?

Only in the last 40 years or so have teachers of writing (both composition and technical writing) and writers in the workplace recognized the need for empirical research in their field. For many years, writing experts believed that good writing is a talent that some people have and others don't. If good writing can only be produced by persons with a gift for writing, then the main duty of teachers of writing is to raise the level of correctness of the ordinary writer by pointing out his or her errors. This view of teaching writing dominated composition instruction in America during the 19th and early 20th centuries, and it is still widely held today. For example, in 1990 Sharon Crowley estimated that each semester more than one-and-a-half million college freshmen were being taught by college English teachers with this philosophy (Crowley, 1990, p. 139).

A review of the concepts of writing presented in *College English* over the years since its inception in the early 1900s shows that, from time to time, dedicated teachers of writing have questioned the current traditional view that teaching writing consists mainly of pointing out errors; however, real change did not begin until after World War II. Then two phenomena occurring within a few years of each other began to move writing instruction beyond what Braddock, Lloyd-Jones, and Schoer (1963) called a state of development similar to what the field of chemistry experienced as it began to abandon alchemy. The first phenomenon was the explosion of technology in World War II: as weaponry became more complicated, so did its repair and maintenance, with the result that the need for how-to manuals produced a demand for good writers. For example, Duffy (1985) explains that 1,800 pages were needed for mechanics to maintain a 1950 fighter plane, whereas 260,000 pages were needed to maintain a fighter plane in 1975. No doubt maintenance manuals for modern fighter planes are even larger. Moreover, the military is increasingly aware that poorly written manuals result in faulty maintenance, so the demand for good writers has grown to the extent that many colleges and universities now offer degrees in professional writing, and many business schools require their students to take a course in writing. With this growth has also come growth in research as the military and other government agencies have funded projects to learn more about literacy and what constitutes effective design of instructional texts (see, for example, Duffy, 1985; Meyer, 1986).

The second phenomenon which had a major impact on the way writing is taught was the influx of returning veterans into college composition classes following World War II. Many of these veterans exhibited serious deficiencies in their writing skills; their compositions were plagued with errors in spite of the years of grammar instruction they had in elementary and high school classes in which teachers taught writing by pointing out errors in student essays and assigning handbook exercises. Mina Shaughnessy (1977) was one of the first college teachers to realize that it was important to find out *why* these students were making the same errors over and over. Other writing teachers and researchers, especially in composition, were beginning to examine other aspects of writing such as the characteristics of expert and novice writers (e.g., Flower, Hayes, Carey, Schriver, & Stratman, 1986; Gould, 1980), what goes on in a typical student's writing process (e.g., Emig, 1971), how writers determine and define the problems they want to deal with (e.g., Flower & Hayes, 1980), and the strategies writers use in a writing task (e.g., Flower & Hayes, 1977; Hayes & Flower, 1980). Much of what is now taught in professional writing courses is based on findings in the last 20 to 30 years of research in composition and cognitive psychology, not research in technical writing.

Even though research in composition and cognitive psychology has contributed much useful information to the field of professional communications, Beard and Williams (1992) found that 68% of the technical communicators who responded to a survey measuring practitioners' attitudes toward research agreed or strongly agreed with this statement: "To further evolve as a discipline, technical communication needs to substantially increase the body of research in the field" (p. 575). However, only very recently have professional writers, both writing teachers and writers in the workplace, begun to research areas of concern in technical writing and document design. For example, an examination of the papers presented over the last 20 years at the annual conference of the Society for Technical Communication revealed that between 1972 and 1981 only 4% of the papers presented were based on empirical research projects, but from 1982 to 1991 this percentage had risen to 11.7% (Mac-Nealy, 1992a). While the rise in papers based on empirical research projects is encouraging, the amount of research in technical writing being carried out today is still too low.

Sadly, the idea that empirical research in writing has helped improve the teaching of composition and technical writing is often rejected by traditionalists. Instead, such research is often blamed for diverting attention from teaching "basic" skills—a claim I often hear from adherents of the current traditional paradigm. Since the inability to "write a coherent paragraph" has plagued college students at least since 1866, when Alexander Bain wrote a manual explaining (among other things) how to write a coherent paragraph for his students who were largely products of an upper-class upbringing and formal schooling, one can hardly ascribe the blame for the students' failure to write coherent paragraphs to modern theories of teaching writing.

Unfortunately, current traditionalists in composition are not alone in scoffing at the need for research in writing. Not too long ago, a technical writer wrote a letter to the editor of *Technical Communication* complaining about the journal's shift to publishing more academic papers "with zillions of footnotes and arcane references" (West, 1992, p. 326). To make matters worse, a subsequent issue of *Technical Communication* (May, 1993) had three letters supporting this view and none opposing it, and all three referred to the uselessness of such articles for technical communicators in the real world (Economou, 1993; Lanyi, 1993; Schrengohst, 1993). Interestingly, of the twelve other letters to the editor published in that May, 1993 issue, four dealt with usage problems such as compound verbs and hyphens. While incorrect usage can certainly hinder communication, the overemphasis on usage turns our attention away from research into aspects of writing which could facilitate communication. We especially need to be investigating visual aspects of documents, and I include in the word "documents" such mundane items as street signs.

Street signs provide a good example of the need for more research and the importance of disseminating the findings. For instance, research has well established that words in all-caps take longer to process than words in mixed case letters, and that readers use cues other than serial processing of the letters to comprehend a word (Just & Carpenter, 1987). Why then do many street signs give the names of streets in all caps? Some effort is being made to make street signs easier to read: at some busy intersections, signs bearing names of intersecting streets are now hung above the entrance to the intersection rather than placed on posts at the corner. Overhead signs bearing street names would certainly help a person wanting to make a left turn onto a particular street because driving in the curb lane in order to read signs on posts would hinder access to the left-turn lane on streets with two lanes in each direction. Wherever they are placed, street signs should be in mixed case rather than in all caps because people use the overall shape of a word to help them decipher the words, and this shape is lost when the word is in all caps.

A recent personal experience confirms the research in text processing and the difficulty facing drivers coping with street names in all caps, even when the signs are hung overhead near the traffic lights. While driving on the left side of the street and manipulating a stick shift with my left hand in busy city traffic in New Zealand, I had to rely on my companion's help in spotting the street I was looking for. Interestingly, my companion frequently made comments such as "No, not the next intersection. I can't read the street name from here, but I can see that it is too short to be Fendalton Road." Although word length provides some visual cues to decoding, the

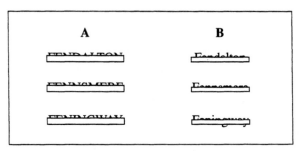

FIGURE 1-1   **Effect of All-Caps on Word Shape**

ascenders and descenders of lower case letters give the word a shape that readers also rely on. For instance, had the street sign said "Fennsmere," the name would have been just as long as Fendalton, and the outer shape of the two words looks the same in all caps, as Figure 1-1(a) shows. Thus a driver cannot quickly decide whether the name is Fendalton or Fennsmere. If mixed case is used, a reader can quickly see that Fennsmere (Figure 1-1(b), middle word) is too flat on the top to be Fendalton (Figure 1-1(b), top word). Likewise, when mixed case is used, a name such as Feningway (Figure 1-1(b), bottom word) is too flat on top and uneven on the bottom to be mistaken for Fendalton.

Not only will research in technical communication help technical writers communicate more effectively with their readers, but research also helps build the professional image of a discipline. Too often business and technical writers are perceived as clerical workers rather than as trained professionals. For example, one of the letters to the editor in the May, 1993 issue of *Technical Communication* tells of a job applicant who said, "I worked as a secretary before but thought that this [technical writing position] would pay more" (Wetterhan, 1993, p. 196). Similarly, I often have heard literature majors, who have to take my course Theory and Practice in Teaching College Composition in order to become graduate teaching assistants, say something like, "I thought this was going to be a pedagogy course—never dreamed there were all these journals, so much research, and so much to learn about teaching writing." Certainly, a good many experts concerned about the development of writing as a discipline and as a profession, both in composition and technical writing, have pointed to the need for more research in the field, and technical writers often find that they can more easily persuade clients that their design choice is the most effective one if they can cite research which backs them up.

ARE EMPIRICAL METHODS APPROPRIATE FOR SCHOLARS IN THE HUMANITIES?

The practice of using empirical methods for research in the humanities is relatively new, and it is still viewed with a good deal of suspicion. Humanities scholars often see their discipline as incompatible with science, believing that there is no relationship between numbers and aesthetic concerns. On the other hand, scientists often think of literature and other humanities scholars as operating in an ethereal realm not well understood by a pragmatist. In other words, both sides tend to believe that the two areas are just too different for empirical methods to be appropriate for scholars in English departments, and academic folklore supports this view. For example, there is the oft-repeated notion that people with strong verbal skills have trouble with math: witness the belief that poets and other creative writers cannot balance their checkbooks without help.

Even more damaging to the acceptance of the importance and validity of empirical research in the humanities is the fact that numerical data have often been manipulated to achieve wrong-headed ends—a practice that exacerbates suspicion of statistics in general (see, for example, Huff, 1982). I am reminded of an article in the *New Yorker* that carried this manipulative tendency to hilarious conclusions by reporting that the first step writers should take if they want to become successful poets is to change their first name to William because an analysis of 400 anthologies of "Top Poems" revealed that one third of the poets who had ten or more poems included in these works were named William (Pollitt, 1993).

However, the humanities and the sciences are not so disparate as many have been led to believe. Although some have argued that numbers simply aren't important or appropriate in the humanities, if a literary critic were to argue for a new interpretation of why Hamlet sent Ophelia to the nunnery and gave only one line from the play as evidence, the critic would be laughed at by responsible literary scholars. Thus, numbers are important to literary scholars. In a like vein, music is generally regarded as a purely aesthetic experience, totally unrelated to science, yet a melody can be described very precisely with numbers. In fact, equipment that plays music which has been recorded digitally (i.e., numerically) is reputed to be the equipment of choice for serious listeners who want the highest quality of reproduction. Finally, even philosophy owes much of its development and theory to numbers witnessed by the important role zero plays in logic.

WHAT DO WE MEAN BY RESEARCH?

Recently the academic community has begun to move toward interdisciplinary studies. This movement has been particularly strong in the writing discipline. Writers interested in how readers process their written texts have turned to research in other fields, such as cognitive psychology, for answers to their questions. Also, literary critics wanting to better understand the construction of texts have begun to employ scientific methods of analysis: a group of literary scholars have formed a society for the empirical study of literature (IGEL, i.e., *Internationale Gesellschaft für Empirische Literaturwissenschaft*). One temptation some scholars may encounter is the tendency to dismiss non-empirical research as not being *true* research. On the other hand, some writing teachers, scholars, and practitioners tend to denigrate empirical research because they don't understand or approve of it. Even more distressing is the tendency of some empirical researchers to value quantitative research over qualitative research or vice versa. These attitudes impoverish the field of studies in writing, and if these attitudes persist, they will hinder the development of the field into a fully accredited academic discipline.

In a later chapter, I will discuss the split in attitude between some quantitative researchers and qualitative researchers. For now, I want to try to bring both those who do empirical research and those who do traditional literary research to a clearer understanding and appreciation for each other's work by examining the foundations of the two types of research. One difficulty in bringing the two sides together is vocabulary. In dealing with this problem, Lauer and Asher (1988) suggest the term "rhetorical research" as a label for traditional or non-empirical scholarship. While "rhetorical" is nicely balanced against "empirical," it places a limit on the understanding of "empirical," since one could empirically examine rhetorical strategies. For example, Kreuz, Roberts, Johnson, and Bertus (1996) designed an empirical project to identify the most common literary figures used in American short stories. On the other hand, one could refer to the two types of research as "traditional" and "empirical," but this terminology creates emotional overtones of "old-fashioned" versus "modern."

Still another possibility would be to follow the practice of the American Educational Research Association, which uses the term "conceptual inquiry" to refer to the kind of scholarship traditionally carried out by literary scholars and the term "research" to refer to empirically based scholarship. However, restricting the use of the word "research" to empirical work seems to denigrate the work of traditional literary scholars who also think of their work as "research." Thus, the polarity and suspicion between the two groups is exacerbated.

To avoid negative nuances of value, in this book research will be categorized as "library-based" and "empirical"; the term *library-based* refers to research efforts largely carried out in libraries, both personal and institutional. For example, such scholars often search for sources of allusions in a work, biographical details about the author of the work, details about the sociological and/or historical setting of the work, information about the author's contemporaries, variations between drafts and published versions of a particular work, and so forth. Although a more detailed description will be given in Chapter 3, the term *empirical* refers to research that carefully describes and/or measures observable phenomena in a systematic way planned in advance of the observation. For example, in the empirical project designed by Kreuz et al. (1996), the researchers first defined a representative sample of contemporary American literature as stories appearing in two annual collections: *Best American Short Stories* and *O. Henry Awards,* published between 1978 and 1991. Next the researchers randomly selected 16 out of the possible 28 volumes, and from each volume they randomly selected two stories. From each story, they randomly selected three pages to come up with 96 pages to analyze. Contrast this precisely specified step-by-step procedure of selecting the material to be analyzed with the procedure typically used by literary scholars in which the researcher selects a single short story he or she is interested in and analyzes that story for its use of figurative language.

Both approaches are valuable, but they also rely on very different methods. Here, I would like to acknowledge that while the term "library-based research" may avoid some negative overtones, it could also create some confusion because empirical research can be done in a library. For example, one could design and carry out a systematic observation to determine whether blue or black book bindings predominate in a particular library. Although the location of such research is the library, the methodology may be empirical; thus, in this case it would be fair to label the research project "empirical." An additional example of the labeling problem is the research carried out by Kreuz et al. (1996), mentioned above. In this case, the researchers obtained copies of anthologies of American short stories from the campus library as a data source; yet, both the method used to determine which pages of which stories to include in the study and the method used to examine the pages were empirical.

A similar problem with using the label "library-based" to distinguish non-empirical from empirical research is that even in the most rigorous of scientific disciplines, considerable library research must be done in order to write the literature review which provides the rationale for doing an empirical study. In this example, both library-based and empirical methods are used, but the research findings and implications are based on empirical methods. Although the library-based work plays an important part, it is not the primary research method. Then the project deserves the label "empirical." Table 1-1 provides a comparison of the two methods under discussion here. Note that many of the steps are essentially the same. One major

TABLE 1-1   **Research Types**

Library-Based Research	Empirical Research
1. Encounter a dissonance	1. Encounter a dissonance
2. Define the problem	2. Define the problem
3. Define the research question(s)	3. Define the research question(s)
4. Plan search of published ideas and observations of others	4. Plan for systematic collection of directly observed activities, products, and other phenomena
5. Search for and analyze evidence Methods: deductive, analogical	5. Collect and analyze the data Methods: descriptive, experimental
6. Propose new theory or insights in a thesis and support essay format	6. Interpret findings in relation to theory and prior findings in an IMRAD format
7. Argue for acceptance & significance	7. Argue for acceptance & significance
Purpose: Build theory	Purpose: Build theory
Result: Theoretical: provide hypotheses	Result: Descriptive: provide or test hypotheses Experimental: test hypotheses

difference is that empirical researchers emphasize a systematic research methodology by reporting details of the research method along with the findings, whereas library-based researchers rarely report details of their research methods, nor do they emphasize the systematic nature of their method. A second important difference between the two methods is that library-based researchers track down and analyze other people's ideas and observations, which have been previously published, whereas empirical researchers directly observe and analyze (often using measurements) actual activities, products, and other phenomena.

Finally, I want to strongly urge you who will be the scholars of the future to be careful that you don't valorize one type of research nor denigrate the other. Writing as a field of study, including composition and technical communication, needs both empirical and library-based research because they add different types of knowledge to the foundations of our discipline.

HOW DOES LORE FIT IN?

The two research methods (empirical and library-based) described above do not account for an additional rich source of knowledge for any discipline: the lore handed down from practitioner to practitioner (North, 1987). *Lore* is often defined as knowledge of what "works" in a classroom or work situation or as wisdom gained through experience. However, most published accounts of what has worked for someone do not include any empirical tests of the strategies involved. As such, lore can be compared to parenting practices handed down from one generation to the next or shared among a group of interested parents. Such ideas are often valuable resources for novice teachers and parents. On the other hand, some lore is just plain false, yet some teachers continue to believe in it even when empirical studies have shown that it is faulty. In the paragraphs which follow, I give examples of the way lore can be helpful and harmful.

On the plus side, an excellent source of ideas for classroom teaching strategies is an experienced teacher. Successful teachers have had to find teaching methods that work consistently, at least in their own classrooms. One common university practice that illustrates the value of lore is the assigning of graduate teaching assistants to office space that appears to be a second class facility: a room full of adjoining desks with few, if any, partitions. Yet graduate teaching assistants repeatedly tell me that their office has been one of their biggest resources for teaching strategies because the closeness of the desks facilitates sharing of ideas and experiences with other teachers. However, one often hears the waggish statement that a particular teacher doesn't really have 20 years of teaching experience—rather, he or she actually has one year of experience repeated 20 times. In some cases, this claim may be true; as in any field, experts tend to reuse those techniques that they believe have been successful over time.

On the negative side is the instance of the experienced teacher who continues with a practice that empirical research has shown to be ineffective. A case in point is the use of grammatical exercises typically found in handbooks. There is not one shred of evidence that assigning these exercises improves students' ability to write well, even though scores of empirical studies have investigated the problem. Teachers who continue to use handbook exercises often claim as evidence in support of this practice the fact that some students in such classes learn how to write proficiently. In fact, I have often heard such teachers claim that they, themselves, were taught with exercises, and since they are good writers, the method "works." However, research has shown that there are just as many, if not more students, in such classes who haven't become good writers (see, for example, Schmidt, 1991).

To make the point another way, one could claim that drinking milk helps people become good writers because most good writers drank milk as children. The situation in this case is somewhat analogous to tossing a coin: if one were to toss a coin 1,000 times in a particular room with fluorescent lighting, the coin will land heads up about half the time. In a room with incandescent lighting, tossing a coin 1,000 times will achieve the same results; thus one cannot claim the type of lighting is or is not responsible for the number of heads-up coins. In fact, the literature on the effectiveness of handbook exercises presents some evidence that giving handbook exercises increases students' anxiety about their writing and that anxiety about errors in writing often leads to an increase in error production (Hillocks, 1986). Thus, although good writers do emerge from classes in which handbook exercises are used, the explanation for these students' writing skills has not yet been found. Given the findings on the possibly negative effects of assigning grammar and usage exercises, it is surprising that so many college handbooks are packed with such exercises.

Sadly, I have often heard experienced writing teachers dismiss empirical findings in favor of lore by claiming that the researcher doesn't know what really goes on in the classroom. This claim may be true in some cases, but it does not invalidate the empirical findings; rather, it suggests areas which need further research. Indeed, lore often precedes research and provides a stimulus for carrying out a specific research project. And a researcher doing controlled laboratory experiments should be among the first to admit that the research lab cannot fully replicate the classroom experience because an empirical researcher designing hypothesis-testing experiments must try to control various aspects of the subjects' experience to eliminate alternative explanations for the results. In other words, the classroom teacher is right—the lab is an artificial setting. But the same argument can be made against laboratory testing of medicine, yet most of us agree that such testing is valuable in deciding which medicines may be harmful or effective.

Let's take a moment to examine more closely the claim about the artificiality of the laboratory setting and its potential effects on the findings by considering a possible idea for laboratory testing. Suppose you wanted to test the effects of incandescent versus fluorescent lighting on students' ability to write. You would have to control for other variables that might influence students' ability, such as the type of paper being used, the type of pencil or pen, the time of day, the type of writing assignment, and so forth. Some of these variables would be fairly easy to manipulate: for instance, you could pass out the paper you want students to use, as is sometimes done in regular classrooms. However, the minute you pass out a certain type pencil or pen everyone must use, some students are going to wonder what's going on. In this case, you will want to tell students that they are participating in a study and give them some reasons why the study is important. You will want to design what you say to them very carefully in order to avoid influencing their behavior. It is quite possible that when students know they are participating in laboratory experiments, their behavior may be slightly affected by that knowledge—perhaps they will feel just a tad uneasy—yet most students who participate in experiments try to follow directions and do not try to wreck the experiment.

In short, I believe that the tendency to valorize or denigrate either lore or findings from empirical studies only hurts our profession. Although this book is intended to help you carry out good empirical research, I would hope that you do not dismiss lore out of hand as being unimportant or not valuable. Instead, I hope you see lore as a rich source of strategies for writing or teaching that are useful in the absence of evidence to the contrary, and as a resource for hypotheses to be tested by library-based or empirical research. Thus, lore can contribute significantly to the building of coherent theory in a discipline.

WHY DO WE NEED THEORY?

Let me begin to answer this question with an example from my teaching experience. I frequently teach a course called "Theory and Practice of Teaching Composition in College." My students are usually graduate students who have been assigned to teach their first course in freshman composition. Not unnaturally, these graduate students are filled with anxiety: they want to know what to *do* in the classroom. They tell me they don't want to be bothered with theory. I agree that knowing what to do in a classroom is vital to any teacher, and any tips from an expert should be welcomed. However, I like to point out that all teachers have to make choices: Should I assign exercises or not? Should I ask students to keep journals or not? Should I grade on the curve or not? Making good choices depends on defining effective criteria and then analyzing the choices to see which measure up. Effective criteria are theory-based criteria. When one knows the theory in an area, one has a foundation for evaluating choices.

For example, I would argue that asking whether one should use exercises in the class is probably the wrong question. The better question is: Will exercises help me teach "X"? Thus, if the goal is to teach students to pass competency exams on usage, the answer is probably "yes" because such exams rely heavily on fill-in-the-blank and multiple-choice questions—a task analogous to that of editing sentences composed by someone else, as handbook exercises require students to do. If the goal is to teach students to write texts in which their own sentences are correctly punctuated, the answer is probably "no" because the task of the exercises (recognizing and correcting errors made by someone else) is not analogous to composing a sentence of one's own. My reasoning in this case is theoretical (by analogy), but I can also cite empirical studies which have demonstrated that the transfer of skills from one task to another depends to a large extent on whether the tasks are isomorphic, that is, identical in form and structure (see, for example, Gick & Holyoak, 1983; Smith, 1986).

Perhaps before we go much further, we should agree on a definition of the word *theory*. What does theory mean and what do we use theory for? Put simply, theory in the situation I described above can be defined as a belief that is the basis for actions. This definition accords, more or less, with the first definition in *Webster's Third International Dictionary*. Of course, theory can be stated in a fuller, more complex manner, as in a subsequent definition listed in *Webster's* 3. a, (2): "the coherent set of hypothetical, conceptual, and pragmatic principles forming the general frame of reference for a field of inquiry." Thus, theory is foundational: it provides explanations of and connections between observed phenomena such as systematically collected data and/or personal experiences. Theory can also provide explanations and connections between mental constructs (i.e., individual ideas or concepts), hypothetical examples, and received lore. Finally, theory can provide connecting links between observable phenomena and mental constructs. Research produces and shapes theory; conversely, theory generates hypotheses for research to test. Thus, theory plays an important role in the research enterprise whether the research is library-based or empirical. Theory often provides the stimulus to do a certain research project; and when the project is complete, its findings must be shown to refute, support, refine, or have no effect on the theory that set the research project in motion.

A final reason for learning theory is that theory provides an effective foundation for solving problems that arise in the classroom and the workplace. A lore-based teaching tip which works wonderfully for one teacher may be a complete fizzle in another teacher's hands or with a different set of students. Similarly, techniques which work well in one technical writing task (e.g., writing a computer user's guide which will be disseminated via printed pages) may be inappropriate for another technical writing task (e.g., writing a computer user's guide which will be disseminated online). What does one do when problems arise in a writing or teaching situation and when recommended strategies fail? The person who is well-grounded in theory has a foundation for solving such problems. And the problem solver builds credibility by presenting the solution not just on the idiosyncratic basis of "It seems good to me," but rather on the basis of research findings that can be cited as supporting evidence—as I did two paragraphs ago when I cited the literature on transfer in learning. Another example of the value of learning theory would be a writer who wants approval of new designs for street signs. Rather than supporting his or her design with the weak rationale that it "looks better," he or she can cite theories such as those stating that readers use multiple cues when decoding words. This theory is based on the results of empirical studies of typography and other visual aspects of text processing (see, for example, Just & Carpenter, 1987; Tinker, 1963).

HOW DO RESEARCHERS FIND
RESEARCH TOPICS?

Ironically, this is a question which needs more research to provide a comprehensive answer. However, some research, both library-based and empirical, has been done on this question. For example, Richard E. Young has posited Leon Festinger's theory of cognitive dissonance as an explanation for the stimulus to creative activity (Young, 1981). Young noticed that some important scientific discoveries seem to have resulted from an encounter with a problematic situation—"a felt difficulty." As an example, Young cites the testimony of Karl von Frisch who discovered that bees dance in the hive to communicate the location of good sources for pollen. Von Frisch explained that when he read a fellow scientist's claim that insects are color-blind, he "could not believe it," and therefore he set out to test the theory that bees are color-blind (Young, 1981, pp. 61–62). In another example, Young describes how the discovery of the source of contagion in typhus came about because a doctor (Charles Nicholle) noticed some hospital patients who did not fit the commonly held theory about the transmission of typhus and set out to find the reason for it (Young, Becker, & Pike, 1970, pp. 78–79).

When confronted with the question of how literary scholars find or choose the topics they write about, I searched the literature on problem-finding and found that empirical studies of poets and artists lend weight to Young's theories. Next, I interviewed 28 literary scholars from three different post-secondary institutions. I found that their descriptions could be classified into one of four kinds of cognitive dissonance: a clash between beliefs, an expectation violated, a gap in knowledge, or a previously unnoticed connection between two phenomena (MacNealy, 1991). Follow-up analyses of articles published in technical communications journals have produced further evidence: the introductory segments of the articles could also be grouped into one of the four categories of dissonance (MacNealy, 1992b). As a result, I advise my students to be alert for these types of dissonances when they read for their classes, when they listen to lectures and participate in discussions, when they observe the actions of others, and when they reflect on their own habits and actions.

As students begin to notice dissonances, ask questions about them, and think about possible methods for researching them, the next step should probably be to make an appointment to discuss the problem with a professor who might be interested in it. Some of my students have been reluctant to take this step, believing they must have the whole project mapped out before discussing it with a faculty member. But my colleagues support my contention (grounded in Zoellner's 1969 Talk/Write theory of discovering and clarifying ideas through orally explaining one's thoughts to an interested or sympathetic listener) that discussing the project with a faculty member will often help define the problem and point to the methodology. The third step I recommend is a library search to see what others have found about the problem. This third step is covered in more detail in the next chapter. Subsequent chapters lay out the principles underlying good empirical research and possible strategies for use in empirical research projects.

REFERENCES

Bain, A. (1866). *English composition and rhetoric: A manual.* London: n.p.

Beard, J. D., & Williams, D. L. (1992). A survey of practitioners' attitudes toward research in technical communication. *Technical Communication, 39,* 571–581.

Braddock, R., Lloyd-Jones, R., & Schoer, L. (1963). *Research in written composition.* Urbana, IL: National Council of Teachers of English.

Crowley, S. (1990). *The methodical memory: Invention in current traditional rhetoric.* Carbondale, IL: Southern Illinois University Press.

Duffy, T. M. (1985). Readability formulas: What's the use? In T. M. Duffy & R. Waller (Eds.), *Designing usable texts* (pp. 113–143). New York: Academic Press.

Economou, S. (1993). Relevancy of STC publications [Letter to the editor]. *Technical Communication, 40,* 192.

Emig, J. (1971). *The composing processes of twelfth graders.* Urbana, IL: National Council of Teachers of English.

Flower, L., & Hayes, J. R. (1977). Problem-solving strategies and the writing process. *College English, 39,* 449–461.

Flower, L., & Hayes, J. R. (1980). The cognition of discovery: Defining a rhetorical problem. *College Composition and Communication, 31,* 21–32.

Flower, L., Hayes, J. R., Carey, L., Schriver, K., & Stratman, J. (1986). Detection, diagnosis, and the strategies of revision. *College Composition and Communication, 37,* 16–55.

Gick, M. L., & Holyoak, K. (1983). Schema induction and analogical transfer. *Cognitive Psychology, 15,* 1–38.

Gould, J. D. (1980). Experiments on composing letters: Some facts, some myths, some observations. In L. W. Gregg & E. R. Steinberg (Eds.), *Cognitive processes in writing* (pp. 97–127). Hillsdale, NJ: Erlbaum.

Hayes, J. R., & Flower, L. (1980). Identifying the organization of writing processes. In L. W. Gregg & E. R. Steinberg (Eds.), *Cognitive processes in writing* (pp. 3–30). Hillsdale, NJ: Erlbaum.

Hayes, J. R., & Flower, L. (1983). Uncovering cognitive processes in writing: An introduction to protocol analysis. In P. Mosenthal, L. Tamor, & S. Walmsley (Eds.), *Research on writing: Principles and methods* (pp. 206–220). New York: Longman.

Hillocks, G., Jr. (1986). *Research on written composition: New directions for teaching.* Urbana, IL: National Conference on Research in English and ERIC/RCS.

Huff, D. (1982). *How to lie with statistics.* New York: W. W. Norton.

Just, M., & Carpenter, P. (1987). *The psychology of reading and language comprehension.* Boston: Allyn & Bacon.

Kreuz, R. J., Roberts, R. M., Johnson, B. K., & Bertus, E. L. (1996). Figurative language occurrence and co-occurrence in contemporary literature. In R. J. Kreuz & M. S. MacNealy (Eds.), *Empirical approaches to literature* (pp. 83–97). Norwood, NJ: Ablex.

Lanyi, J. (1993). Relevancy of STC publications. *Technical Communication, 40,* 191–192.

Lauer, J. M., & Asher, L. W. (1988). *Composition research: Empirical designs.* New York: Oxford University Press.

MacNealy, M. S. (1991). Creativity in literary scholars. In E. Ibsch, D. Schram, and G. Steen (Eds.), *Empirical studies of literature* (pp. 281–288). Amsterdam: Rodolpi.

MacNealy, M. S. (1992a). Research in technical communication: A view of the past and a challenge for the future. *Technical Communication, 39,* 533–551.

MacNealy, M. S. (1992b). Getting published: Experts tell how to. Paper presented at the Association for Business Communication, Western Region Meeting, San Diego, CA.

Meyer, B. D. (1986). The ABC's of network publications. *Technical Communication, 33,* 16–20.

North, S. M. (1987). *The making of knowledge in composition.* Montclair, NJ: Boynton/Cook.

Pollitt, K. (1993, February 22). Poetry secrets of Attila the Hun. *The New Yorker, 69,* 180–182.

Schmidt, L. P. (1991). *Improving students' surface errors in writing: An empirical study and a program proposal.* Unpublished master's thesis, Memphis State University, Memphis, TN.

Schrengohst, J. (1993). Relevancy of STC publications [Letter to the editor]. *Technical Communication, 40,* 192.

Shaughnessy, M. (1977). *Errors and expectations.* New York: Oxford University Press.

Smith, S. B. (1986). An analysis of transfer between tower of Hanoi isomorphs (Doctoral dissertation, Carnegie Mellon University, 1986). *Dissertation Abstracts International, 48/09,* 2808B.

Tinker, M. A. (1963). *Legibility of print.* Ames, IA: Iowa State University Press.

West, M. (1992). Journal berated [Letter to the editor]. *Technical Communication, 39,* 326–327.

Wetterhan, R. (1993, May). Why we must have professionals [Letter to the editor]. *Technical Communication, 40,* 195–197.

Young, R. (1981). Problems and the composing process. In C. H. Frederiksen & J. F. Dominic (Eds.), *Writing: The nature, development, and teaching of written composition* (pp. 59–66). Hillsdale, NJ: Erlbaum.

Young, R. E., Becker, A. L., & Pike, K. L. (1970). *Rhetoric: Discovery and change.* New York: Harcourt Brace Jovanovich.

Zoellner, R. (1969). Talk-write: A behavioral pedagogy for composition. *College English, 30,* 267–320.

▶ 2

Library-Based Research

WHAT IS LIBRARY-BASED RESEARCH?

Library research is an essential part of any scholarly research project. If your pro-posed paper, thesis, or dissertation is going to be library-based, then of course you will do most, if not all, of your research there. However, if your research project is an empirical one, you will still have to do a sizable amount of library-based work for the literature review. Thus, whether you are writing a library-based research paper or an empirical one, you need to get to know your library. Because libraries differ, this book cannot tell you what you need to know about the resources to be found in libraries available to you. Most of that information you will need to find out on your own or with the help of a library employee.

However, you can avoid the all-too-common mistake of thinking that your school library is your best or only resource. It may be your best resource, but some-times city libraries are treasure troves for the researcher. For example, many city libraries have a whole section or floor devoted to local history with archival material you can't find anywhere else. In some cases, city or public libraries have borrowing agreements with other public libraries in the area so that you can order a book to check out at little or no cost from one of the area's other public libraries participating in the borrowing program. Borrowing from libraries across the nation is also possi-ble through the interlibrary loan program offered by most college and university libraries. This program enables you to borrow books for short periods and order pho-tocopies of individual articles from scholarly journals for a reasonable fee. Another good source of information on local history is the local newspaper morgue which usually maintains clip files by subject matter. Given this wide access to resource material, you can understand why your teacher probably has little patience with the excuse, "Our library doesn't have anything on this topic."

To help you in your own use and exploration of the libraries available to you, this chapter will explore the issue of source credibility: what kinds of sources—books, newspapers, journal articles, and so forth—are generally perceived as having scholarly authority. The next three sections provide tips on how to track down material, how to collect information, and how to organize a literature review for an empirical project.

SOURCE CREDIBILITY

In selecting the materials to read in preparation for writing, you want to avoid wasting your time on materials to which your readers will attach little credibility. Because your work is going to be read by scholars, you need to consider which sources will carry the most scholarly weight. There are four issues to consider: type of research on which the source is based, place of publication, principal author, and recency of publication.

Type of Research

If you are doing library-based research, your sources can often include both library-based and empirical sources. For example, in the February 1993 issue of *College Composition and Communication,* Michael Pemberton's article, "Modeling Theory and Composing Process Models" is an integrative piece which contains references to both library-based and empirical works. The empirical studies cited include books and articles by Carl Bereiter and Marlene Scardamalia and by John R. Hayes and Linda Flower, all of whom have made major contributions to the discipline of writing by searching empirically for answers to questions such as: How do writers plan? and How do experts and novices differ? Examples of library-based work cited by Pemberton include books and articles by Kenneth Bruffee, James Berlin, and Lester Faigley, all of whom have made major contributions to writing theory by reasoning out the answers to questions such as: What effect does the social context have on the writing task and product? Furthermore, Pemberton's reference list includes work that is primarily based on personal experience, like that of Peter Elbow, whose vivid accounts of his own writing practices have prompted writing teachers to adopt new attitudes and strategies in the classroom.

In certain types of library-based research, you should use mostly (if not exclusively) empirical sources. For example, the goal of some library-based studies is to integrate findings from prior empirical research in a subject area. This type of work can make a valuable contribution to the field. For instance, document design is a relatively new area in the field of technical communications, so little empirical research has been done into it by technical communicators. However, there is a good bit of empirical research in related disciplines, such as instructional design and cognitive psychology, that could contribute to document design theory if someone were to tie it together in an integrated presentation. An early work of this type is Felker's *Document Design: A Review of Relevant Literature* published in 1980 by American Institutes for Research. The reference section of this book contains 314 references to journal articles, in addition to books, articles in anthologies, technical reports, dissertations, and conference papers. The text is organized into chapters that review the empirical research findings in specific areas such as typography, psycholinguistics, and human factors. Felker may have found some non-empirical sources while working on this book, but he did not include them. The decision as to whether an article is empirical or not can be made fairly easily by skimming an article to look for evidence of an empirical methodology. A more recent review of empirical research in document design is Schriver, 1993. Her purpose, like Felker's, is to integrate the findings of empirical projects from a wide variety of disciplines.

In a slightly different case, in the literature review section of an empirical project, you may use some of each type of source, but the sources should be predominantly empirical. The reason lies in the purpose of a literature review: to lay the foundation for your particular empirical research project. Thus, if you want to examine the effect of fluorescent versus incandescent lighting on writers at work, you will use the literature review to show that this is a problem worth considering, and to describe prior empirical research that addresses this question. In the sections where you try to show the importance of the problem, you may want to cite an authority on writing who has described this question as important or who has specifically called for research in the area even if the opinions of these authorities were published in library-based works. But you do not want to make the mistake of building most of the literature review around library-based sources when your main task in the literature review is to create the foundation for an empirical project. Rather, to build credibility in your skill as an empirical researcher, you should demonstrate that you are acquainted with all the major empirical research done in your area of study, and you should explain how your research project fills a gap or resolves a conflict.

For example, if you were investigating the effects of lighting on writers, you would probably include empirical research on halogen as well as fluorescent and incandescent lighting. Moreover, you would probably cite some empirical studies that find effects for one type of light used in a particular line of work other than writing, perhaps in a sewing factory or a computer-chip assembly line. Also, you may cite studies showing how other environmental factors in the workplace (e.g., glare from computer screens or ergonomics of chair design) contribute to writer fatigue and error production. Keep in mind that the purpose of your literature review is to describe what has been done by prior research on lighting and what still needs to be done in order to establish a rationale for your project.

Source of Publication

While newspaper and magazine articles often report findings of empirical research, these sources often lack credibility in the eyes of a scholarly audience because the information they present about the research is usually incomplete and, in some cases, the findings are presented out of context so that they appear to support a particular stance on an issue of concern to the general public. Although none of you would be tempted to cite an article which begins "Talking Light Fixtures in Chicago Classroom Turns Teacher's Hair White," you might want to track down the original source of information for a newspaper article which claims that researchers have found a significant number of cataracts among workers in factories using purple light bulbs. In this imaginary case, you need to read the original research report to determine, among other things, who did the study, how carefully the study was designed, and who paid for it. So, while secondary sources such as newspaper and magazine articles may alert you to research projects, you should take care to read and cite the primary or original source—i.e., the one in which the findings were first published.

Other secondary sources carry a little more weight. For example, if you come across a brief description of pertinent research findings in someone else's literature review, you can include this information in your work by citing both the primary source of publication and the source in which you discovered it. However, you will build more credibility for yourself if you take the time to track down the primary source, read it, and cite it. You will probably gain from this little bit of extra work because you will have a better understanding of the details of the methodology and data, and you will be better able to evaluate the validity of the findings and how they fit into what you are doing. What is more, you may find that the reference section of the primary source can point you to other sources you need to know about.

Although primary sources carry the most weight in the scholarly community, there are additional factors which affect their credibility. One such issue is whether the publication is a book or an article. Although books are heftier than articles in terms of number of pages, they may not carry as much scholarly weight as some articles reporting on empirical projects because articles can be published more quickly than books, and thus, important findings can be quickly disseminated. Most scholarly journals also submit articles to experts for review before deciding to publish them, but I will say more about this later.

Books

Because of the amount of scholarship involved in producing them, books carry a lot of scholarly weight. However, one important factor in determining credibility, especially for books, is the reputation of the publishing company. Generally, university presses and large textbook firms are given the highest status because it is assumed that they will have experts review a book before the decision is made to publish it; however, the volume of potential sales often influences publishing decisions more strongly than does quality of the material. You should also watch out for vanity presses—publishing companies that will publish nearly anything if an author is willing to pay for it. Sometimes authors also set up small presses of their own when they cannot get a book accepted by a reputable firm. A good way to check the credibility of a publishing source is to compare it with those most frequently cited in other works in that discipline. However, in recent years, some very reputable book publishing companies have been purchased by rivals, with the result that some well-respected names in book publishing have more or less disappeared. If you are in doubt about a publishing company's reputation, you should ask your faculty advisor. Librarians on college campuses are also knowledgeable about which publishing companies have reputations for producing quality texts.

The scholarly weight accorded to a book depends also on the type of book. Some books are designed for the mass market (i.e., big sales, large profit) even though the author is a person with a scholarly reputation. For example, there are a number of writing manuals aimed at novice or insecure writers; the flashy titles of such "trade" books are usually a clue to their credibility in the scholarly community. You know the type of book I mean: *Power-Writing Made Easy!* or *Writing Your Way to the Top.* Some large publishing companies retain marketing specialists who are assigned to help authors choose a catchy title. Occasionally reputable scholars will write such books, probably for the chance to have their ideas considered by a wider audience, and the opportunity to supplement academic salaries. In such cases, you should realize that this kind of book will add less credibility to your list of sources than will a more scholarly treatment of writing by the same author.

Textbooks are another type of book which do not carry much scholarly weight, although there are exceptions such as Young, Becker, and Pike's *Rhetoric: Discovery and Change* (1970). Originally intended as a textbook for freshman composition courses, this book has become a classic resource for rhetoric scholars interested in modern theories of invention. In it, the authors apply a theoretical approach grounded in linguistics and physics to the development of a new model—tagmemic rhetoric—for writers to use in exploring their topics.

However, as is the case with trade books, potential sales and profit often determine what is put in a textbook. For example, the market for undergraduate writing textbooks is a potential gold mine for publishers. Consider that at universities with a student population of 20,000, the number of students required to take freshman composition (and thus having to buy the required book for the course) will be in the neighborhood of 4,000 to 5,000 per year. Because many students drop out during or shortly after their freshman year, the number of freshmen is almost always more than one fourth the student population. Thus, some 150–175 sections of the course will probably be taught each year at a medium to large university, and as Sharon Crowley (1990) has pointed out, the persons who design these courses are often firmly grounded in the current traditional practices of focus on essay modes (comparison/contrast, classification, and so forth), concern with surface errors (grammar and usage), and stylistic issues. So to appeal to those in charge of textbook adoptions for these courses, most freshman writing textbooks contain at least some material on grammar, usage, and traditional modes of essay organization even though the primary thrust of the book may be based on findings from empirical research.

Also, although textbooks may be based on solid scholarship, that basis may not be obvious because textbook authors usually do not cite sources for the content. In some cases, such as Houp, Pearsall, and Tebeaux's *Reporting Technical Information* (1995), the textbook authors do list sources in a chapter-by-chapter reference list at the back of the book. Other authors (e.g., Linda Flower in *Problem Solving Strategies for Writing,* 1993) provide a list for "further reading" at the end of each chapter. However, these instances are the exception rather than the rule. Perhaps at this point, you are wondering, as did one of my students, why many textbook authors do not cite sources. I can only speculate, but my guess is that some authors and publishers believe that in-text citations could be distracting to student readers. Another reason could be to save space and thus cut the cost of the book. Finally, for a special category of books, citing sources would be nearly impossible since the source of the ideas presented is the author's own life. A good example is *Writing Without Teachers* which argues for practices derived from its author's personal experiences as a teacher and writer (Elbow, 1973). For instance, Elbow tells in a first-person narrative how dissatisfied he was with various methods he tried for commenting on student papers when grading them. Eventually he developed a different approach—the classroom as a community of writers in which all members, teacher and students, write and share their writings with each other.

Articles

Articles are affected by some of the same credibility constraints as books. Articles that appear in the popular press (e.g., the supplement to the Sunday newspaper) do not carry the weight of articles published in more scholarly sources. One issue in the amount of weight assigned to articles is peer review. If the publishers send manuscripts of articles out for review by experts in the area before publishing them, then the credibility attached to the article is higher because the contents have received the approval of independent scholars. Most issues of scholarly journals undergo a peer review, and the names of the reviewing staff are often listed on the front or back pages of the journal. This list can also add weight to the value of the source if the list of reviewers contains well-known names in the field because it is assumed that persons with prominent reputations will reject work that isn't competently done.

Peer review, however, is a murky area because to be totally fair, it should be blind—the reviewers should not know the name of the author so that they won't be swayed by friendship or by the author's reputation, and so forth. However, blind reviews are sometimes not so easy to achieve. Some critics have charged that even when the peer review process is blind (author's name removed), peer reviewers favor certain high-profile authors whose style or internal references are recognizable. Especially if the author refers to his or her previous work or findings using first person pronouns, anyone familiar with those findings will know who the author is (Ceci & Peters, 1984). For example, there are only a few researchers working in document design at the present, so if I had been called on to review "Quality in Document Design: Issues and Controversies" which appeared in the May 1993 issue of *Technical Communication,* I would have wondered from the beginning if the author was Karen Schriver, a leading researcher in this area. By the time I read the third paragraph, I would have strongly suspected that the author was indeed Schriver because here the author refers to "an ongoing study I am conducting to explore document design practices in the United States and Japan," and I know that Schriver has done a lot of work on document design in Japan. Eight pages later, I would have known my guess was right because the author explains, "We recruited 200 consumers within a 50-mile radius of Pittsburgh....," and Pittsburgh is where Schriver lives and works. I don't cite this example as a criticism of Schriver, who is, in my opinion, the leading spokesperson in this area, but the example does show how difficult it is for a review to be totally "blind."

Peer review is so important to establishing the credibility of a source that articles and research reports published for the first time as part of a collection in a hardcover book do not have quite the credibility of articles published in journals with a peer review policy, because the book's editor selects, on his or her own, those articles and reports to be included in the collection. This latitude seems contrary to what one would expect since a book is a source seemingly more durable and more widely disseminated (people other than scholars buy books) than a soft-cover journal (read primarily by scholars). A similar situation arises when a scholarly journal publishes a "special issue" on a certain topic. If the editor has asked a certain expert to write an article for the special issue, the article is sometimes not subject to peer review (Stanton, 1997). On the other hand, some special-issue editors call for submissions and then put those received through a peer review process to select the ones to be included. Unfortunately, the journal editors in such cases often do not indicate which practice has been followed, so some scholars tend to question articles published in special issues of scholarly journals.

Less weighty in scholarly authority are those articles published in the proceedings of meetings or conferences. The reason is fourfold:

1. The selection of conference speakers is rarely a blind process. In most cases, would-be speakers send in abstracts, and the group in charge of the conference decides which will be accepted. The Conference on College Composition and Communication (CCCC) is a notable exception (because it uses blind review and has a rejection rate of 50–70%)—for the regular sessions, that is, not the preliminary and post conference workshops. However, to date, no proceedings are published for this conference, but writers sometimes cite an unpublished conference presentation. It is hard to say whether an unpublished presentation at CCCC carries more weight than a presentation at a conference such as ITCC (Annual Conference of the Society for Technical Communication), which hasn't always had blind review but which does publish proceedings (for a fuller discussion, see Heseltine, 1989).

2. The selection of speakers for conferences is often made on the basis of submitted abstracts or summaries rather than full papers (ITCC is an exception here, although there is some evidence that the rule is not strictly enforced).

3. The proceedings often have a standard page limit each article must meet regardless of the quality of the scholarly effort or the size of the research project. For

example, articles in the ITCC proceedings have usually been limited to four pages; for 1994, the limit was just three pages.

4. The attendees at conferences of professional organizations are frequently more interested in "How To" articles which help them solve problems in their workplaces rather than articles that report research findings. Although research-based articles lead to general principles that apply to numerous workplace tasks, conference goers tend to prefer those presentations that dwell on how a certain task is carried out at "ABC company." (A notable exception in the field of writing is the American Educational Research Association, but like CCCC, it doesn't publish proceedings.)

On the other hand, in a developing discipline such as technical communication, proceedings often carry the first reports of new scholarly work. Your job as a scholar, then, is to be a knowledgeable and discriminating reader when seeking sources of information on your research topic.

Another useful source of articles that often carry less scholarly weight is ERIC (Education Resources Informational Center). ERIC is especially useful for those who were unable to attend a professional conference for which no proceedings is published (e.g., CCCC) because ERIC regularly solicits copies of presentations from conference speakers. However, in the scholarly community, conference papers are generally given less weight than articles published in journals for the same reasons that proceedings are less powerful sources in establishing credibility. On the other hand, ERIC sometimes also provides copies of articles that have been published elsewhere.

Principal Author

From the Schriver (1993) example given above, you can see that an author's name can lend credibility to a source. How can you tell if the authors of the sources you are consulting will lend additional credibility to your citations? This is one area where your professor or thesis advisor can be a big help, especially if you have chosen someone knowledgeable in the area for your advisor. Sometimes authors publish a work so important to the discipline that you leave them out of your references only at your own peril. For example, it is extremely unlikely that you will find an article that discusses problem solving in freshman writing without citing Linda Flower (1993), or an article on typography that doesn't cite Miles Tinker (1963). You need to check with your advisor to be sure you haven't overlooked such principal authors.

Another clue to an author's reputation is the number of times that author is cited by others who are writing in the area. Thus, you will see Linda Flower's name in list after list of references in the literature on research in writing, both in composition studies and technical writing studies. Likewise, articles on document design will cite Karen Schriver, and often Ginny Redish and Charles Kostelnick. If you keep running into a certain name in the area you are researching, it is probably worth your while to look up that author to see what else he or she has published which might be important to your research effort.

Recency of Publication

The comparative recency of publication is another factor that lends credibility to a possible source. As mentioned above, you will want to include anyone who has published some seminal work in the area even if the date of that publication is fairly old. For example, most of Miles Tinker's work on typography was published in the 1960s, yet his work is so important that you shouldn't ignore it. In the case of other authors, however, findings published more than ten years ago have probably been superseded by more recent work, and in fact, the more recent work may have disproved the findings published earlier. On the other hand, if you want to show the how an idea has developed over time, then using early sources is appropriate.

Judging whether a source ten or more years old is important enough to cite in a research paper or literature review can be a problem for novices, as one of my students pointed out when reading a draft of this chapter: "When students begin research, they don't know what sources published in the 60s and 70s have been discounted, so they make copies of *every* article. Is there a way of finding out who does *not* carry academic clout before citing that author?" In answer to this dilemma, I would suggest you work backward. First, read the most recent work and note any earlier sources which the recent work describes as problematic. Then read the earlier source and decide which of the two makes the better argument. If you decide in favor of the earlier source, you may have uncovered a topic worth pursuing in anticipation of possible publication—in other words, if you can find a way to refute the criticism in the more recent article or find a middle way between the two positions, you can join in the academic conversation yourself.

Another strategy which I mentioned earlier, is to note which sources are cited over and over. Chances are, these sources represent an idea or finding so well known by people in the field that failure to cite them may suggest superficial research on your part. In some fields, important studies fade from reference lists because the author's name becomes almost synonymous with an idea or process. The best example of this case is probably Darwin's theory of evolution; many people cite Darwin without ever having read anything by him.

Other Factors Affecting Credibility of Sources

Other factors affecting credibility of sources will be covered in more depth in the chapters on empirical research designs because poor design of the research method usually calls the reported findings into serious question. However, one factor you should be very alert to is the possible adverse effect on credibility resulting from the source of funds which paid for the research effort. All research is expensive. The researcher and his or her assistants must be paid for their time; laboratory equipment must be rented or purchased; and some supplies must be bought.

For example, students often think that a survey is a relatively easy research project to carry out because they haven't fully looked into the issues of survey methodology or the costs involved. To get maximum return and thus increase validity of results, postage is required for the return envelope as well as the initial one. Also, the postage on the initial envelope may cost more than a single first-class stamp because of the size of the survey instrument and the fact that a cover letter and return envelope must also be included. Finally, researchers conducting surveys often find that they must send out reminder cards or letters to get respondents to return the completed survey. Thus, postage is probably going to be a minimum of $1.00 per addressee, which quickly mounts up with even a short list of 100 or so addresses, and that does not count the cost of envelopes, paper, address labels, printing, or labor involved in stuffing envelopes and tabulating returns.

No wonder, then, that researchers frequently look for financial support for their work. However, sometimes the persons most interested and willing to pay for the research are those most interested in obtaining favorable results from the project. For example, a project which found that incandescent lighting causes eyelashes to grow thicker and longer would lose credibility if a major manufacturer of such bulbs paid the research costs. Of course, many important products (e.g., medicines) have been developed by research laboratories owned and operated by manufacturing firms. In such cases, a reader would need to look very closely at the research methodology in deciding how much credibility to attach to the findings.

HOW TO TRACK DOWN MATERIAL

Card catalogues used to be the main source for finding books in a library, but most libraries are switching to computerized catalogues because they allow information to be retrieved much faster. However, budget constraints often mean that many libraries still rely on their card catalogues for finding books acquired before the installation of the computerized system. Thus, you may need to know the date the library stopped cataloging books on cards to determine which system (computer or card catalog) to use in hunting for a particular book or books by a particular author. In such libraries, when you are tracking down books on a particular subject, you will probably have to use both the card and the online catalogues.

Online Searches in the Library

Computer search facilities are expanding rapidly—too rapidly to be discussed here as the information is apt to be outdated before this book is a year old. However, most reference librarians enjoy introducing novices to their collections and helping scholars track down materials. Many libraries have acquired CD ROM collections of data.

These are compact disks (CD) with "Read Only Memory" (ROM)—meaning that a user can read the information stored on the disk by its producer, but the user can make no changes to that information. Because writing is a newer discipline, useful sources are not limited to those CD ROMs traditionally used by English department scholars. The Modern Language Association CD ROM does contain some work relevant to writing, but the disk is largely a tool for literary scholars. *The Humanities Index* and *The Social Sciences Index* online searches both go back to 1983. *Arts and Humanities Search* covers some 1,300 journals since 1980.

Databases from other disciplines such as cognitive psychology, education, and business may prove even more fruitful for technical communication scholars. For example, *PsycINFO* covers about 1,000 journals from as far back as 1967, and some research in discourse processing can be found there. *Dissertation Abstracts Online* covers American dissertations in most disciplines as far back as 1961. If your library has UNCOVER, you will be able to browse the table of contents in a variety of journals, but as yet, UNCOVER includes only very recent publications. Scholars in technical communications can find many good suggestions about online search resources in Elizabeth Smith's 1996 article in *Technical Communication Quarterly.*

One big advantage of many of the online facilities is that you can print out the information on the screen to take with you. Such printouts can help you avoid transcription errors which so often creep into handwritten bibliographic information. Frequently you can also print out abstracts of the articles you are interested in. On the other hand, you probably should not rely completely on computer searches at this time simply because they are not yet comprehensive. Eventually information scientists may begin cataloguing work from the past as well as that currently being produced, but the information explosion is such that keeping track of current work involves a major commitment of a library's time and money.

Resources via the Internet

Persons who have a personal computer with a modem and access to an Internet server can do much of their searching without ever physically visiting a library. In fact, the Internet allows you to view the catalogs and data bases of libraries all around the country and even some in other countries. Many universities now provide computer labs in buildings other than the library where students can access the Internet and the World Wide Web (the Web), and some universities provide research software which allows students to dial up the university's computer network, and use it to access the Internet. I hesitate to say much about the various programs you can use to conduct your search because computer software is often outdated almost as soon as it is distributed. GOPHER is one of the oldest of search software packages, and it is still being used at many schools. The information about participating sites in GOPHER is arranged hierarchically, so you travel to other libraries by calling up one menu, selecting an option from it which will give you access to another menu from which you select an option, and on and on until you arrive where you want. To get to my school, you would follow this path: World/ North America/United States/Tennessee/University of Memphis. GOPHER also allows you to do keyword searches.

The World Wide Web is also a potentially valuable resource for researchers. Like the Internet, the Web is usually accessible through a university's computer network and commercial servers such as America Online and CompuServe which charge fees to users. The Web, however, is organized differently from the Internet. Instead of a hierarchy of menus, the Web allows you to follow its links in many directions. For example, if you access someone's Web page, you can often go from there directly to someone else's page (if the links are available) without having to call up a series of nested menus. Because it is so easy to jump from one Web page to another, Web users often find they can't keep track of how they reached a certain page. Two ways of dealing with this problem are "bookmarks" and "URLs." A bookmark works something like the crumbs Hansel and Gretel dropped along their path to help them find their way back, but unlike bread crumbs, bookmarks can be confusing if you put too many along the path. A URL, or Universal Resource Locator, is an address which enables a Web user to go directly to a particular location without having to make a series of jumps from one site to the next in order to get there.

Two long established Web browsers are LYNX (which is available at many universities but does not have graphics capabilities) and MOSAIC (which is also available at many places and does have graphics capabilities, although they are somewhat limited). Two recently developed Web browsers are Netscape Navigator (a very much improved version of MOSAIC) and Internet Explorer. Because Web browsers allow you to jump quickly from one site to the next and on and on, it is easy to lose track of where you've been or the path you used to get where you are. One helpful answer is to visit Internet directories such as Argus, Yahoo, and Excite which help you track down information with keyword searches. But all of this changes rapidly, so if you don't already know how to get around on the Web, you might want to buy a how-to book such as *Connections: a Guide to On-Line Writing* by Anderson, Benjamin, and Paredes-Holt (1997). In addition to explaining how to use the Web and how it can help writing students, the authors provide a Web page where you can get updated information in this area.

One interesting feature of the World Wide Web is that it is becoming a publication site. Some authors (and some journals) are now publishing articles electronically. This source of publication is too new to assess its scholarly credibility. Because it is relatively easy for people to create their own Web page and publish their own article there, researchers must exercise judgment. A good example is a recent posting on the Web of a graduation address supposedly written by Kurt Vonnegut, which it turned out Vonnegut had never even seen. Thus, electronically published articles are already running into some of the same kinds of credibility problems many hardcopy conference proceedings now face.

Library Search Resources in Hardcopy

The library reference room should contain several hardcopy indexes that can help you track down research findings relevant to composition and technical writing. The following is only a partial list:

> *Education Index,* since 1929
> *Psychological Abstracts,* since 1927
> *Business Periodical Index,* since 1958

The business index is particularly helpful to technical communicators because *Technical Communication* is one of the journals included. Some indexes have changed their names and focuses over the years. For example, MLA indexes include the *MLA American Bibliography* from 1921 to 1955 and the *MLA International Bibliography* since 1956. Another index with a changing name and focus covers the humanities and social sciences:

> 1907 to 1965: *The International Index*
> 1965 to 1974: *Social Sciences and Humanities Index*
> 1974 to present, separate indexes:
> > *Humanities Index*
> > *Social Sciences Index*

By the time of this book's publication, these hardcopy indices could be online; however, online versions of indices tend to cover only fairly recent years.

Government documents are often a rich resource for technical communicators because various government agencies have produced style manuals for use in designing documents produced by or submitted to them. For example, the Department of the Treasury, IRS produces two handbooks for writers: *Effective Writing: A Workshop Course* and *Effective Revenue Writing.* Similarly, the departments of Agriculture, Commerce, and Interior have produced materials to help their employees improve their writing skills. Also in government documents are environmental impact statements which are sometimes interesting models of document design. The *Monthly Catalogue of United States Government Publications* is one place you can search for material on a certain subject. Again, the librarian is an invaluable resource.

Additionally, there are a number of standard reference books that can be of help; *The Guide to Reference Works* is probably a good place to begin. Other reference books that may be helpful in finding research relevant to writing are as follows:

> *Encyclopedia of Education,* (Deighton, 1971)
> *Encyclopedia of Education Research. World Survey of Information,* (Mitzel, 1982)
> *Encyclopedia of Psychology,* (Eysenk, Arnold, & Meili, 1972)
> *Dictionary of Psychology and Related Fields,* (Beigel, 1971)
> *International Encyclopedia of the Social Sciences,* (Sills, 1979)

Finally, annotated bibliographies are a rich resource for writing researchers. The *CCCC Bibliography,* published every year since 1987, can be purchased from Southern Illinois Press. Because of the amount of work involved in producing these volumes, each one covers material published 18 months or so previously. Also of interest to composition researchers are the annotated bibliographies published in the May and December issues of *Research in the Teaching of English.* These cover research in writing published the previous year. Similarly, an annotated bibliography of research in technical communication is published yearly in the fall issue of *Technical Communication Quarterly.*

Personal Detective Strategies

You can also track down sources through two strategies I think of as personal detective strategies because they involve looking for clues much like detectives do. These sources are called ancestry and invisible colleges. *Ancestry* is a source you encounter as you read articles on a particular topic because scholarly articles almost always include references to scholarly work done in the past. You should examine reference lists for titles that seem related to your topic and authors who have published in that area frequently. When you track these down, you will probably find some that are not really pertinent. On the other hand, ancestry research can help make you aware of seminal works—those that are repeatedly referred to by other researchers.

Invisible colleges are informal networks of scholars who are interested in the same area or particular type of research. Sometimes invisible colleges consist of people who have gone to graduate school together or worked together on a project, or even persons who share mutual friends. For example, Art Graesser of the Psychology Department at my university is a cognitive scientist interested in discourse processes, among other things. I often attend his research seminars, and he often sends one of his students over to talk to me if that student is interested in writing research. I also send my students who are interested in cognitive processes to see Art. Similarly, I send some students over to see Gary Morrison in the Education Department if they are interested in online help because Gary has done a lot of research in screen design. You can tap into an invisible college by going to see a professor who is interested in the topic you are researching because that professor probably knows others interested in the same area.

HOW TO COLLECT INFORMATION

Many textbooks give very specific instructions for collecting information (e.g., use a separate note card for each fact or idea). However, I have never found a published system I was entirely committed to, mostly because they seem too restrictive and nitpicking. In this section, then, I'm going to propose some general principles that you can carry out in your own way.

1. Provide yourself with easily sortable and portable information. Photocopies of articles or pages from a book are handy for rereading, but they are not easily sortable nor portable. Nor are the highlighted sections on a photocopy. For example, 50 photocopied articles are harder to carry back and forth from home to school than 50 3 × 5 or 4 × 6 cards. Notes taken in a spiral-bound notebook are very portable, but they are not very sortable. Highlighting prominent ideas in articles means you may have to sort and resort articles, skimming each article again for the idea you are looking for. Cards can be more easily sorted. For example, you might want to pull out all information on incandescent light for work on one section of your paper and later write a section on fluorescent light, again sorting your information for that aspect of your topic. (On the other hand, if you photocopy an article, you can reread the whole article at your convenience instead of having to rely on the summary on a note card.)

2. Avoid having to return to the library for additional information from or about each source. For example, I used to be in such a hurry to get to the material itself, that I would write down only the barest bibliographical information. As a result, I often wasted valuable time returning for a missed page number or journal issue number. Now, I am very careful to get the publication data right the first time. If you photocopy articles or pages from a book, also photocopy the cover page of the book or journal and be sure the date and all other essential bibliographic information is written on it. Also, be sure the photocopies of the individual pages have legible page numbers—you will need this information when you use quotes or cite specific data. When taking notes, you should be extremely careful about the accuracy of quoted material. If you decide the author's words on a certain topic are worth using, put these words in quotation marks and follow them with the page number.

Many sources recommend note cards: small ones for bibliographic information and larger ones for notes. Whether you use different size cards or some other system, it is probably a good idea to at least record the full bibliographic citation for sources you have examined even if you decide not to take notes from that source. Then if you run across a reference to that work later, you will know that you've already examined it. One of my colleagues keeps an alphabetical list of examined sources in a computer file because it is so easy to check to see whether a reference he encounters while reading is one he already has looked at. Lap top computers no doubt simplify the whole note-taking process. In any case, you can probably set up a system that suits you. For example, Figure 2-1 is a copy of the front of one of my note cards used to gather information for my article on research reported at ITCC over the last twenty years (MacNealy, 1992). At the top of the card, I list information to direct me to the photocopy I have: the authors' last names, the initial page number, and the year. Note that this card does not carry the complete bibliographic information (for example, it does not list the name of the article), but it does carry enough information for me to pull the complete citation off the ITCC list in my computer. I put ITCC at the top to indicate that this card belongs in the ITCC set, because I have

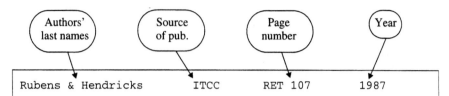

Rubens & Hendricks   ITCC   RET 107   1987

The authors tested 2 principles of program instruction:
(1) small step size (Skinner) vs. large step size (Pressey),
and (2) active responding (Skinner) vs. passive (Pressey).
Subjects completed either online or hardcopy tutorials on
elements of BASIC programming language and editing skills on
IBM PC. All subjects had both type questions, but only 1 of 4
step sizes. All completed a post-test 5 days later. In the
post-test, the online subjects' scores were significantly
higher than the hardcopy ones, and the active responding
group scores were significantly higher than the passive
group. The larger step sizes, however, took less time, a
puzzling result for which the authors present several
possible explanations.

FIGURE 2-1   **Front of Note Card**

other sets of cards from other projects. Next is a summary of the article; here I tried to put in the basic methods and findings as objectively as I could.

3. Collect your reactions to things you read, but be sure these reactions are separated from the actual information found in the source. For example, to insure that I use sources fairly, I try to present the author's main points in a short summary on one side of a 4 × 6 card, as shown in Figure 2-1, and then on the back I write my reactions (see Figure 2-2). As Altick explains, "To be a good researcher, one must be a thoroughgoing skeptic" (1981, p. 23). For example, on the back of the card on which I wrote the summary, I wrote a comment about a lack of information in the article— "no info on participants, etc.," and a question I would ask the authors if I ran into them.

Since this card was part of a set of cards in a project assessing research in technical communication, I also entered some brief coded notes at the bottom of the back of the card, and I highlighted them according to a color code to help me do quick sorts. The word "experimental" (on the right) is highlighted in green, as an indicator of the research method, and "CAI" (on the left) is highlighted in blue, as an indicator of the subject investigated. My combination of location of information and highlight color made it easy for me to sort all the cards into either subject investigated (I used the left side and blue for education, orange for manuals, and so forth), or type of research (I used the right side and blue for case studies, orange for surveys, green

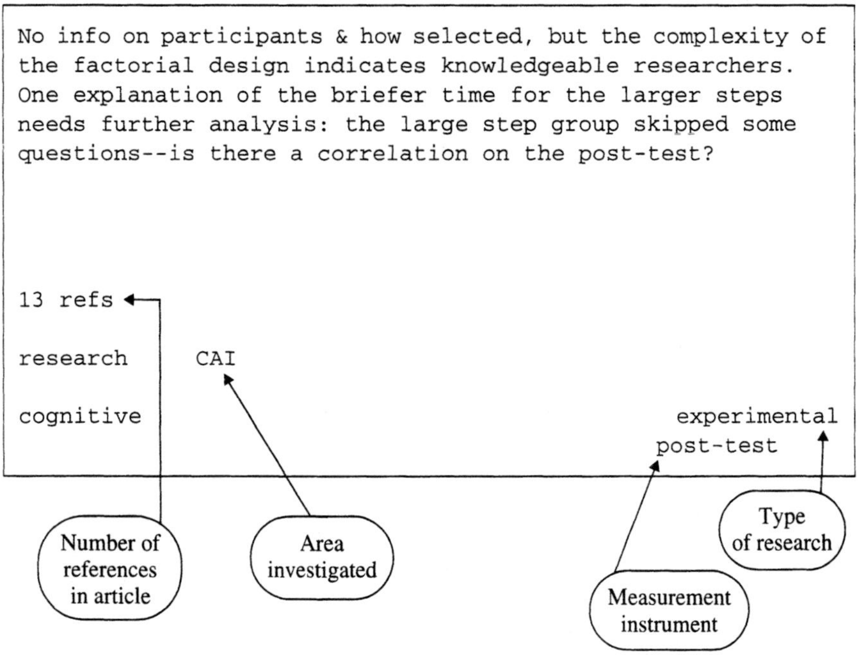

No info on participants & how selected, but the complexity of
the factorial design indicates knowledgeable researchers.
One explanation of the briefer time for the larger steps
needs further analysis: the large step group skipped some
questions--is there a correlation on the post-test?

13 refs

research   CAI

cognitive   experimental
                                              post-test

Number of   Area   Type
references   investigated   of research
in article
                                   Measurement
                                    instrument

FIGURE 2-2   **Back of Note Card**

for experiments, and so forth). On a set of cards for a different project, I would use a different set of codes, depending on what sorts I think I might want to make. Some researchers put library name and call number in places such as this in case they want to find the source again quickly.

ORGANIZING THE LITERATURE REVIEW

Organizing the material you find in your sources is frequently more challenging than you might think. I notice students often organize around their sources so that the opening sentences in their paragraphs focus on a particular source rather than the connection of that source to the issue under discussion. In other words, the name of the author of the source appears in the subject position of sentences rather than in the citation in parentheses at the end of the sentence. Placing the author's name in the foreground may work well in instances when the name is very recognizable as an authority in the area, but otherwise you will help your reader process your discussion of an issue if you place the *issue* rather than the *source* of the information you are providing on that issue first. Furthermore, in a discussion of issues, your reader can follow your points more easily if you integrate material from your sources in support of an idea, and then, in the in-text citation at the end of a sentence, you list several sources.

For example, in a section of a hypothetical paper on research in technical communication, I might be discussing research focusing on computers. To include the findings of Rubens and Hendricks shown in Figure 2-1, I could begin a new paragraph this way:

> Rubens and Hendricks (1987) investigated the application of two different principles of instructions: small step size proposed by Skinner versus large step size proposed by Pressey. Subjects were....

This opening begins with the *researchers,* not the findings. Beginning paragraphs this way makes the paper read like a laundry list—Smith and Jones in the first paragraph, Rubens and Hendricks in the second, and so on.

On the other hand, in this paper I could describe some studies which show that computer-assisted instruction increases students' test scores in Math and then begin the next paragraph as follows:

> Although several studies support the belief that computer-assisted instruction increases students' test scores in Math, it is not clear whether the computer delivery or the design of the instruction delivered by the computer is responsible for the increase. In other disciplines, the educational principle underlying the design of computer-assisted instruction has been found to make a significant difference (Rubens & Hendricks, 1987). In particular, a design which includes active responding...

Note that in this paragraph, I use the opening clause *Although several studies support the belief that computer-assisted instruction increases students' test scores in Math* to sum up information I've given in preceding paragraphs, and I use the second clause *it is not clear whether the computer delivery or the design of the instruction delivered by the computer is responsible for the increase* to introduce a new topic. In the second sentence, I support the new topic by mentioning a finding and its source: *In other disciplines, the educational principle underlying the design of computer-assisted instruction has been found to make a significant difference (Rubens & Hendricks, 1987).* In the third and subsequent sentences, I would give particular details of the findings.

If I know of more than one study with a finding similar to that of Rubens and Hendricks, I would add that to the citation following the second sentence in this way:

> In other disciplines, the educational principle underlying the design of computer-assisted instruction has been found to make a significant difference (Rubens & Hendricks, 1987; Smith & Jones, 19xx).

Then my third sentence would have to include the information that I will talk about the Rubens and Hendricks study in detail. For example,

> In other disciplines, the educational principle underlying the design of computer assisted instruction has been found to make a significant difference (Rubens & Hendricks, 1987; Smith & Jones, 19xx). In particular, Rubens and Hendricks (1987) found that a design which includes active responding...

The basic principle to keep in mind when organizing a literature review is that you should focus on ideas, not sources. The citations should be thought of as aids to readers wanting to know more details; thus, citations should not be the focus of the text, but they should be as accurate as possible to make it easy for your readers to find the sources for themselves.

REFERENCES

Altick, R. D. (1981). *The art of literary research* (3rd ed. revised by J. J. Fenstermaker). New York: Norton.

Anderson, D., Benjamin, B., & Paredes-Holt, B. (1997). *Connections: A guide to on-line writing.* Boston: Allyn & Bacon.

Beigel, H. (Ed.). (1971). *Dictionary of psychology and related fields.* New York: Frederick Ungar.

Ceci, S. J., & Peters, D. (1984). How blind is blind review? *American Psychologist, 39,* 1491–1494.

Crowley, S. (1990). *The methodical memory: Invention in current traditional rhetoric.* Carbondale: Southern Illinois University Press.

Deighton, L. C. (1971). *Encyclopedia of education* (Vols. 1–10). New York: Macmillan.

Elbow, P. (1973). *Writing without teachers.* New York: Oxford University Press.

Eysenk, H. J., Arnold, W., & Meili, R. (Eds.). (1972). *Encyclopedia of psychology* (Vols. 1–3). New York: Herder.

Felker, D. (Ed.). (1980). *Document design: A review of relevant literature.* Washington, DC: American Institutes for Research.

Flower, L. (1993). *Problem solving strategies for writing* (4th ed.). New York: Harcourt Brace Jovanovich.

Heseltine, E. (1989). Bringing conference proceedings into the light. *CBE Views, 12,* 24–26.

Houp, K. W., Pearsall, T. E., & Tebeaux, E. (1995). *Reporting technical information* (9th ed.). Boston: Allyn & Bacon.

MacNealy, M. S. (1992). Research in technical communication: A view of the past and a challenge for the future. *Technical Communication, 39,* 533–551.

Mitzel, H. E. (Ed.). (1982). *Encyclopedia of education research. World survey of information* (5th ed.) (Vols. 1–4). New York: Free Press.

Pemberton, M. (1993). Modeling theory and composing process models. *College Composition and Communication, 44,* 40–58.

Rubens, B. K., & Hendricks, R. (1987). The psychological advantage of online instruction. *Proceedings of the 34th International Technical Communication Conference.* Arlington, VA: Society for Technical Communication, RET:107–RET:110.

Schriver, K. (1993). Quality in document design: Issues and controversies. *Technical Communication, 40,* 239–257.

Sills, D. L. (Ed.). (1979). *International encyclopedia of the social sciences.* New York: Macmillan.

Smith, E. O. (1996). Electronic databases for technical and professional communication research. *Technical Communication Quarterly, 5,* 365–385.

Stanton, D. C. (1997). Editor's column: What's in a name? Revisiting author-anonymous reviewing. *PMLA 112,* 191–197.

Tinker, M. A. (1963). *Legibility of print.* Ames, IA: Iowa State University Press.

Young, R. E., Becker, A. L., & Pike, K. L. (1970). *Rhetoric: Discovery and change.* New York: Harcourt Brace Jovanovich.

▶ 3

Overview of
Empirical Methodology

Readers unfamiliar with empirical methodology sometimes groan at the necessity of learning new terminology. For some readers, the terms used by empirical researchers sound like arcane scientific jargon with the result that readers tend to dismiss empirical research as too complex to understand. At the risk of sounding unscientific and occasionally even simple-minded, I hereby promise to try to explain the concepts of empirical research in very ordinary terms and with very basic (even ridiculous) examples. In fact, when I mentioned that I intended to write this book, one of my former students suggested I might want to call it *All About Eyelashes.* You can judge for yourself whether that would have been a better title as you read on.

On the other hand, in almost any area of life, it is difficult if not impossible to talk about concepts and endeavors without using jargon. One good example is the field of teaching English grammar: can it be done without using such familiar words as noun, verb, and adjective? In discussing empirical studies, you need to know what constitutes qualitative and quantitative methods and specialized terms such as *participant observer, validity* (both internal and external), *reliability, significant difference,* and so forth. As a first step, this chapter provides some basic characteristics and categories of empirical research.

ADVANTAGES AND DISADVANTAGES
OF EMPIRICAL RESEARCH

At its most basic level, empirical research can be defined as recorded observations of events. In some cases, certain aspects of the events being observed are controlled, as in laboratory experiments; in other instances such as case studies, events are observed in their natural settings. The foremost advantage to empirical work is its power to persuade. The best example of this power is its use (and misuse) in advertising: e.g., "four out of five dentists recommend brand X." The persuasive power in this ad has two bases: numbers, which most people believe can't be argued with (i.e., "numbers don't lie"), and scientific authority (doctors, dentists, researchers, and other professionals who are assumed to be very knowledgeable and ethical). The power to persuade is often crucial to the success of proposals for a change in procedure or for funds to implement programs. For example, a technical writer who wants her supervisor to permit her to use lists rather than paragraphs in a certain piece of writing can use evidence from empirical research, such as that by Tenenbaum (1977), to show that lists are easier to process and that their content is remembered longer and more accurately.

The major disadvantages of empirical research are four: in spite of the perception of the power of numbers to persuade, some audiences distrust numbers; some audiences suspect researchers of bias; some audiences believe that results are not applicable because scientific methods lose sight of the human element; and carrying out an empirical project usually has a high cost in dollars and time. Note that the first three disadvantages are problems of audience perception, so a researcher may also be able to reduce the negative effects of these perceptions to some degree by the way she writes up the description of the methodology and the findings. After I describe each disadvantage, I offer a suggestion for reducing this effect.

Distrust of Numbers

Audience distrust of numbers is often a reaction to the belief that "numbers don't lie." Ads such as three out of five doctors or dentists or whoever may be made up out of thin air. Or the doctors/dentists/whoever who were asked about the product may be friends of the investigator or paid by the investigator in some way. Furthermore, folk wisdom holds that data can be made to support whatever you want it to, and most people are acquainted with at least one instance of such abuse. Thus, those empirical projects that use numbers to report their findings (e.g., experiments and surveys) may be viewed with some distrust.

Also related to the suspicion of numbers is the notion that there are verbal people and nonverbal people. Verbal people, according to this belief, can write and speak easily, but they cannot perform numerical tasks such as balancing their own checkbooks. Probably the right-brain/left-brain theory has intensified this belief. Right-brain/left-brain theory aside, the faulty reasoning is apparent when one considers that it is not necessary to fully understand the statistical procedures to accept as highly probable the results of a particular empirical project. For example, scientists could use a set of fairly complicated statistics to demonstrate that there is a high probability that the sun will rise tomorrow morning. The going gets stickier in the case where statistical procedures indicate that the sun probably won't rise tomorrow. We would rightly be suspicious of such findings, but we might also want to say a few prayers. In other words, numbers *can* lie, and our common sense and prior experience can alert us to possible cases when numbers are being made to lie. But it is also the case that when multiple empirical studies produce results that point to strategies that could help us carry out important tasks or make important decisions, it seems ridiculous to denigrate such results (in the absence of evidence to the contrary) simply because they were arrived at through numerical procedures. A case in point is the assignment of grammar and usage exercises in college writing classrooms. In spite of a number of empirical research projects whose findings have cast doubt on the probability that such exercises teach people to express themselves well in writing (Hillocks, 1986), many teachers continue to assign such exercises. One could argue that such assignments don't hurt students even if they don't help them. But such assignments do take time that might better be devoted to something which has a stronger possibility of helping students learn to write well.

One way to cope with this disadvantage is to reduce the use of numbers in an article. Certainly journals such as *College Composition and Communication* and *College English* rarely, if ever, print articles that use the IMRAD (Introduction, Method, Results, and Discussion) format and contain statistics. In other journals, such as *Research in the Teaching of English* and most technical writing journals, statistics and the IMRAD format are welcome. Even in articles submitted to these journals, however, you could possibly reduce the frequency of numbers in the text itself by placing them in tables that readers can skip if they are turned off by numbers.

Distrust of Researchers

The second disadvantage commonly associated with empirical research—researcher bias—is somewhat related to the distrust of numbers. In this case, researchers themselves are suspected of biasing the results. Folk wisdom says that researchers usually find what they are looking for, and we have all seen evidence of this. For example, a local newspaper article described new EPA strategies "to curb illness from secondhand smoke" (Press Services, 1993, p. A-11). The main strategy described in this article is a new "brochure which explain[s] the findings that the EPA announced in January when it officially classified secondhand smoke as a serious cancer threat" (Press Services, 1993, p. A-11). The last two paragraphs of the article are as follows:

> *Meanwhile, the House Agriculture subcommittee on specialty crops and natural resources took testimony from four scientists who said EPA's work on secondhand smoke was fraught with manipulated data, statistical irregularities and an effort to make the science fit a preconceived anti-smoking goal.*
> *The scientists who testified are paid consultants of The Tobacco Institute.* (Press Services, 1993, p. A-11)

It may be true that the four scientists have found serious flaws in the empirical work on which the brochure is based. Unfortunately, flaws in methodology seem to creep into the best of plans, and if the flaws are serious, one should definitely be wary of accepting the findings. On the other hand, the fact that the four scientists are being paid by The Tobacco Institute certainly causes one to worry about a possible bias in their approach—are the flaws they mention ones that would seriously affect the findings, or are they minor technicalities that reasonable scientists (and possibly even the four scientists mentioned in this article) would ignore in considering the results of studies in other areas?

The suspicion of researcher bias may be even stronger in those empirical research projects carried out in natural settings where the researcher, as a participant-observer, is part of the group being studied as well as the person doing the studying. For many years, teacher research has suffered from perceptions of bias, but of late such research is receiving more favorable attention. You can read more about teacher research in Chapter 12. One way to counter the disadvantages of reader perception of research bias is to plan your research carefully and describe your methodology in enough detail that readers can see that you are aware of the possibility of bias and are trying to avoid it. For example, if you are coding (categorizing) segments of interviews or observations, you could enlist the help of another researcher to code a subset of the data and then tell your readers the rate of agreement between you and the other coder.

Distrust of Empirical Methods

The third disadvantage connected to empirical research is related to both of the first two: the general public and those involved in aesthetic pursuits tend to question the appropriateness of empirical research methods. In this camp are those who dismiss empirical research (especially quantitative methods such as experiments) as being too positivistic—they point out that laboratories don't replicate the real world and people are not similar to rats or cornfields, so they believe that the findings arrived at in laboratories are questionable. Certainly, a reasonable person must admit that laboratories are artificial settings as I explained in Chapter 1. However, in areas other than writing research, results produced in laboratory settings are usually accepted as valid. For example, most reasonable people accept as valid empirical findings that smoking adversely affects health, that yellow fever is spread by mosquitoes rather than bad air, and so forth. Thus, the charge that empirical research is too positivistic seems to be selectively applied.[1]

---

[1]This term is difficult to define in just a few words because some people who use it to criticize research in English studies use it in a pejorative sense. If you would like to read more about this issue, I recommend two articles in *Research in the Teaching of English* 27 [1993]: Richard Larsen's "Competing paradigms for research and evaluation in the teaching of English," pp. 283–292 and John R. Hayes' "Taking criticism seriously," pp. 305–315. Another helpful explanation can be found in J. Kirk and M. L. Miller (1986). *Reliability and validity in qualitative research.* Newbury Park, CA: Sage.

One strategy experimental researchers often use to counter reader suspicion or dislike of laboratory methods is to present the findings with caveats and hedges. For example, many research reports contain a paragraph or two describing limitations of the study, including an acknowledgment of how the research setting or method could have affected the findings. Also, researchers can use a tentative rather than a positive stance when reporting the findings. For example, instead of stating boldly that assigning grammar exercises harms students, one could say something like, "These findings strongly suggest that assigning grammar exercises could harm students."

High Costs of Empirical Research

The fourth disadvantage to empirical research—the cost—cannot be denied. Empirical research costs typically include large amounts of time and money. It is not uncommon for medical projects to be carried out over a five year period. For example, one of my students (a chemist) has been assigned by his firm to a new over-the-counter drug development project that is expected to last five years. If the drug under development were a prescription drug, the project would probably take eight to 12 years. Research into writing costs time also: time to plan carefully, time to carry out the project, and time to write up the results. Such projects also cost money, such as salaries for the research staff and costs of equipment and supplies.

One way to cope with costs is to look for outside resources. For example, grants can sometimes be obtained from the government, from charitable foundations, and from professional societies (e.g., The Society for Technical Communication) that might be interested in the topic.

An additional hazard, particularly in hypotheses-testing projects, is that the results of such expenditures can be disappointing; often journals are reluctant to publish articles about experiments in which no significant differences were found between the experimental and control groups. For example, I once designed a project to determine whether students would improve the quality of their papers if they revised on a computer after receiving teacher feedback on their drafts. This project involved, among other things, finding teachers who would cooperate by giving specified assignments and requiring computer-produced revision, training, supervising, and paying a team of evaluators to judge over 100 drafts and revisions, and statistically analyzing the data. In addition to the planning time, the project took a whole semester to carry out. The results showed no significant difference between those who used computers to revise and those who didn't. The results don't mean that computers don't facilitate revision; rather, they only mean that, *in this particular instance*, the evidence in either direction was not strong enough to support a claim of a cause/effect relationship between revising on a computer and producing a quality essay no matter how intuitively right such a relationship seems to be.

When a research project produces results that are counter-intuitive, the researcher may want to examine the methodology to see if some confounding factor may have been responsible. If so, a second project could be carried out. One good example is a project by Tammy Bourg (1996), that investigated possible benefits of teaching students strategies for empathy-building when reading literature. Bourg used two short stories in an experiment in which one group of students (the experimental group) were taught the empathy-building strategies before reading the stories and another group of students read the stories without having been taught any empathy-building strategies. To Bourg's surprise, there was a significant difference between groups for one short story but not the other. Bourg's next step was to try to track down the cause of the discrepancy by doing a systematic analysis of the structure of the two stories.

In summary, to counter the suspicions with which empirical research findings are often greeted, researchers must make sure that their research projects are well designed. Researchers in writing should be aware that they can adversely affect the standing of writing as a respected profession and academic discipline if they fail to use rigorous research strategies.

ESSENTIAL CHARACTERISTICS OF EMPIRICAL RESEARCH

So what, in plain language, are the essential characteristics of good empirical work? First, an empirical study is *planned in advance* of the data collection. For example, you may, while driving to work, notice that most of the cars you pass contain only one person. In fact, you may decide to start counting just to see if your observation holds true during the rest of your drive to work. However, since you didn't plan this study in advance, it cannot be counted as a good empirical study for reasons which will become obvious as you read the rest of this chapter. Or in another example, you may be a person who takes aspirin quite regularly. Given this fact, when someone mentions that you have the longest eyelashes of anyone in the class, you could conclude that the aspirin might be the cause, so you ask your classmates how much aspirin they take in order to confirm that you are the biggest aspirin user in the class. No doubt you immediately see the flaw in this reasoning (as you probably will in subsequent eyelash studies described in this book). But, again, your study has flunked the first test for being a real empirical study—it was not planned in advance.

A second essential characteristic of an empirical study is that the *data are collected systematically*. In the eyelash study described above, you did use a system for collecting data: you asked every member of your class about aspirin usage. However, in the description of the study of single-occupant cars above, there is no way to know whether you collected data systematically or not. Did you look in every car in the city, every car you passed, or every car coming in the opposite direction? Could it be that, at other times of the day, cars routinely contain more than one person? As you can see, if you do not have a systematic plan for collecting data, then your findings are subject to a multitude of questions.

The third essential characteristic of an empirical study is that the method of *data collection produces a body of evidence that can be examined by others.* By providing others with access to the data, you reduce the likelihood that the findings are based on researcher bias. So unless you took photos of the cars in the single-occupant study and tape-recorded or took field notes as you questioned your classmates about their aspirin use, the two studies described above could not be considered as meeting minimum requirements for an empirical study.

PURPOSES AND BASIC DESIGN PRINCIPLES

Empirical research projects are usually carried out to answer one of these questions: What details best describe something such as a person, event, or community? To what degree are two phenomena related to each other? and Is there a causal relationship between two phenomena? Researchers usually try to answer the first question with a study that collects thick description, a *qualitative* study such as a case study or an ethnography. Although the second question can be partially answered with a descriptive study, if we want to know the degree of relationship, we will have to collect some *quantitative* data that can be used in a statistical analysis. Even then, we cannot say with *certainty* that there is a relationship between two occurrences; however, statistical procedures can tell us how likely it is that the degree of relationship is a matter of pure chance. For example, most researchers accept that a relationship between phenomena is significant if the probability that the relationship could have occurred by chance is less than one out of 100 times. Similarly, the third question (Is there a *causal* relationship between two phenomena?) requires quantitative data and statistical procedures if we want to know whether a difference in the performance of two groups is a result of a special treatment given to one of them. Again, statistics will show whether the difference is significant enough to indicate that the special treatment is the cause of the difference in performance or whether the difference is probably just due to chance.

In collecting data for questions involving measurement (as in experiments), two principles are acknowledged by most good researchers. In the first place, no matter how carefully a researcher designs a study, he or she must recognize that *all instruments of measurement are imprecise.* For example, though we may tend to believe otherwise, an oral thermometer commonly used to measure body temperature can really only indicate the approximate body temperature. In writing research, imprecision of measuring instruments is even more of a problem. For example, what instrument can be used to measure how "good" a piece of writing is? For many years, teachers commonly counted the number of grammatical or usage errors as a basis for judgment. But even a grammatically perfect piece of writing can still be considered "poor" if it doesn't achieve its purpose—a quality much harder to measure precisely. In the case of a sales document, we might say we can determine the document's effectiveness by counting the sales that followed its publication. But we cannot be sure that some of the sales occurring after publication of the document weren't the result of the buyer's prior resolve to buy the product because he or she had had long service from the same brand. Even if we were to ask the buyer whether the sales document was the major influence in the decision to buy the product, we are faced with defining *what percentage* of the decision can be attributed to the major influence of the sales document.

The second important factor, the *control of confounding variables,* is closely related to the first. To go back to our body temperature question, suppose that we believe that the temperature of the blood accurately matches the temperature of the body (an assumption which needs proof in itself, but which we will accept for the moment). How can we measure the temperature of the blood? If we don't have a thermometer small enough to insert easily into a blood vessel, we might decide to withdraw some blood with a hypodermic needle and then measure it with the most precise thermometer known, but the process of withdrawing the blood may affect its temperature. Suppose we did have a thermometer as tiny as a hypodermic needle, into which blood vessel would we insert it? In other words, does blood in the feet have the same temperature as blood in the brain? Thus, there are aspects of any situation which could affect the result, and many of these aspects are extremely difficult to control. Writing researchers must also be aware of factors which could affect the results of a research project. For example, suppose we think that using a computer facilitates revision of drafts. In planning a research project to investigate this idea, some factors we would have to be watchful for are student alertness when at the computer, fear of computers, prior experience with computers, and poor typing skills, among other things.

COMMON CATEGORIES OF EMPIRICAL RESEARCH

We've already introduced the idea of qualitative and quantitative categories applied to empirical projects. Projects which are predominately *qualitative* are those which do not rely on numbers. For example, personal interviewing (a major strategy for both case study and ethnographic research) is a qualitative methodology. In most cases using personal interviews, little emphasis is placed on being able to count details in order to carry out statistical procedures. Instead, the researcher tries to ask questions that will prompt the interviewee to provide many details, both those that at first seem important and those that seem unimportant. (The importance of certain details may only become apparent after a good deal of information has been collected.)

Another example of qualitative research might be an ethnographic study of some community in an attempt to better understand its culture. In such studies, a researcher often amasses more data about a community than he or she could possibly use in an article reporting on the research. This data could consist of field notes of observations, transcriptions of tape-recorded interviews, activity logs, and so forth.

From all this data, the researcher selects that material which is most helpful in describing important aspects of the community. The researcher then uses quotations, paraphrases, and summaries of the data as evidence in support of the conclusion he or she has reached about the important aspects of the community.

On reading the previous two paragraphs, one of my students commented that a literature review is very similar to a qualitative research project because the purpose of a literature review is to collect and integrate information on all previous relevant work done in the area. As in interviewing, a person doing research for a literature review may collect many articles based on what the titles of the articles seem to promise. Later, the researcher has to sort out which articles are truly relevant and authoritative, and then he or she integrates material from the articles through paraphrases or quotations into discussions of issues. Thus, a literature review is very similar in method to a qualitative study; however, persons doing a literature review rarely plan the details of their method in advance, and the method used to collect information for a literature review is very seldom, if ever, described in the review itself.

A literature review also differs from some empirical studies in at least one essential way: the data for a literature review are usually not collected systematically. For a literature review, the researcher most often tracks down books and articles mentioned elsewhere, sources mentioned by colleagues, articles listed in bibliographies and computer data bases, and so forth. The researcher does not try to set up a plan for collecting a representative random sample of the materials (as a text analysis researcher does), nor can the literature review researcher realistically plan to examine all possible sources. Thus, a typical literature review never contains statements implying that the method used was quantitative. For example, the statement, "Seven out of the ten articles found on this subject were..." implies that the researcher has used some kind of quantitative method (e.g., random sampling) in the search for articles, and that the purpose of the research is a quantitative text analysis rather than a literature review.

Projects that are predominately *quantitative* rely heavily on collecting data that can be counted and statistically analyzed. For example, surveys collect much information that can be easily assigned a numerical value (e.g., 1 for yes and 2 for no). Even open-ended survey questions are frequently quantified when raters are asked to put the answers into one of two or more distinct groups or categories (e.g., 1 for complaints, 2 for compliments). When doing a quantitative text analysis, a researcher should first choose a representative sample to analyze, as do Kreuz, Roberts, Johnson, and Bertus (1996) when they investigate how often figurative language occurs in modern American literature and whether certain types of figurative language tend to occur together. Next, the researcher should count occurrences of the phenomena under study.

To give another example, Stohrer and Pinelli (1981) solicited examples of reports from 611 organizations selected from the membership list of the Society for Technical Communication and the distribution list of NASA. Then, they analyzed a sample (99 reports) to determine which report components (e.g., title page, table of contents, etc.) were used in 50% or more of the reports in the sample. This project, like the Kreuz et al. (1996) project, used survey methodology to select the texts to be analyzed and to conduct the analysis.

Although research projects can be categorized as mainly quantitative or qualitative, many projects use some data of each kind. For example, in an ethnographic study of writing in a particular workplace, researchers might collect field notes describing observed work habits and interviews with the workers (qualitative data), but the researcher might also collect usage time for each employee on each piece of equipment, or the amount of time equipment is unavailable for use because of maintenance or repair (quantitative data). Thus, there are other classification systems that are not based on the qualitative/quantitative distinction. Some of the more common ones are classification by data source and classification by purpose of project.

Classification by Data Source

Because both quantitative and qualitative research strategies are used in many empirical projects, often projects cannot be sorted into just one or the other of these two types. Thus, some authorities divide empirical research into four categories according to the source of the data used: historical, descriptive, experimental, and meta analysis. To illustrate these categories, I will first introduce a ridiculous eyelash example. Then, I will briefly describe an actual piece of empirical research in writing.

Historical Studies

Historical studies refer mostly to work with archival material as the primary source of data. Both qualitative and quantitative methods can be used. For example, suppose you had reason to believe that creative persons tend to pay a lot of attention to their eyelashes. To test this hypothesis, you could examine archival records on famous writers such as Shakespeare, Browning, and Hemingway. You could look through medical records, personal diaries, personal correspondence, and accounts written by contemporaries for any mention of eyelash length. You would not only count the references to eyelashes (quantitative), but you would describe the information provided in the different sources, quoting some and paraphrasing others (qualitative).

On a more serious note, I recently examined 20 years of the proceedings of the annual conference of the Society for Technical Communication to determine what percentage of the papers presented each year were based on empirical research (MacNealy, 1992). I wanted to determine whether there has been any increase in the amount of empirical research over time (quantitative). But I also examined the empirical papers in the proceedings for evidence of good and poor research methodology (qualitative assessment).

Descriptive Studies

In descriptive studies, the researcher attempts to preserve the natural setting when collecting data. Thus, the researcher gives up the goal of trying to control variables.

In this category are both those studies which collect mostly qualitative data (e.g., interviews or field notes in ethnographies and case studies) and those which collect quantitative data (e.g., surveys and text analyses that enable the researcher to identify patterns of behavior). Descriptive studies often provide a rich understanding of some phenomenon, person, or community. When no quantitative data are collected and no statistical procedures are used, the researcher relies on his or her experiences as a participant in the community to help in interpreting the observational data. When making comparisons or considering possible causal relationships, the researcher relies on reasoning skills rather than on statistical methods.

To examine the question of eyelash length and concern over eyelashes among famous authors, you could visit all the authors whose work appeared last year on the *New York Times* list of best sellers. During the visit, you could measure the author's eyelashes (quantitative data), and you could ask in a personal interview questions such as whether the authors are more attracted to people with long eyelashes or not, whether they would be interested in using an eyelash lengthening cream or other substance, and so forth (qualitative data).

A good example of research in writing is a study by Pinelli, Cordle, and McCullough (1985) in which a random sample of technical report writers were asked to submit samples of reports they had written. The researchers then examined 50 of those submitted to see which features were most prevalent: ragged right or justified margins, font type and size, indented vs. non-indented paragraphs, and so forth (quantitative data). In another case, Pinelli, Cordle, Glassman, and Vondran (1984) sent questionnaires to over 1,000 report users to determine which features they preferred (qualitative data). Although answers about preferences are qualitative, the answers can be counted, so this kind of data is sometimes referred to as "quantitative descriptive" (Lauer & Asher, 1988). Perhaps the most famous descriptive research in writing is Heath's (1983) study of children's writing in an ethnographic study of two working class communities, one of which was primarily African American (Tracton) and one Caucasian (Roadville) in the Carolinas. Heath not only examined the children's school writing, but she collected data about the types and frequency of writing done in their homes. You can read more about descriptive research in Chapter 7 on discourse analysis, Chapter 8 on surveys, and Chapters 10, 11, and 12 on qualitative research.

Experimental Studies

In experimental studies, the researcher usually does not try to collect data in natural settings because he or she is very concerned about controlling variables that might provide alternative hypotheses for the findings. Most such studies compare the results between a control group (no treatment given, or treatment given is a placebo) and an experimental group (treatment of interest given). The researcher usually administers treatment or no treatment, tests for results, and compares the results of the two groups with an eye to determining causality. Thus, conditions for data collection are highly specified and somewhat artificial. The data are statistically analyzed to determine what role, if any, chance played in the results. In the eyelash question, you could assign a sample of students to experimental and control groups, and then measure their eyelashes before giving the experimental group an aspirin and the control group a sugar pill each day. At the end of three weeks, you would measure their eyelashes again to see if the aspirin treatment caused any lengthening of the eyelashes. Sometimes, qualitative data are also collected in an experiment because such data can be useful in explaining or illustrating the findings.

A report that exemplifies some of the pitfalls in conducting experimental research is Davis' 1975 paper at the International Technical Communications Conference. Davis reported on three experiments to determine the effect of departures from standards (misspellings, subject/verb agreement problems, long sentences, shifts in point of view, etc.) on the effectiveness of technical documents. One group received a writing that was considered up to standard and the other group received a writing in which standards were not met. Effects were measured in terms of comprehension, reading time, judgment of the author's competence as a writer, and judgment of the author's knowledge of the subject matter. The results were mixed. significant results were found in both directions, but there was some tendency for more positive results from the group who read texts that had not been altered to make them substandard. However, because of the large variety of errors introduced into the substandard texts, it is hard to tell which error (if any) was responsible for the adverse effects. Maybe it was the combination of all of them. To conduct an effective experiment, the researcher must limit the number of variables which could be responsible for the results. You can read more about experimental methodology in Chapters 4 and 5.

Meta Analysis Studies

Meta analysis studies are closely related to experimental studies because meta analysis relies heavily on statistical procedures. These procedures enable the researcher to integrate the data from several different prior empirical research projects in the same area even though the projects used different methodologies and materials. You might be in real trouble if you want to do a meta analysis on eyelash studies because it is unlikely that there are many prior studies to provide the data you will need.

In composition, however, quite a number of experimental studies have been conducted in various areas. In 1986, George Hillocks published a meta analysis of experimental studies in writing to compare results across such dimensions as grade level, mode of instruction, and effects of feedback. To give you an example of his findings, let's consider the issue of instruction that focuses on grammar and mechanics versus instruction that focuses on other aspects of writing such as heuristics for helping students discover what they want to say (e.g., freewriting). Of the 14 studies using grammar in experimental or control conditions, the pre-test to post-test mean effect size was .06—a very low amount indicating almost no effect from the grammar instruction (Hillocks, p. 214). Of the five studies focusing on grammar and mechanics, the effect size was –.29—an amount so far below zero it suggests that the focus on grammar actually *adversely* affected student writing (p. 215). In contrast, the pre-to-post mean effect size for instruction that did not mention grammar (based on 75 studies) was .44, indicating that the procedures helped students write better (Hillocks, (1986), p. 214). In interpreting these statistics, it may be helpful to consider that Lauer and Asher claim that an effect size of .20 to .50 is very respectable, that is, the results should be considered important (Lauer & Asher, (1988), p. 163). As Hillocks explains, the difference in effect sizes regarding instruction in grammar and mechanics is quite significant because the probability of this difference occurring by chance is only one in a million ($p < .000,001$). Most writing researchers accept a finding that has a probability of occurring five times out of 100 as significant ($p < .05$). Thus, Hillocks concludes that grammar and mechanics as a focus of instruction may have a negative effect on students' ability to write. In fact, Hillocks goes on to say "that nearly anything else [as a focus of instruction] is more effective [than focusing on grammar and mechanics] in increasing the quality of writing" (Hillocks, (1986), p. 214). You can read more about meta analysis research in Chapter 6.

Classification by Purpose of Research

Yet another way of categorizing empirical research is based on the purpose of the research or the type of knowledge the research project contributes to the discipline. The major categories are basic, applied, and evaluative.

Basic Research

Basic research projects are often motivated by curiosity, and the questions they try to answer are usually long-range ones. For example, you could probably find out as a matter of curiosity whether *thicker* eyelashes (more lashes per inch) are likely to be *longer* eyelashes, but there really isn't any practical use for such information, at least not now.

In terms of writing research, my study into the stimuli for creative work by literary scholars was a result of curiosity. A colleague from cognitive psychology asked me one day in a casual conversation, "How do those literary types in your department choose the topics they write on?" I admitted that I didn't know. And the more I thought about this question later, the more my curiosity moved me to do something about it. So I interviewed 28 literary scholars. I also looked up research on problem finding in other disciplines. After analyzing the responses I obtained from the interviews, I then began to wonder what their implications were for teaching writing. I could have written up the results simply as information adding to the body of knowledge on problem finding or creativity, but given my own interest in helping students learn to write well, I ended the article with questions about the implications for teaching writing (MacNealy, 1991). Thus, what began as a piece of basic research was reported in a way that somewhat blurred the distinction between basic and applied research.

Applied Research

Applied research is that which tries to answer an immediate question of concern in a particular area. Usually, the researcher is looking for information that can be of practical use, for example, will rubbing eyelashes with cold cream at bedtime each night make them grow thicker and longer? An example of applied research in writing is a project that investigates whether computers facilitate revision. This question arises out of the frustrations of writing teachers who are puzzled by students' inability or lack of desire to revise. One reason experts have advanced for students' poor attempts to revise is that revising requires a lot of work. Therefore, if there is a way to reduce the workload, students might be more willing to revise and be more successful at it. Revision is an area that several researchers have been looking into, but the results have been mixed to date. For example, Duin and Jorn (1989) investigated the effects of collaboration aided by telecommunications. They found that students in the experimental group (the one using telecommunications in their collaborative efforts) spent significantly more time planning and revising than did the control group, but independent holistic evaluations of the writings produced by both groups revealed no significant difference in their quality.

Evaluative Research

Evaluative research projects are usually undertaken to evaluate some procedure or product. This research could be considered applied, but instead of looking for possible future answers to immediate concerns, evaluative researchers check to see if a product meets specifications. Here, for example, you could research the staying power and appeal of several types of mascara. Evaluative research is often funded by major manufacturers. For example, producers of computer software are very interested in the usability of the manuals they must provide with their software. Manuals are an expensive accessory; if they are not satisfactory to users, the product will usually be unsatisfactory as well. A famous example of this problem is Coleco's Adam computer, one of the first personal computers on the market. The computer was placed in stores in the fall, and the company experienced terrific sales as Christmas approached. In January, customers returned the computers in droves, to the point where the Adam division was forced into bankruptcy. The reason most customers gave for their dissatisfaction was inability to operate the computer; the manuals, they said, were hard to follow. Now large computer companies budget sizable amounts for testing manuals on groups of typical users before printing manuals to include with the software.

A project in writing research that well illustrates the evaluative approach is Duin's 1990 study comparing manual types: use of a minimal manual versus use of instructional cards to teach novices how to use a telecommunications system. Subjects were randomly assigned to the two conditions, and performance was measured in terms of time on task, error rate, and questions asked. Duin also administered an attitude questionnaire at the end of the experimental period and a follow-up assessment of frequency of use of the system. Although subjects in the cards condition made more typing errors, they were better at manual/display coordination, and they used the system more and felt more comfortable with it in the follow-up task. Otherwise, there was no significant difference between groups.

Developmental and Instrumental Research

Developmental and instrumental research play a minor role in research in writing. Developmental research attempts to build or develop new products. In these projects, researchers design and test prototypes or models (e.g., Should false eyelashes be made of human hair or horse hair?). In this respect, developmental research into computer software can provide insights into problems in writing (e.g., Does the shape of the computer keys affect the number of typing errors?). Instrumental research is done for the sake of demonstrating competence in research methods. For example, the professor in your research strategies class might tell you to design a study of eyelash length even though no one is really interested in the results of such a study. Although instrumental research projects are sometimes required as part of the work done toward a degree in the sciences, I am not acquainted with any degree-granting programs in writing which require instrumental research. In my classes, I often ask students to design a hypothetical research project, but I suggest that they do so as a sort of design trial run in an area of interest. Sometimes these designs are later modified by the student and actually carried out, but that is not the purpose of the assignment.

Action Research

Action Research has only recently been used in research in writing. In the past, it appeared more often in other disciplines such as marketing, education, and the social sciences. In this type of research, there is a double-faceted goal: to find answers to questions while possibly influencing the subjects to think or behave in new ways. For example, a researcher could design a survey to find out about mascara buying habits while also hoping to make consumers aware of Brand X mascara in the hopes that they might then buy it. Or a social science researcher might collect information about attitudes toward people with physical disabilities while also intending to help the respondents see that lack of handicap access in buildings needs to be rectified. In writing, a teacher may want to determine whether computers facilitate revision while at the same time encouraging students to see that revision is an important component of the writing process.

In recent years, action research techniques have been used in research in writing by feminists and teacher/researchers. Both groups are interested not only in acquiring new knowledge but also in effecting change. Feminists try to raise awareness to stimulate changes in social and economic policies which hinder the development of the potential of women as well as other groups which are traditionally marginalized by society. Similarly, teacher/researchers hope to change their own classrooms and the school systems in which they are located so that their students become participants in planning and carrying out their own education. Most teacher/researchers also are interested in learning from their students in order to improve their teaching practices. You can read more on these topics in Chapter 12.

REFERENCES

Bourg, T. (1996). The role of emotion, empathy and text structure in children's and adult text comprehension. In R. J. Kreuz & M. S. MacNealy (Eds.), *Empirical approaches to literature and aesthetics* (pp. 241–260). Norwood, NJ: Ablex.

Davis, R. M. (1975). Does expression make a difference? Three experiments. In *Proceedings of the 22nd International Technical Communication Conference* (pp. 171–177). Arlington, VA: Society for Technical Communication.

Duin, A. H. (1990). Minimal manuals vs. elaboration in documentation: Centering on the learner. In *Proceedings of the 37th International Technical Communication Conference* (pp. RT:77-RT:80). Arlington, VA: Society for Technical Communication.

Duin, A. H., & Jorn, L. A. (1989). Writing in communication contexts: Research on collaboration and telecommunication. In *Proceedings of the 36th International Technical Communication Conference* (pp. RT:11-RT:14). Arlington, VA: Society for Technical Communication.

Heath, S. B. (1983). *Ways with words.* Cambridge: Cambridge University Press.

Hillocks, G., Jr. (1986). *Research on written composition: New directions for teaching.* Urbana, IL: National Conference on Research in English and ERIC/RCS.

Kreuz, R. J., Roberts, R. M., Johnson, B. K., & Bertus, E. L. (1996). Figurative language occurrence and co-occurrence in contemporary literature. In R. J. Kreuz & M. S. MacNealy (Eds.), *Empirical approaches to literature and aesthetics* (pp. 83–97). Norwood, NJ: Ablex.

Lauer, J. M., & Asher, J. W. (1988). *Composition research: Empirical designs.* New York: Oxford University Press.

MacNealy, M. S. (1991). Creativity in literary scholars. In E. Ibsch, D. Schram, and G. Steen (Eds.), *Empirical studies of literature* (pp. 281–288). Amsterdam: Rodolpi.

MacNealy, M. S. (1992). Research in technical communication: A view of the past and a challenge for the future. *Technical Communication, 39,* 533–551.

Pinelli, T., Cordle, V. M., Glassman, M., & Vondran, R. F. (1984). Preferences on technical report format: Results of a survey. *Proceedings of the 31st International Professional Communications Conference* (pp. RET:65-RET:68). Arlington, VA: Society for Technical Communication.

Pinelli, T., Cordle, V. M., & McCullough, R. (1985). Typography and layout of technical reports: Survey of current practices. In *Proceedings of the 32nd International Professional Communications Conference* (pp. RET:49-RET:52). Arlington, VA: Society for Technical Communication.

Press Services. (1993, July 22). EPA recommends ban on smoking at home, work. *The Commercial Appeal,* pp. A1, A11.

Stohrer, F., & Pinelli, T. (1981). The technical report as an effective medium for information transmittal. In *Proceedings of the 28th International Technical Communication Conference* (pp. E:99–E:101). Arlington, VA: Society for Technical Communication.

Tenenbaum, A. B. (1977). Task-dependent effects of organization and content upon comprehension of prose. *Journal of Educational Psychology, 69,* 528–536.

OTHER USEFUL RESOURCES

Jaeger, R. M. (1990). *Statistics: A spectator sport* (2nd ed.). Newbury Park, CA: Sage.

Kraemer, H. C., & Thiemann, S. (1987). *How many subjects? Statistical power analysis in research.* Newbury Park, CA: Sage.

Sommer, B., & Sommer, R. (1997). *A practical guide to behavioral research: Tools and techniques* (4th ed.). New York: Oxford University Press.

▶ 4

Concepts Basic to Quantitative Research

WHAT IS QUANTITATIVE RESEARCH?

Quantitative research uses numbers in collecting and interpreting data. The two primary methods of quantitative research are experimental studies (including both true and quasi experiments and meta analysis) and quantitative descriptive studies (including surveys and discourse analysis) all of which are described more fully in subsequent chapters. Fundamental to good quantitative research methodology are five basic concepts: reliability, validity, randomization, probability, and the null hypothesis. As you read further, you will encounter these concepts over and over. Therefore, it seems worthwhile to sort them out now, before we go any further in our discussion of empirical research. Reliability and validity are qualities that affect the degree to which scholars grant credibility and importance to the results of a quantitative research project. These qualities are also important, but to a lesser extent, in qualitative research (Kirk & Miller, 1986). Scholars examining your work will consider how reliable the findings are—(i.e., Would similar research projects produce similar results?). Further, in examining your findings, scholars will ask whether the procedures you used can be considered accurate measures for the phenomena you tried to measure and whether there are alternative hypotheses arising from a problem in the design of your project. The validity of your findings is based on the answers to these questions.

   Thus, for findings of quantitative research projects to be widely accepted by knowledgeable people, research projects must be carefully designed to minimize threats to the reliability and validity of the findings. Although the two aspects are sometimes interrelated, they are easier to understand if considered separately. Therefore, this chapter first considers threats to reliability and then threats to validity.

Interestingly, many threats to validity and reliability are greatly reduced by the use of random sampling, the third concept I will discuss in this chapter. Finally, I discuss the concepts of probability and null hypothesis because they are central to experimental design.

RELIABILITY

Quantitative research results are counted as reliable to the degree that the same results will be found when the project is repeated with similar people in a similar situation. Thus, the threat that must be eliminated or controlled in the research design is the possibility that the findings are idiosyncratic, in other words, resulting from some factor in the design that cannot be replicated in a subsequent project. Reliability contributes to validity because it affects the degree to which one can generalize from findings.

Perhaps an inherent threat to reliability can best be illustrated if we look for a moment at a non-quantitative empirical research method—the case study. A case study, by nature, is an investigation of a specific event or person or small group of people at a particular period, so it is rare that a case study can be replicated exactly. That is not to say that a case study cannot make an important contribution to knowledge in a field, but one must be careful not to generalize case study findings because a second case study carried out in exactly the same way may produce different results simply because it was carried out a little later in time or with different subjects (Kirk & Miller, 1986).

On the other hand, experimental studies are frequently replicated. And if the replication does not succeed, the original researcher's work is challenged (e.g., scientists tried, but could not replicate the cold fusion findings). Of course, a replication of a quantitative study carried out some years after the original may also produce different results because people, conditions, and language change. For example, if you carried out two writing research projects using identical methods in the same school but separated by 20 years, you would probably get at least slightly different results. For one thing, neighborhoods change, and economic factors influence how much access students have to resources that could affect their writing skills. For another thing, language changes—words such as "bad" when used by young people today mean something entirely different from what they meant 20 years ago. However, when we talk of the reliability of the results of an experiment, we generally mean that if we repeated that experiment in a comparatively short period of time with a very similar group of people, we would probably get very similar results.

An example of reliability is standardized tests such as the SAT and ACT, which are considered reliable predictors of student performance in college because they have been given over and over to thousands of students, and the results have been quite similar. However, some researchers have raised questions about whether these tests (and others such as IQ tests) are biased against some segments of the general population. Certainly, one would want to use additional information and not just test scores to determine who should qualify for admittance to college or some special program. However, because standardized tests have established some reputation for reliability, you might want to consider using one as part of a particular research project rather than designing a test yourself. For example, if you believe that creativity is closely linked to ability to revise, you may want to obtain the Torrance Tests of Creative Thinking (Lexington, MA: Personnel Press) to use as one of your measuring instruments. You might also want to search the literature (especially dissertations) to see if you can locate a good system for evaluating revisions such as that devised by Faigley and Witte (1981). The advantage to you is that these measurement instruments have already established some degree of reliability.

On the other hand, it may be that you cannot find a standardized test to use to measure the construct you are interested in. In such a case, you may be able to adapt one that you find in the literature, again taking advantage of whatever reliability the previous test has established. A good example of adapting previous measures is a recent study by Charney, Newman, and Palmquist of epistemological style and attitudes toward writing (1995). For their measurement tool, these researchers made some changes to an instrument used in a previous study (Palmquist & Young, 1992) which in turn had adapted some items from a well-established test of writing anxiety—the Daly Miller Test (1975). When Charney et al. explained their methodology, they gave the results of a statistical test they had run to see how closely the results of their test matched the results of the earlier tests—in other words, they carefully established the reliability of their measurement instrument.

The reliability of the measurement tool is often an issue in empirical research. For example, in a study that compares the effect of some treatment (e.g., use of a word processor) on the ability to do a task (e.g., revise an essay), there has to be some way to measure the results. In this revision example, researchers would probably not ask a teacher to grade the papers and use that grade as a measurement of the treatment effects because grades given by different teachers on the same paper are rarely the same. Instead, the researchers would probably use holistic rating procedures in which a group of trained raters would holistically rate a stack of essays (some of which were revised with a word processor and some without). Holistic rating of student writing was pioneered by the Educational Testing Service, and variations of the process are used in many disciplines. Basically, each rater is trained by reading papers which have been chosen as models of various levels of skillful writing. Then each rater reads the papers to be evaluated and assigns them a score (usually between 1 and 4). In some cases, three raters read each paper and the scores are averaged; in other cases, two raters read each paper, and if their scores differ, a third reader is used. Generally, if the raters are well-trained, the scores of the different raters match most of the time.

Later the researcher may also analyze the holistic judgments made on the essays to see if the raters were consistent with each other in the ratings they gave to the essays. In such cases, when researchers report their findings, they usually determine the degree of inter-rater reliability with a statistical procedure and report this score as well as the findings on the essays.

Finally, consistency of results is also a concern *within* a research study: the findings are considered reliable if the results in one area of a test are consistent with those in another. For example, some standardized tests of personality include questions that essentially measure the same thing (e.g., truthfulness). In this instance, a question measuring truthfulness will often be included in a section in which subjects are asked to choose which of the several actions listed they would take in a given scenario. Then, in another section of the test, subjects might be asked to check off (from a list that includes truthfulness) those characteristics which describe themselves. Or subjects could be asked to rank order a list of characteristics indicating those that are most important in choosing a friend—and the list will include truthfulness. If the test is reliable, the subjects' answers in these various areas should match.

In general, researchers can do much to control the reliability of a study by using careful research designs. In particular, methods for selecting the subjects who will be studied affect reliability. Random selection of subjects will be discussed more fully later in this chapter. For now, remember that it is a powerful tool in assuring that your findings will be considered reliable.

VALIDITY

This aspect of quantitative research is more complex because there are two types of validity, internal and external, each with several subtypes (See Figure 4-1). In simple terms, validity is the degree to which a specific procedure actually measures what it is intended to measure. Threats to *internal validity* can be described as issues affecting the determination of causal relationships; in short, these threats are sources of rival hypotheses or rival explanations of the results found in the study. Threats to *external validity* consist of aspects of the study affecting the degree to which the situation or subjects are representative of the population in question; in short, they are those factors which affect the generalizability of the findings (i.e., the degree to which one can generalize from the behavior of the research subjects to the behavior of the population of interest or to other populations). While both internal and external validity are important to consider in designing a quantitative research project, threats to internal validity are most important because they determine whether the findings can even be considered valid for the specific subjects in the research project, let alone those in the general population.

Threats to Internal Validity

Because internal validity is so crucial to good research, the next several pages are devoted to specific threats to internal validity. Most of these threats affect research that investigates the results of a treatment. In such projects, it is necessary to compare

---

Threats to Validity

Internal   *External*

- History   • Bias
- Maturation   —Subject Bias
- Instrumentation/Measurement Tools   —Self-Selection
- Statistical Regression to the Mean   —Subject/Researcher Relationship
- Mortality   • Random Sampling Fluctuation
- Diffusion   • Interaction Effects
- Testing Effects   —Pre-Test/Treatment Interaction
- Treatment Interactions   —Treatment/Selection Interaction
    —Testing/Treatment Interaction   • Specificity of Variables
    —Treatment/Selection Interaction   • Reactive Arrangements
- Differential Selection   —Subject/Testing Reaction
- Selection Interactions   —Setting/Treatment Reaction
    —Maturation/Selection Interaction   —Multiple Treatment Interference
    —History/Selection Interaction

FIGURE 4-1   **Threats to Validity: Internal and External**

two groups, so these groups should be shown to be equal before the treatment is administered in order to reduce the possibility of an alternative explanation for the results of the treatment. Random assignment of subjects to the experimental and control conditions usually resolves threats to internal validity, but sometimes researchers use scores from standardized tests such as the SAT or ACT to further establish that the subjects in the experimental and control groups were essentially the same before treatment was administered to the experimental group. In such a case, the experimenters do not administer the standardized test to their subjects, but rather they obtain the scores subjects previously made on these tests from their school's records office. A good example of this use of standardized tests is the Wallace and Hayes (1991) study.

To counter threats to internal validity, it is also necessary to control for events other than the treatment that could affect the behavior of the subjects. If this definition seems a little vague to you right now, the examples provided with the description of each threat in the pages that follow should help you grasp the concept of internal validity. Moreover, understanding the various threats to internal validity can make you a more critical reader of research reports. You will soon be identifying faulty research designs with labels such as *history, mortality, selection,* and so forth

History

This threat refers to an event or events outside an experiment (or in some cases, events inside the experiment other than the treatment under investigation) that may affect subject behavior during the experiment. For example, one could ask whether the poor quality of the revision efforts in a particular project happens to be the result of the school cafeteria not being open for breakfast. In another example, if the control group met at 8:00 A.M. and the experimental group met at 10:00 A.M., one might suspect that the poorer performance of the experimental group was due to the big test most of them had just had in their 8:00 or 9:00 classes. A history threat could also happen during the experiment if something occurred in one of two classes that was likely to have affected the students' performance. For example, if one of the students in the experimental class clowned around to the point that everyone was distracted, the experimental class might do more poorly than the control group in spite of the very good teaching techniques being tested. This threat can be controlled by having four or more groups meeting at consecutive or very similar times, in which case, if something occurred in one of the classes that could affect performance, there would still remain an experimental and control group that hadn't been affected. Most of the time, you will not have to worry about a history threat taking place during an experiment involving two or more classrooms if all teachers stick to the prepared script and maintain a friendly attitude.

Additionally, if the research project consists of two or more data collection points or times of observation (as in a pre-test, post-test), then a researcher should consider that the longer the time between the data collection points, the greater the possibility of an effect from an outside event. Thus, history rather than treatment can provide a strong rival hypothesis (i.e., alternative explanation) for the effects found. Generally, random assignment of subjects to conditions, testing subjects individually instead of in groups, and varying the times when data are collected will control for history; but if an event is likely to have affected the performance of all subjects (as when the death of a popular hero distracts the subjects to the point that they perform badly no matter which condition they have been assigned to), the researcher may want to replicate the experiment at a later time with another set of subjects.

Maturation

This threat refers to changes that have occurred in subjects between a pre-test and post-test due to biological or psychological processes unconnected with external events (e.g., growing older, more tired, or more bored, and so forth). The longer the period between the tests, the greater the possibility that maturation will affect the behavior of the subjects. For example, a writing researcher could count errors in subjects' writings at the beginning of the semester and again at the end, but the researcher would have to be careful not to assume that fewer errors in the writings at the end of the semester were solely a result of the teaching methods. If the subjects were elementary school students, maturation in eye-hand coordination could account for fewer misspellings, especially if the misspellings were largely due to accidents in transcription rather than lack of spelling knowledge.

In another example of maturation effects, the better spelling in the post-test could be due to psychological factors. Perhaps at the end of the semester students were less anxious about writing, so they made fewer transcription errors. Generally, random assignment to experimental and control conditions will reduce the threat of maturation because any effects of maturation should show up in both groups, thus negating its influence and helping to establish that the difference between the groups at the end is due to the treatment.

Instrumentation/Measurement Tools

This threat to validity results from the possibility that changes in the measuring instrument between a pre- and post-test could affect the results. For example, in trying to determine the quality of essays produced, experimenters often use raters as the measurement instrument. These raters are trained to grade holistically or to grade on the basis of a set of criteria. Once the raters have been trained to use the system, it is not safe to assume that history or maturation have not affected the raters between the time of the rating of the first set of essays and that of the second. Raters can become tired, impatient, or even more experienced, so they may make swifter and thus less accurate judgments in the second rating session. One way to control for this effect is to wait until the experiment is over and then randomly mix the pre- and post-treatment essays so that, even if the raters have to work in two or more rating sessions to get through all the papers, they will grade some papers from each set each time they work (without knowing which papers came from which session). Usually, experimenters also train or rehearse the raters before each rating session to try to get them to achieve consistency in their ratings. Using statistical procedures, the experimenter can also show that the raters have a high inter-rater reliability that increases the internal validity of the project.

Mechanical instruments can also wear out or malfunction during the second set of measurements. Since a comparison of two groups rests on all things being equal except for the treatment, measurement tools should be essentially the same for post-tests as for pre-tests.

Statistical Regression to the Mean

This mathematical phenomenon has been demonstrated by research to be a threat to internal validity. Simply stated, this threat is caused by the tendency of post-test scores to shift toward the mean. For example, in any subject pool there are usually subjects whose scores fall at the extreme ends of the bell curve. If a mean were calculated for the group of low scorers on a pre-test and another mean calculated for the group of high scorers on that test, those two group means will shift toward the mean for the whole group in the post-test. The mean for the group at the low end of the pre-test scale will rise a bit in the post-test, and the mean for the group at the high end of the pre-test scale will drop a bit in the post-test. Experts in statistics claim that this shift is a result of inaccuracy of the measurement instrument; remember that no measurement instrument is perfect, and the error rate of measurement instruments follows a predictable curve.

For example, if you believe that assigning multiple spelling exercises over several weeks will improve the ability of poor spellers in the third grade, you will need to take into account the possibility of regression to the mean. In other words, the mean post-test spelling score for the poor spellers is going to rise, at least a little, above their mean pre-test score no matter whether you give them spelling exercises or not because of the tendency of the mean score of a subgroup at either end of the scale to shift toward the mean score for the whole population—a mean score that will be higher than the mean for the subgroup because the mean score of the whole group includes the good as well as the poor spellers in the third grade. Likewise, the mean post-test score of an experimental group at the other end of the scale (i.e., the good spellers) will drop a little, shifting toward the mean of the overall group. Because regression to the mean is often seen in projects that focus on subjects clustered at one or the other end of a scale (e.g., remedial students or gifted students), you will probably want to consult a statistician if you are designing a project involving students whose scores tend to be grouped at one end of a particular scale (e.g., low ACT or SAT scores).

Mortality
This threat to internal validity occurs when subjects drop out of an experiment between the pre- and post-tests. The problem is that the subjects who dropped out may have dropped out for a similar reason; thus, the remaining subjects in the groups being compared may no longer be equal in an area affecting the results. For example, if you are studying the effects of a teaching strategy on student control of grammatical error and the subjects who dropped out of one group are the ones who tend to make the most grammatical errors, or the ones who tend to worry about the number of errors they make, the group with the dropouts is now a special group of either those who tend to make few errors or those who don't worry much about their errors. Thus, results could be skewed so that a possible explanation of the results is that make-up of the group, rather than treatment, is the cause of the results.

Mortality is a particularly serious threat when the dropouts tend to be those from one group, either the experimental or the control group, because then you would be comparing dissimilar groups. Mortality is especially serious if the reasons for dropout are similar within a group and possibly related to performance (e.g., test anxiety). However, if the dropouts resulted from events unrelated to the investigation (e.g., hospitalization, new job, or car trouble), then mortality is not a serious threat. Thus, it will often be beneficial for you to track down the reasons subjects dropped out of your experiment. In any case, responsible researchers always report the amount of mortality when writing up the results of their study.

If reasons for dropout are potentially related to the research question, one possible way to argue that mortality hasn't compromised your results is to show that the subjects who dropped out of the control group are very similar to those who dropped out of the treatment group by showing that their pretest scores are similar. Or, the effects of mortality can be reduced by showing (perhaps with scores from standardized tests) that the subjects remaining in the two groups are very similar. As with other threats to internal validity, random assignment to conditions also helps counter threats from mortality. Random assignment or selection of subjects is so important to experimental validity that I devote a whole section to randomization later in this chapter.

Diffusion

This threat to validity (a threat that is very hard to control) occurs when the subjects are in close contact with each other outside the experiment (e.g., freshman students who frequently see each other in classes or in dorms) because then their conversations can contaminate the performance of other subjects. For example, when there is limited lab space, subjects are usually tested individually or in small groups at various times over a period of a couple of weeks. If the subjects who were early participants discuss their experiences in the study with friends, those friends' knowledge of the research procedures or research questions could influence the way they behave when they participate in a later session of the same experiment. Or if a teaching technique is being tested and the teachers involved mention it to friends who try it out in their classrooms, discussion between students in the two classes could bias the performances of the students in the study and thus skew the results.

Researchers often try to control the threat to validity from diffusion by asking participants to refrain from discussing any aspects of their experience for a limited time (e.g., two weeks); however, cooperation with the request may vary according to levels of maturity, peer pressure, and individual personalities. Jaeger (1990) suggests that teachers are more likely than factory workers to cooperate in avoiding possible diffusion because they understand the reason for doing so, but I don't know of any research that supports this belief.

Some researchers try to control for diffusion by putting all subjects in the same room at the same time. Still, this arrangement can also pose a reactive threat to the generalizability of the results (*external* validity) because subjects can have their performance affected by the proximity of other subjects. For example, when you ask a roomful of subjects to revise a piece of text, if several subjects complete the task quickly and leave the room, the subjects remaining may hurry through their task rather than doing it in the way they usually would.

Testing Effects

This threat often results from repeating or taking similar tests. Research has shown that most subjects do a little better the second time they take an achievement or personality test (Campbell & Stanley, 1966, p. 9). Thus, the researcher must control for this effect when designing pre- and post-tests. Often, researchers design several versions of a test so that subjects don't repeat a particular test as the post-test. However, preliminary trials of the separate versions of a test are needed to show that the different versions of the test are truly equal. Also, random assignment to control and experimental conditions will help reduce this threat. If the number of different versions of the test are limited, the researcher can reduce the threat from testing by splitting the groups (randomly) and counterbalancing the tests as is illustrated in Figure 4-2.

Testing effects have also been found to result from just the experience of participating in an experiment. You don't have to worry too much about effects on internal validity if subjects in *both* the experimental and control groups are changed in some way (e.g., made nervous by their participation in the pre-test) because both groups will be essentially the same before the treatment and post-test are given. However, testing effects from pre-tests can affect the generalizability of the findings, as will be discussed in the section on external validity.

Testing/Treatment Interaction

In the case of this type of testing threat, the pre-test sensitizes the subjects in some way so that the effects of the treatment are either exacerbated or diminished. For example, suppose you wanted to know whether a teaching technique of giving exercises to simulate reader response would help professional writers become more aware of readers' needs when they plan their writing. In your research design, you first plan to measure how attuned writers are to readers' needs with a pre-test before introducing the teaching technique of simulation exercises; then you administer the simulation exercises; and finally, you administer a post-test to find out how attuned subjects are to needs of prospective readers. In other words, your design looks like the one in Figure 4-3.

For the pre-test, you ask a group of writers to read a description of a writing task and then fill out a questionnaire on how they would carry out the task. One of the questions on the questionnaire asks which of the following they usually consider when planning a piece of writing: how the reader will use the document, the reader's educational level, how to arrange the document so the reader can find information easily, and so forth. Next, you involve the experimental or treatment group in a simulation of reader response. Finally, for the post-test, you give *all* the subjects a written description of a specific writing task and ask them to plan their writing aloud

Control Group (n = 100)	Group A (n = 50)	Group B (n = 50)
	Pre-Test = Test #1	Pre-Test = Test #2
	Post-Test = Test #2	Post-Test = Test #1
Treatment Group (n = 100)	Group A (n = 50)	Group B (n = 50)
	Pre-Test = Test #1	Pre-Test = Test #2
	Post-Test = Test #2	Post-Test = Test #1

FIGURE 4-2   **A Counter-Balanced Research Design**

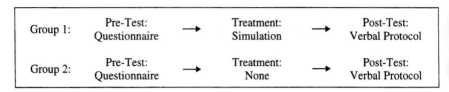

| Group 1: | Pre-Test: Questionnaire | → | Treatment: Simulation | → | Post-Test: Verbal Protocol |
| Group 2: | Pre-Test: Questionnaire | → | Treatment: None | → | Post-Test: Verbal Protocol |

FIGURE 4-3   **A Pre-Test/Post-Test Design**

(verbal protocol). In the written description, you give enough details (e.g., educational level of the readers and probable use of the document) so that the writers can consider their readers' needs when planning. In this case, you may find that the subjects will immediately see a connection between the question about readers' needs on the pre-test and the details about the readers in the description of the writing task; and based on this connection, the subjects will all say a lot more on readers' needs in their protocols than they would normally. The result could be that there is very little difference in the amount of attention to readers' needs between the treatment and control groups because the pre-test sensitized the subjects to your research question. (This design could also cause a threat to external validity or generalizability of the results as will be discussed below.)

One way to avoid the possibility of the rival hypothesis that the pre-test sensitized the subjects to the treatment is to drop the pre-test and do what is called post-test only. In such a case, your research design (a post-test-only design) would look like that in Figure 4-4. If the subjects have been randomly assigned to the two groups, you can assume that they were equal before the treatment, so any difference in the post-test should be due to treatment. In many cases, a post-test only design is the best choice a researcher can make given his or her research question (Campbell & Stanley, 1966).

Treatment/Selection Interaction
This threat to validity can occur with a post-test only design if the control group receives nothing in place of the treatment. To illustrate this threat, let's consider the notion that an aspirin a day might help writers make fewer usage errors. If you gave aspirin to one group and nothing to the other, there is a possibility that merely receiving *some* kind of treatment caused the one group to do better than the other (Hawthorne effect). To reduce this threat, you might give the control subjects a placebo

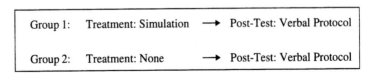

| Group 1: | Treatment: Simulation | → | Post-Test: Verbal Protocol |
| Group 2: | Treatment: None | → | Post-Test: Verbal Protocol |

FIGURE 4-4   **Post-Test Only Design**

(the strategy in medical research in which a pill is made of an inactive ingredient to look and taste like the pill being tested). Or in the experiment to test the effect of reader response simulation exercises described above, notice that the control group was given no treatment. To eliminate the treatment/selection interaction, you could give the control group a treatment placebo by giving them a task commonly assigned by writing teachers (e.g., a set of usage exercises) to do before the post-test. The research design would look like that in Figure 4-5. The trick in this situation is to design the placebo so that both groups have experienced a treatment, but the placebo treatment is a very ordinary treatment—one from which no effects would be expected, as is the case with usage exercises, and the treatments are different enough that there is a real possibility for different results. This design is also often used to test which of two choices (in curricula, document format, etc.) is better. One difficulty with the design is that there is no way to measure the *amount* of gain in skills or awareness.

Another answer to the treatment/selection problem, the *Solomon Four-Group Design* shown in Figure 4-6, is more powerful, but also a little more complex. This design permits the experimenter to measure the gain from pre- to post-test, and it controls for both effects of pre-test and for pre-test/treatment interaction. To measure the results of the gain, you would compare combined results of groups 1 and 2 with combined results of groups 3 and 4. To control for pre-test/treatment interaction, you would check to see if the results of groups 1 and 3 (treatment group with pre-test and treatment group without pre-test) are the same, and if the results of groups 2 and 4 (Pre-test/No Treatment, and No Pre-test/No Treatment) are the same; if they are, then any difference in gains between the two sets of combined groups is not due to interaction between pre-test and treatment.

Differential Selection

This threat to internal validity occurs in studies that compare two groups when there is a possibility that the groups are not similar *before* the treatment. If the groups are different before the treatment, then it is difficult to argue that the *treatment* caused a difference in the results of the experiment. Random assignment of subjects to conditions controls for threats to internal validity from selection. Differential selection is particularly a problem when the research project investigates the effectiveness of classroom techniques because students are not assigned to classes randomly. For example, in comparing the ability to revise among students in two different classes

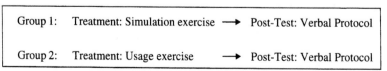

FIGURE 4-5   **Post-Test Only Design with Placebo**

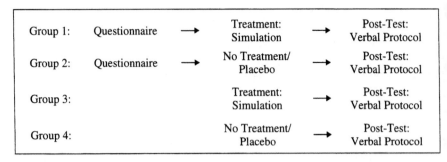

FIGURE 4-6   **Solomon Four-Group Design**

in freshman composition, a researcher needs to be aware of the possibility that the time the class meets could result in dissimilar populations in the two classes. It is possible that certain types of students sign up for early classes and other types sign up for later classes. As an illustration, consider that at some schools, students with good grades are allowed to register early; thus, it is possible that classes meeting at a popular time (e.g., 10:00 A.M.) have more students with a higher motivation or higher IQ than students in less popular class times (e.g., 8:00 A.M.). So if the treatment is given to the 10:00 class, and they do better than the students in the 8:00 class, it could be that the two groups were not equal *before* the treatment.

The ideal solution to this hazard is to randomly assign the students *in each class* to the treatment and control groups so that each group has students from each class. But, you may ask, how can only half the class be exposed to the procedure being tested while the other half (the control group) does not receive the treatment? One answer is to divide each class into two groups to which students are randomly assigned, and then take one group out of the classroom for a limited period. However, then there is the threat from students being aware that some classmates are receiving different treatment (reactive arrangement, a threat that will be discussed under external validity). But studies can be designed to circumvent these problems.

For example, in a study I conducted with Reta Douglas (Douglas & MacNealy, 1993), we were able to split each of four classes in the study into two random groups of approximately half the class each: A and B. We were careful not to mention that the groups would receive different types of training; we simply removed one group at a time to go to the computer lab, explaining that the lab was too small to accommodate the whole class at one time. In some classes, group A (who received training with written instructions) was taken to the computer lab to receive training on the computer on a Tuesday and was asked to carry out a writing task (testing the training) the following Tuesday. On Thursday of the same weeks, we took the other half of that class to the lab for training and testing. During the lab sessions, the regular classroom teachers led students remaining in the classroom in peer feedback on drafts of a paper in progress. So every member of the class received training in the same week and testing in the same week. However, we did not refer to the second visit as a testing visit. In other classes, Group B (who received training with oral instructions) went on Tuesdays and Group A on Thursdays, so we counter-balanced for the effect of the day of the week. Thus, our experimental groups (A—those who received written instructions) and control groups (B—those who received oral instructions) were set up as shown in Figure 4-7.

Because students were highly focused on learning to write with computers and because the treatment in the computer lab varied only slightly, students were not aware that they were in an experimental or control group. Notice, also, that because we had four each of control and experimental groups and that we used counterbalancing to schedule the groups into the lab on different days and times, we controlled for history affecting either group A or B.

Of course, some experiments involve longer periods than two one-hour sessions, one week apart, in which case it is not feasible to split a class into two groups. In this instance, researchers do use entire classes as experimental and control groups. Usually, researchers in these projects try to minimize the effects of differential selection by using standardized test scores to show that the students in the two classes were similar before the treatment. In such cases, it is important to show that students in the two classes or two groups of classes are similar in *a way that relates to the area being researched.* For example, in a study investigating writing ability, it would be pointless to try to show that students in the two groups are similar because they have eyelashes that are similar in length because there is no evidence to link eyelash length to writing ability. Thus, as I mentioned earlier, researchers in writing often use SAT or ACT verbal scores for this purpose (see, for example, Wallace & Hayes, 1991—a study discussed in more detail in Chapter 5), but of course, obtaining these scores requires permission from university authorities. The threat to validity from differential selection can also be reduced by including several classes rather than just comparing one intact class to another.

Selection Interaction

This threat to internal validity results when non-random selection procedures pose the possibility that one group had some potential to outperform the other in the area

	Tuesday in the lab	Thursday in the lab
Section 004 at 8:00 A.M.	Group A (written)	Group B (oral)
Section 005 at 9:00 A.M.	Group B (oral)	Group A (written)
Section 006 at 10:00 A.M.	Group A (written)	Group B (oral)
Section 007 at 11:00 A.M.	Group B (oral)	Group A (written)

FIGURE 4-7   **Research Design for Douglas & MacNealy, 1993**

being tested. For example, in a *selection/maturation interaction* there is a possibility of a different level of maturation in subjects in either the control or treatment group. As an illustration, consider an experiment that compared performance on end-of-term tests at two universities, one of which operated on the semester system and the other on the quarter system. Because semesters can last 15 weeks and quarters ten weeks, students in the semester condition will be more experienced in certain areas than the students in the quarter condition by five weeks even though time in class was the same because the semester students met for one hour twice a week and the quarter students met for one hour three times a week. This difference creates a threat to validity from a selection/maturation interaction.

To control for the effect of selection/maturation interaction, *individuals* rather than whole classes should be randomly assigned to conditions. However, if random assignment is impossible, then researchers should consider whether some factor such as maturation may influence the performance of a certain segment of the population being investigated. Thus, in the case of semester versus quarter classes, the researcher who can't randomly assign individual students to conditions will be careful to put both a semester and quarter class in each condition.

Another possible selection interaction is termed *history/selection interaction* which is what happens when a disruptive or distracting event occurs while a whole group is gathered for a post-test. The event, rather than the treatment, then becomes a possible explanation for the results. For example, suppose that during a post-test, such as an essay test, one subject in the control group fainted. The other students in that group could become so anxious that they do poorly on the test; thus, the performance of the experimental group (the group which received the treatment) could look much better than it otherwise would when compared to the performance of the control group. The solution is to test subjects individually rather than in groups.

Threats to External Validity

External validity is concerned with generalizability: Do the results of a particular study apply beyond conditions of that study? Are the results applicable to other persons or in other contexts? Generalizability is obviously of particular importance to applied research, but it is also a matter of concern in basic or evaluative research. Although basic research is often carried out to satisfy a researcher's curiosity, readers of research reports often see possible applications to practical situations. For example, my study of the source of creativity in literary scholars (1991) was undertaken as a result of curiosity. Readers of this study might decide to try to help freshman students become better writers by teaching them to be alert to the kinds of dissonances I identified in the study. Likewise, reports of findings on the design of a particular computer manual (evaluative research) have application to designers of computer manuals in other places because such research findings are often used to build theories and principles of document design. Thus, researchers must consider threats to external validity as they construct their research designs.

Bias Error

This threat occurs when subjects in an experiment or respondents in a survey are different in a systematic way from the population they are supposed to represent. There are three common types of bias error: subject bias, self-selection, and subject/ researcher relationship. *Subject bias* is often a matter of concern in research in discourse processing. Most of this research has been carried out in universities, and the subjects have usually been college students who receive some course credit for participation, so the question is sometimes raised as to whether college students represent a typical adult population. Do college students read in the same ways as other adult readers? When the research methodology has a biological foundation (e.g., tracking eye movements while the subject is reading), the generalizability seems stronger than when the foundation is psychological (e.g., type of reading material chosen by people in a waiting room).

A famous example of subject bias error occurred in 1936 when a survey that had over two million respondents revealed that presidential candidate Alf Landon would easily beat Franklin D. Roosevelt. The researchers used the phone book, car registration lists, and the subscription list of a literary magazine as the sources of names of persons to be surveyed. They overlooked the fact that the sample did not include anyone from the large number of voters in the population who didn't own a phone or a car, or who didn't subscribe to a literary magazine. These less affluent voters (and there were many of them at the height of the Great Depression) tended to support Roosevelt, who won the election, much to the embarrassment of the pollsters. Obviously, this problem could have been avoided had researchers considered the possibility of data collection methods biasing the results.

Another source of bias error is *self-selection*. While some people will volunteer to participate in a study and others will agree to participate when asked, some subjects in a population will simply refuse to cooperate. For instance, some persons just won't be bothered to return questionnaires, others will refuse to answer certain questions (e.g., questions on age, income, sexual preferences, and so forth), and still others will refuse to answer any questions over the phone. Thus, the sample used in a study may not be truly representative of the population as a whole. To reduce the number of refusals to participate, researchers often explain in cover letters or introductory paragraphs at the top of the questionnaire the probable benefits of the study either to humanity in general or to a group the potential participant may have some interest in (e.g., students). For example, when the cover letter sent with a questionnaire states that the letter writer is asking for information to help a student who is writing a thesis, many recipients will fill out the questionnaire because they feel some pity, empathy, or a desire to help students obtain an education. The design of the survey instrument itself can also encourage recipients to participate; design issues are discussed more fully in Chapter 8 on surveys.

Bias error can also result when the researcher is acquainted with the subjects (*subject/researcher relationship*). In this case, the researcher may interpret the results differently because he or she "understands" the subjects, or the subjects may perform differently because they understand what the researcher is looking for. A good check on the possibility of biased interpretation of results is to have an outside person independently rate the results. To avoid biased performance of subjects because of subject/researcher relationship, a researcher can enlist someone else to carry out the project and not disclose that he or she is involved in any way. Obviously, researchers will also want to avoid the possibility of bias error by choosing subjects randomly rather than by recruiting friends and acquaintances as participants.

Random Sampling Fluctuation

This threat to external validity occurs when the mean score of a sample does not accurately represent the mean score of a whole population. Mean score can be either actual scores on a test or a mean arrived at by measuring some feature such as shoe size, age, height, and so forth. Thus, the results cannot be generalized beyond the subjects in the experiment. For example, if the mean eyelash length of the subjects in your study of eyelashes is 1.75 inches, you can be sure you have somehow acquired a very unusual group of subjects, a group that is not at all representative of the population as a whole. This error is particularly likely to happen when sample sizes are small. Some methods for dealing with random sampling fluctuation are careful selection of subjects (discussed more fully below), conducting a pilot study before carrying out the full project, and consulting a statistician for procedures which could compensate (e.g., power analysis for small samples).

Interaction Effects

Interactions between various factors not only affect internal validity as was discussed above, but they can also threaten external validity or the generalizability of the results. Some common interaction threats are pre-test/treatment interaction, history/treatment interaction, and selection/treatment interaction. *Pre-test/treatment interaction* may result when the pre-test given to subjects alerts them to the researcher's interest, thus skewing their performance. They become a non-typical sample of the population because subjects in an experiment want to cooperate by doing their best, and knowing what the researcher wants may lead subjects to behave in ways they wouldn't ordinarily. Research has shown that subjects often want to help the researcher confirm his or her hypothesis, so they will try to guess what the hypothesis is and then cooperate to help prove it. Research has also shown that another factor that prompts subjects to try to guess the research question and cooperate is the desire to look good—to behave in ways that are professionally or socially commendable. Whether subjects react in these ways deliberately or unconsciously, the result is the same: a threat to external validity (generalizability of the results). One way to help reduce this threat is to design the experiment so that subjects are so busy or involved with their assigned tasks that they have little time to try to puzzle out the researcher's hypothesis. In classroom research on the effectiveness of certain teaching methods, researchers sometimes don't mention the fact that research is being conducted. However, Federal law requires clearance with school authorities in such cases. To gain clearance, researchers usually submit a detailed description of their methodology and show that there is no possibility of physical or mental damage to subjects as a result of participating in the project. Protection of human subjects is discussed more fully in Chapter 5.

Another interaction that limits generalizability is *treatment/selection interaction.* This threat to external validity occurs when a treatment works better with one type of subject than with another. For example, if you tested the reader response simulation training in a professional writing firm where the majority of the writers happened to be female, it is possible that the strong results you obtained are not applicable to male professional writers. Or it is possible that your strong results were due to some aspect of the particular firm where the female writers worked. Obviously, to counter this threat, you need to replicate the experiment at other firms and at firms with a larger percentage of male writers. In fact, you may want to design your research project to identify gender for the data you collect; and then sort the data into male and female groups and test for differences. Gender issues are the focus of much interesting current research. For more information about research on gender, see Chapter 12.

Specificity of Variables

This threat to external validity means that results are not generalizable because some facet of the research is not applicable to the general population. For example, suppose you tested your reader/response simulation exercise in a government facility. Would the results be applicable to writers in the entertainment industry? Maybe. Let's consider a more extreme example to illustrate this problem. Suppose you tested the reader response simulation exercise on technical writers who work from 11:00 P.M. to 7:00 A.M. in Japan. How generalizable would those results be?

Reactive Arrangements

Reactive arrangements can occur in a multitude of situations in which some aspect of the study affects the feelings and attitudes of the subjects involved to the extent that the results produced would not be the same as results produced by the same study in a different place or with different subjects. For example, in the reader response simulation exercise, you might need to investigate whether the simulation scenario involves events that are culturally acceptable to Japanese. Or in another example, would middle-aged Japanese female homemakers feel comfortable performing the verbal protocol that you are using as your testing instrument? One might especially question whether these subjects would feel comfortable with this research technique if a young, white, male researcher were present during the taping of the protocol. If an aspect of the study unduly affects the feelings or attitudes of the subjects, the results may be disappointing and not generalizable beyond the participants in the study.

Other threats to external validity include *setting/treatment interaction* (something about the setting intensifies or diminishes the treatment) and *multiple treatment interference* (in studies with more than one treatment, an earlier treatment may affect the results of a later treatment). The findings in these situations cannot be generalized beyond the subjects in the experiment.

RANDOMIZATION

In reading the definition and example of various threats to internal and external validity in experiments, you may have noticed that in case after case, a recommended solution is random assignment of subjects to conditions. In fact, *randomization* is the single most important strategy in good quantitative designs. Randomization helps rule out rival hypotheses (i.e., alternative explanations for the results) and controls threats to reliability and validity (internal and external). It is so powerful that if it is used in experiments designed to test a treatment, no pre-test is needed. Random assignment of subjects is also the major characteristic that distinguishes experiments (sometimes called "true experiments") from quasi experiments. In the sections which follow, I discuss some randomization issues and strategies which apply to experiments. In Chapter 7 on discourse analysis and Chapter 8 on surveys, I say more about randomization issues and strategies commonly associated with quantitative descriptive research; however, you might like to skip ahead and read those sections now if you are interested in getting a more complete picture of randomization procedures.

To fully understand the principle of random selection, we need to first define two related terms: population and sample. A *population* is a group of people, organisms (e.g., plants or animals), or objects (e.g., books, cars, snowflakes, etc.) that have at least one characteristic in common. For example, a population of people might be characterized as children or adults, residents of a place or visitors, and so on. In most cases, it is impractical, if not impossible, to study all the people or objects in a population. For example, not all residents of a place are listed in the telephone directory or city directory, and even if they were, studying every single resident would be very expensive except possibly in the case of a small village. Therefore, most research is conducted on a *sample* (subset) of that population. However, for the researcher to generalize that the research findings apply to the whole population and not just to the sample investigated, the sample has to be chosen carefully so that it represents the population as completely as possible.

Similarly, in any project that tests the effectiveness of a treatment, whether it is a teaching technique, a tool, or some other item that can potentially affect behavior, it is critical to show that the group receiving the treatment is not significantly different from the group not receiving the treatment to rule out alternative explanations for the result of the treatment. In this case, random assignment to the groups involved in an experiment assures some degree of equality among the subjects prior to treatment.

Randomized selection, in simple terms, means that subjects in a particular sample are essentially representative of a larger population and that subjects in two or more groups in an experiment are essentially alike—or at least not unequal. Although randomization will not produce a perfectly representative sample nor experimental groups that are perfectly identical, we can assume that if a group or sample has been selected randomly, then all members of a population had an equal (50/50) chance of being a member of the sample, and all members of the sample had an equal chance of becoming a member of a specific group (control or experimental) in the experiment. Therefore, the possibility that the majority of the members of a certain group or sample will be different from the population of interest in an important way (e.g., nearsighted, unable to spell, or non-native speakers of the language common to the population as a whole) is very low.

Randomizing procedures can range from a simple procedure (e.g., writing names on slips of paper, dumping them in a hat and shaking them well, and then drawing out a certain number without looking in the hat) to a more complex procedure (e.g., entering the names into a computer program and asking it to produce a random list or using a computer spread sheet program to produce a random number table). One common procedure is to number the names or objects in some way, blindly choose a starting point on a random number table, and then follow the numbers across or down the page to select from the numbered list. However, in using a random number table, the researcher must make some decisions in advance. For example, what numbers are needed in the random number table. The best solution is to ask a computer whiz to generate a random number table using the digits between X (e.g., 1) and Y (e.g., 300). However, if you have to rely on a two-digit random number table in a textbook, you could convert it to a three-digit table by deciding, in advance, that you will use the two numbers in the first column and the first digit in the second column to construct a three-digit number. For example, in Table 4-1, if you needed three digit numbers, your first number (beginning in the upper left corner) would be 861.

Another problem is what to do if the next number you encounter as you move right is one you've already selected? All you have to do is set the rules *before* you begin using the table. Specify where you will start (most people start in the upper left corner), which direction you will read (most people read left-to-right and top-to-bottom), and what you will do when you reach a repeat (go to the next number to the right, or if at the end of the row, to the first number in the next row down).

Researchers doing experimental studies often have to rely on volunteers from the population of interest even though recruiting volunteers can limit the generalizability of the findings. When you post a notice or place an ad asking for volunteers, you run the risk that your sample may not include people who distrust science or empirical research; or your sample may not include extremely busy people. To a large extent, survey research is based on volunteer or self-selection, even when you have carefully chosen your mailing list using the random procedures described in Chapter 8, because not everyone who receives the survey will answer it. Self-selection or volunteer selection is a charge often leveled at experimental research carried on in universities because the researchers rely on students signing up to be subjects. Of course, in some disciplines, participation in a research project is considered one of the course requirements, so in that case a very high percentage of the population will volunteer. But even when participation in a research project is a course requirement,

TABLE 4-1   **Random Number Table from 01 to 99**

86	19	46	87	49	40	24	21	37	53
32	09	68	52	02	71	96	89	31	60
67	33	54	83	13	65	42	16	07	72
75	47	23	69	29	05	95	74	20	81
45	10	76	12	34	18	58	01	25	14
30	92	27	91	63	43	26	64	44	88
28	61	94	59	79	85	90	35	70	38
03	51	57	77	55	98	15	82	73	93
22	06	78	17	04	36	39	08	11	80
41	99	66	50	56	84	62	48	97	

there is usually the option for students to do an extra report of some kind as a substitute for participating in an experiment. And in most cases, students required to participate in an experiment can choose one of several options posted on a bulletin board. Even though volunteer or self-selection can bias results to some extent, careful researchers do make sure that the volunteers are randomly assigned to experimental and control groups.

For example, suppose your research project involves several hundred subjects who have to do some task at a computer. You can't possibly make yourself available at all possible hours in which the computer lab could be used, so you recruit colleagues to help, and you train them in how to handle the subjects. Now a possibility for researcher bias exists; perhaps some of your colleagues seem more reassuring to the subjects, causing those subjects to do better on the task. To reduce effects of this kind of researcher bias, you will need to randomly assign your fellow researchers to different hours and days.

Or suppose you want a group of fellow teachers to rate writing samples. You can't be one of the raters yourself because you can recognize which samples were collected when, but you can split the stack of writings at some random point (e.g., take off what looks to be the top fourth and put it on the bottom); then, beginning with what is now the top paper, you can deal the papers (just like dealing cards in a card game) into the same number of stacks as you have raters, and thus you will have assigned raters to the papers randomly.

So far we've talked about randomization in selecting human subjects, but the same principle is involved if you are studying objects such as textbooks, journal articles, or newspaper obituaries (see Chapter 7 for more on this topic). How will you choose your sample? First you have to define the population you want to make inferences about. Suppose you want to find out what percent of freshman handbooks contain usage exercises. Do you intend to examine all that have ever been printed or maybe only "contemporary" ones? If the latter, you will have to define "contemporary" as published within some time frame. If you decide to look at only those handbooks published within the last three years, where will you find them? Will you examine those which publishers have sent to your thesis advisor as sample copies, or those available in your campus library, or both? Or is there some other source you should consider? Research on texts is more fully described in Chapter 7.

To sum up, probably the single most important strategy for quantitative research is randomization. It helps reduce threats to internal and external validity and threats to reliability. The word "randomization," however, does not mean any system of choices that is more or less haphazard. True randomization is achieved only through a systematic method planned in advance—one that ensures that each member of a population has an equal chance of being selected to be part of the sample for investigation.

PROBABILITY

Probability plays an important role in interpreting the results of an experiment. Researchers use statistical procedures to determine how probable it is that the performance on the post-test occurred by chance rather than as a result of the treatment given. For example, if you wanted to test the idea that an aspirin a day makes eyelashes grow longer, you would measure the eyelashes of all the subjects in your sample; then you would randomly assign members of the sample to an experimental and a control group. The experimental group would receive specified doses of aspirin, and the control group would receive a placebo. At the end of a certain period you would measure all the eyelashes again and compare the measurements in the two groups. Suppose you did find that several subjects in the experimental group had longer eyelashes at the end of the experiment. Could those cases have happened by chance? The answer depends on how much longer the eyelashes are and how many subjects had longer eyelashes. An *analysis of variance* is a statistical procedure which takes account of the longer length and the number of subjects with longer eyelashes and estimates the probability that the longer length occurred simply by chance. These results are reported as either significantly longer or as a *significant difference,* and the researcher states the probability something like this:

The eyelashes of subjects taking aspirin were significantly longer after 60 days than the eyelashes of the subjects in the control group ($p < .01$).

The information in the parenthesis, $p < .01$, means that the probability that the results happened by chance is just one out of 100 cases. Note that researchers must decide in advance what level of probability they will consider significant. Most researchers choose either .01 or .05, but in almost no case are higher probabilities accepted as indicators of significant results. The issues involved with setting a good level of probability are discussed more fully under errors in interpretation near the end of this chapter, and concerns with level of probability are further discussed in Chapter 6 on meta analysis.

THE NULL HYPOTHESIS

This concept is very important to experimental research. Simply stated, it means that there is no evidence that findings of a research project are due to anything other than chance. For example, in an experiment, the null hypothesis means that any differences between the experimental and the control group cannot be attributed to treatment. It is possible that the treatment *did* cause the differences, but if your findings are not statistically significant enough to disprove the null hypothesis, then you cannot claim an effect for the treatment. But you should also be careful not to state that the treatment did *not* cause the results because failure to disprove the null hypothesis does not mean that you have proved it.

Let's consider an example. Lacye Schmidt (1991) designed a careful experiment to test the effects of assigning handbook exercises on student's ability to punctuate correctly. She randomly assigned students to conditions, took steps to ensure against researcher bias, the Hawthorne effect, and so forth. In the control condition, students wrote a journal entry each week on a specified topic. In the experimental condition, students did a set of handbook punctuation exercises. The person who counted the punctuation errors in the diagnostic essays given at the beginning and the end of the semester was not aware which student was in which condition. What Schmidt found was no significant difference between groups at the end of the semester. She could not claim that giving handbook exercises helps students learn to punctuate correctly. She also could not claim that handbook exercises do not help. All she can really say is that this experiment produced no evidence to show that handbook exercises are any more help than writing a journal entry each week.

Unfortunately, some people misunderstand what a null hypothesis is. They assume that the null hypothesis means that if you don't disprove the effectiveness of a common practice, then it must be assumed that the practice is effective because many people believe it. In the case of Schmidt's work, a teacher who was dedicated to handbook exercises assumed that because Schmidt had found no significant difference between the groups, and thus hadn't proved that handbook exercises are ineffective, it must be the case that handbook exercises *are* effective. If this seems complicated to you, it might help to consider the eyelash question. Perhaps there are people who strongly believe that taking an aspirin a day causes eyelashes to grow longer. This belief may be based on their own practice of taking an aspirin a day and noticing that their eyelashes are longer than the eyelashes of many other people. What is the null hypothesis in this instance? No matter how strongly people believe in the effectiveness of aspirin in growing long eyelashes, that is not the null hypothesis. The null hypothesis that a researcher must test in this case is that a daily dose of aspirin does *not* produce longer eyelashes—i.e., aspirin has no effect on eyelash growth. If the researcher finds sufficient evidence to reject this hypothesis, then it can be assumed that the aspirin, not chance, did cause the eyelashes to grow long.

The null hypothesis also plays a role in studies of a possible correlation between two phenomena. Here the issue is not whether a treatment caused an effect, but whether two phenomena tend to occur together. For example, there is ample evidence that when a person has a high SAT score, that person will also earn good grades in college. This does not mean that the high SAT score *caused* good performance in college. In this example, it is easy to see the difference between a correlation (phenomena tend to occur together) and a causal relationship (one phenomenon causes the other). An example of a case in which people tend to misread the findings is the significant correlation between persons who smoke cigarettes and persons who are addicted to hard drugs. There is simply no evidence that I know of that cigarette smoking causes addiction to hard drugs; perhaps both the addiction to cigarettes and the addiction to hard drugs are caused by the same factor—a genetic characteristic, an environmental influence, or some other factor. What a high correlation does say is that if a person is a hard drug user, it is extremely likely that the person is also a smoker—the two seem to go together. Or if you want to find hard drug users, you are more likely to find them among smokers rather than among non-smokers. The null hypothesis in this case would be that there is no statistically significant relationship between smoking and hard drug use. This hypothesis has been rejected because of numerous studies that have found a significant relationship between smoking and the use of hard drugs. This smoking and drug use example helps illustrate the role of the null hypothesis in correlational studies and also what is meant by finding or not finding a correlation between phenomena. You can read more about correlation in Chapter 8 on survey research.

A FEW WORDS OF ENCOURAGEMENT

If your head is swimming from all the terms defined in this chapter, you are not alone. One of my students commented after reading this chapter, "…it's a little overwhelming to think that people have to consider all these factors when doing an experiment." But do not be discouraged. You will meet and get better acquainted with many of these terms again as you read the rest of the chapters in this book. My aim in putting them all together in one place is to set up a central reference section while introducing you to the major problems in the design of quantitative research projects.

At this point, you may also wonder if it is possible to construct a design entirely free of threats to either internal or external validity. My answer is that on a theoretical basis, yes—but on a practical basis, probably no, or at least, rarely. Almost every researcher I know finds some aspect of his or her finished research project which could be improved if the project were replicated. However, writers and teachers have profited enormously from the research carried out over the last 20 to 30 years even though many of the studies have flaws. My hope is that this chapter has helped you to become a discriminating consumer of research findings, as well as a more sympathetic supporter of those tackling difficult research questions. Furthermore, if you intend to design a research project of your own, perhaps you could use this chapter as a kind of checklist for evaluating preliminary designs.

REFERENCES

Campbell, D. T., & Stanley, J. C. (1966). *Experimental and quasi-experimental designs for research.* Boston: Houghton-Mifflin.

Charney, D., Newman, J. H., & Palmquist, M. (1995). "I'm just no good at writing": Epistemological style and attitudes toward writing. *Written Communication, 12,* 298–329.

Daly, J., & Miller, M. (1975). The empirical development of an instrument to measure writing apprehension. *Research in the Teaching of English, 9,* 242–249.

Douglas, R., & MacNealy, M. S. (1993). Effective training techniques: Oral versus written. *IPCC 93 Proceedings—The new face of technical communication: People, processes, products.* New York: Institute of Electrical and Electronics Engineers.

Faigley, L., & Witte, S. (1981). Analyzing revision. *College Composition and Communication, 32,* 400–407.

Jaeger, R. M. (1990). *Statistics: A spectator sport* (2nd ed.). Newbury Park, CA: Sage.

Kirk, J., & Miller, M. L. (1986). *Reliability and validity in qualitative research.* Newbury Park, CA: Sage.

MacNealy, M. S. (1991). Creativity in literary scholars. In E. Ibsch, D. Schram, and G. Steen (Eds.), *Empirical studies of literature* (pp. 281–288). Amsterdam: Rodolpi.

Palmquist, M., & Young, R. (1992). The notion of giftedness and student expectations about writing. *Written Communication, 9,* 137–168.

Schmidt, L. P. (1991). *Improving students' surface errors in writing: An empirical study and a program proposal.* Unpublished master's thesis, Memphis State University, Memphis, TN.

Torrance, E. P. (1974). *Torrance tests of creative thinking: Norms-technical manual.* Lexington, MA: Personnel Press.

Wallace, D. L., & Hayes, J. R. (1991). Redefining revision for freshmen. *Research in the Teaching of English, 25,* 54–66.

OTHER USEFUL RESOURCES

Campbell, D. T., & Stanley, J. C. (1963). Experimental and quasiexperimental designs for research. In N. L. Gage (Ed.), *Handbook of research on teaching.* Chicago: Rand McNally.

Kraemer, H. C., & Thiemann, S. (1987). *How many subjects? Statistical power analysis in research.* Newbury Park, CA: Sage.

Lauer, J. M., & Asher, J. W. (1988). *Composition research: Empirical designs.* New York: Oxford University Press.

Sommer, B., & Sommer, R. (1997). *A practical guide to behavioral research: Tools and techniques* (4th ed.). New York: Oxford University Press.

► 5

Experimental Research

Experimental research is probably the type that you are most familiar with because you have no doubt read newspaper or magazine articles describing medical experiments such as those which have investigated whether vitamin E can help prevent heart disease. This kind of research usually tries to define a cause-and-effect relationship by testing a hypothesis (e.g., people who take one vitamin E pill each day will have fewer instances of heart disease than those who don't). As you know by now, such research relies on careful control of all the factors involved in order to reduce the possibility that any effects noticed (fewer cases of heart disease) are not caused by some factor other than vitamin E intake. Thus, the researcher must compare two groups of people who are very much alike in every way likely to affect heart disease (e.g., amount of exercise, weight, caffeine consumed, etc.) except one: the taking of a certain amount of vitamin E each day.

For the results of an experiment to be accepted by knowledgeable persons, researchers must plan carefully to control, as far as possible, all challenges to validity and reliability described in Chapter 4. In the sections below, I first discuss issues in defining the research question, then various types of experimental research and the associated disadvantages and advantages. In the next two sections, I give techniques for choosing methods, materials, and subjects which will help reduce challenges to the credibility of the results. Then I explain some frequent mistakes and errors. Finally, I suggest statistical procedures appropriate to the various designs.

DEFINING THE RESEARCH QUESTION

As explained in earlier chapters, research questions often arise as a reaction to some perceived difficulty, usually a discrepancy between a situation we encounter and what we had expected to encounter, or a gap between what we know and what we'd like to know. In most cases this perception of difficulty is somewhat fuzzy at first, so an important step in designing an experiment is to ask what it is you want to test because an experiment always involves a test. As a first step in deciding the nature of the test, two concepts must be considered: *constructs* and *variables*—both of which are closely related to the task of defining the question.

Defining the Construct of Interest

We can begin our consideration of *construct* with an illustration from medicine and then switch to one from writing. In testing a medicine, we want to know whether the medicine can cure a disease or improve health. A disease is usually fairly easy to define—in fact, symptoms of a disease can often be visually observed without use of a microscope. So a reduction in symptoms could be taken as an indication that the disease is regressing. On the other hand, good health is a far less precise construct. Good health in a teenager might be evaluated in terms of the number of repetitions of a physical task a subject can do without needing a rest. Of course, we probably could not use the same number of physically demanding tasks to assess the health of elderly persons.

Similarly, in testing a technique for teaching writing, the condition we want to improve may be hard to define. What do we mean by "teaching writing"? Do we want to teach students to produce *good writing?* Then we have to delineate what constitutes good writing. If we define good writing as that which is free of surface errors, that condition is fairly easy to observe and measure; however, if we define good writing as that which persuades readers, we will probably have a much more difficult time devising a measurement device. Going a bit further in considering the construct of teaching writing, we could even define that construct as teaching students to write cursively instead of printing their letters, or we could define the construct of teaching writing as teaching students to use certain writing tools (e.g., a word processor) which could help them revise. In any case, we need to define the construct we want to investigate as precisely or narrowly as possible.

To illustrate the process of defining constructs in the teaching of writing, let's consider an experiment Reta Douglas and I conducted to test whether oral or written instructions are more effective in teaching basic word processing skills (Douglas & MacNealy, 1993). We decided that competency in basic word processing would be defined for this experiment as the ability to produce a paragraph of five lines of text, to move the cursor to a particular point and delete words, to move the cursor to a particular point and add words, and to highlight and center previously entered text. These abilities were easy to assess visually, so we could assign subjects a score as an indicator of their basic word processing skills.

Another example of a construct defined in order to assess techniques for teaching writing can be found in an experiment conducted by Wallace and Hayes (1991) to see if changing students' task definition would improve their performance on a revision task. Students in two classes were randomly divided into experimental and control groups. The control group was taken to another classroom to do the revision task; the experimental group remained in the classroom where subjects received an extra eight minutes of instruction on revision. Students in both rooms were then asked to revise the same problematic text. The completed revisions were evaluated on three dimensions by judges who did not know which group (experimental or control) produced which revision. The three evaluation dimensions were "a global revision analysis, a text quality analysis, and an error correction analysis" (p. 59). The error analysis was, of course, easy to define. The experimenters defined global revisions as those in which students rearranged information, added to or revised sections, and/or added transitions. Quality was measured by having two judges independently rank the texts in order.

Of course I have not given you all the details of the two experiments, but I hope you can see from these examples that clear definitions of the construct led to the development of specific methods for measuring it. For example, in the Douglas and MacNealy (1993) experiment, student-produced texts were measured in terms of the presence or absence of three features, and the scores served as indicators of the level of student ability in basic word processing skills. What I have mentioned, but not discussed at this point, are factors or variables possibly affecting the performance of students on these tests.

Defining Variables

Note that in the paragraph above I mention *factors* that could affect performance. Scientists use the word *variable* when referring to these factors, and they also use the word *variable* when referring to the construct being tested. In short, a variable is a characteristic, quality, or attribute which is measurable. Variables are usually divided into two types: independent and dependent. The *independent variable,* sometimes called *treatment variable,* is the one (or ones) that the researcher manipulates; for example, in the aspirin/eyelash experiment, aspirin is the independent variable. The researcher controls which group gets the pill containing aspirin, the amount of aspirin in the pill, and so forth. In the Douglas and MacNealy (1993) experiment, the independent variable (the one we manipulated) was the type of instruction—oral versus written. In the Wallace and Hayes (1991) experiment, the independent variable was instruction in revision: the experimental group received eight minutes of instruction and the control did not receive any.

The *dependent variable* is the characteristic or attribute that may change depending on how the independent variable is manipulated; it is used to measure the results of the experiment. In the aspirin/eyelash experiment, the dependent variable is eyelash length. In the Douglas and MacNealy (1993) experiment, the dependent variable was ability in basic word processing skills, measured by the presence or absence of three text features. In the Wallace and Hayes (1991) experiment, the dependent variable was revision skill, measured by text quality and amount and type of revision. The dependent variable is also sometimes called the *criterion variable* because it is the variable used to determine the results when testing hypotheses. Another way to think of these two variables is in terms of cause and effect. The researcher manipulates the independent variable to see if the manipulation causes some effect in the dependent variable.

Of course, situations almost always have more than two variables; the other variables are the ones that the researcher tries to control in order to test the effect of the independent variable on the dependent variable. In the aspirin/eyelash experiment, some of the variables a researcher might try to control include when the pill is taken and whether it is taken with food, and so forth. To rule out possible effects of unknown variables associated with characteristics of individual subjects, the researcher will be careful to randomly assign subjects to the two groups. For example, Douglas and I randomly divided each class into two groups: one receiving oral instructions and the other receiving written instructions (Douglas & MacNealy, 1993). (And as you already know, random assignment of subjects helps reduce various threats to reliability and validity.)

A third type of variable often considered in experimental research is a *moderator variable,* by which is meant some characteristic (e.g., gender) that may have an effect on the outcome although it is not the variable of interest. However, a moderator variable cannot be manipulated (you can't change someone's gender in an experiment). The effects of a dichotomous (only 2 possibilities) moderator variable such as gender can be measured by subdividing treatment and control groups so that one subgroup in both the experimental and control groups is made up of all subjects of one sex and the other subgroup subjects are of the opposite sex. Figure 5-1 displays an empirical design with gender as a moderator variable. How do you decide whether to include a moderator variable in the experiment you are planning? Such a decision should be made on rational grounds rather than just adding a moderator variable such as gender because it seems popular at the moment. For example, in the literature on technology and word processing, Douglas and I had seen some questions raised about the effects of gender, so we included that variable (Douglas & MacNealy, 1993). On the other hand, Wallace and Hayes (1991) do not report having considered gender, very probably because the question hadn't been raised in the literature on revision. I will say a little more about a design that includes a moderator variable later in the chapter when we look at factorial designs.

Experimental Group n = 50		Control Group n = 50	
Males n = 25	Females n = 25	Males n = 25	Females n = 25

FIGURE 5-1   **Experimental Design with Gender as Moderator Variable**

TYPES OF EXPERIMENTAL DESIGNS

Experimental research can be classified into various types, each of which has advantages and disadvantages, so it is important to consider which type will best help you answer your research questions. In this section I discuss four categories into which experimental designs can be grouped so that you can compare the two types in each category and determine which type of research design will best help you investigate your research question. As you consider these four categories, note that they are not mutually exclusive; however, the two types within each category are mutually exclusive.

True versus Quasi Experimental Designs

Although the labels of these two types imply some sort of valuing of one over the other (*true* over *quasi*), most researchers do not classify one above the other except in terms of which is the more appropriate choice for use with a particular research question. The labels *true experiment* and *quasi experiment* are assigned based on the control of variables in the design. The major variable to be controlled is disparity in subjects. This variable is so important that an experiment with subjects randomly assigned to treatment and control groups is called a true experiment. These experiments provide the most precise evaluation of treatment effectiveness. However, sometimes the researcher cannot randomly assign group members; for example, in an educational environment, a researcher may want to compare two intact classes. Thus in much empirical research in writing, quasi experiments are used because of the educational environment and access to subjects. In such cases, the project is called a quasi experiment. Although both the Douglas and MacNealy and the Wallace and Hayes experiments we've been discussing used subjects from specific classrooms, they were true experiments because students in each class were randomly assigned to two conditions: experimental and control. As I discuss further aspects of experimental research, I will point out which are true and which are quasi experiments. Remember, each type is appropriate in specific circumstances.

Laboratory versus Field Experiments

Experiments can also be classified into two types according to location: experiments can be either laboratory or field, depending on the setting. For the most rigorous control of variables, researchers use a *laboratory*. One example would be the testing of a new drug or medicine on animals. In such cases, researchers can control variables such as diet, temperature of environment, amount of light, and so forth in the laboratory. Of course, when researchers want to use human subjects in their natural settings, they must give up some aspects of control. Drug tests involving human beings are often called *field* studies because the subjects can go on with their normal lives and routines, but they have agreed to accept some limits. For example, in the aspirin/eyelash study, both groups might be asked to agree to take no pills other than those issued by the researcher and to take one researcher-issued pill each morning. Then the researcher would distribute two pills that look alike and that are alike in all ingredients except one, aspirin—only the researcher knowing which subject received which pill.

The Douglas and MacNealy (1993) study of teaching basic word processing skills could be considered a laboratory experiment because it was conducted in a computerized classroom where it was possible to control a great many variables such as type of computer and software, chairs, lights, distractions, and so forth. On the other hand, the Wallace and Hayes experiment in revision instruction was much more of a field experiment because it made no use of a special room where variables could be controlled. Instead, the experimental group did the revision task in one classroom, and the control group did the revision task in another classroom, so the two rooms could have differed in ways such as the number of windows; but of course, the effect of any such difference on the experiment was probably negligible.

Most laboratory experiments are true experiments; on the other hand, a field experiment can be either a true experiment or a quasi experiment. In a true experiment, the subjects are assigned randomly to the two conditions; in a quasi experiment, one intact group (e.g., a particular 9:00 A.M. class) is assigned to the experimental condition, and a different intact group (maybe also a 9:00 A.M. class meeting in a different room) is assigned to the control condition. Note that the time the class meets may not have any effect on the results, so in either a true or quasi experiment the experimental and control groups do not necessarily have to be held at the same time. On the other hand, if the experimenter believes that class meeting time might have some effect on the result, then the researcher will try to schedule the experimental and control groups at very similar times.

Univariate versus Factorial Designs

Still another way of classifying experiments is on the basis of the number of variables investigated. So far in this chapter, we have discussed *univariate* designs in which there is only one independent variable of interest (e.g., the taking of an aspirin or the type of instructions used to teach basic word processing skills). However, sometimes a researcher believes that some other characteristic or treatment may interact with the treatment of interest and thus affect the results. When more than one independent variable is used or when a researcher is interested in a treatment (e.g., taking an aspirin each day) and a moderator variable (gender), the experimental design is called a *factorial* design. I discuss factorial designs more completely later in this chapter.

Hypothesis Testing versus Product Testing

Researchers who use any of the types of experiments described above are most often interested in testing the effects of some variable on some condition or activity, fo example, the effects of aspirin on eyelash growth or revision instruction on student writing. In such cases, the researcher hypothesizes (based on related studies conducted previously) that the independent variable will have an important effect on the dependent variable (e.g., giving students specific instructions in revision techniques will help them revise more effectively). However, experiments can also be used to evaluate commercial products such as user manuals for computer programs. Although such experiments are often funded by the manufacturer of the product, they are no less valuable in terms of building a body of knowledge in technical communication if the products differ along some dimension that can become a principle in manual design.

For example, an experiment could be conducted to determine whether a newly designed manual is better than the one usually shipped with a particular software package. Naturally, the manufacturer will want to know the answer before investing in the substantial costs of printing the new manual. Such an experiment could also help build the body of knowledge in technical communication if the manuals differ in a particular way such as using the second person pronoun, "you," rather than third person or no pronoun, as in imperative statements (see, for example, Soderston & German, 1985). The question of when to use "you" in formal writing is an interesting one—some of my students tell me that their high school teachers told them they must *never* use "you" in formal writing. However, Houp, Pearsall, and Tebeaux, whose textbook for teaching technical communication in college is now in its ninth edition, have long recommended using what they call a "you attitude" when writing business letters (Houp, Pearsall, & Tebeaux, 1995, pp. 325–327). When writers adopt a "you attitude," they use the word "you" to address their readers directly, and they try to focus on their reader's concerns rather than looking at a situation solely in terms of how it affects themselves. For example, a person writing a job application letter will not simply say, "I have two years experience with WordPerfect." Instead, the applicant might say something like this: "My two years experience with WordPerfect will enable me to learn whatever word-processing your employees use very quickly." As far as I know, no one has ever tested the effects of Houp et al.'s "you attitude" style.

Advantages and Disadvantages of the Various Types

The biggest reward gained from experiments is the power to infer causal relationships. For true experiments, an additional advantage is precision of the results; laboratory experiments also allow for more precision because of the strict control of factors that might affect the results. However, laboratory experiments tend to be more expensive because of the laboratory space and equipment required; and laboratory experiments are often criticized because the setting is artificial.

On the other hand, field experiments and quasi experiments allow a researcher to work in a natural environment. Quasi experiments also permit research with intact groups that have not been assembled just for experimental purposes. Although field experiments have the advantage of not requiring special facilities and they produce results that may be more generalizable because of the natural setting, their results are often regarded as less precise because the researcher has less control of environmental variables which could affect performance. Similarly, results of quasi experiments are less precise because it is possible that some characteristic of one of the two groups involved may affect group performance. As with any research, costs can also be a disadvantage to field or quasi experimental research whenever specialized equipment or personnel are needed.

TECHNIQUES FOR DESIGNING METHODS, MATERIALS, AND MEASUREMENTS

In the three sections that follow, I explain in more detail some of the issues involved in selecting experimental designs, materials, and measurements. As we consider these issues, I will continue to refer to the three experiments mentioned in this chapter: aspirin/eyelash, Douglas and MacNealy (1993), and Wallace and Hayes (1991), but at times I will suggest possible variations on these three experiments to illustrate certain points. I will also introduce a fourth experiment that tested the effects of line length on the psychological reality of the paragraph (MacNealy & Hedges, 1996).

Selecting the Design

In considering the most frequently used designs, it will be helpful to first define some symbols and terms that will be used over and over in graphic presentations of designs. Although you have seen some of these designs in a different form in the previous chapter, in this chapter I will use symbols to represent the various conditions because they may help you to see more quickly the differences in the designs.

The first of these symbols is "n" for number of subjects, as in Figure 5-1. The second symbol is a subscript "$_R$" which indicates random assignment of subjects. When randomization is impossible, as in a quasi experiment, a horizontal line of dashes is used (see Figure 5-2). The third symbol is "M" for measurement (as in eyelash length or as in pre-test and post-test). The fourth symbol you will need to recognize is "T" which stands for treatment; for example, in the aspirin/eyelash study, the T would stand for aspirin. In a case such as Douglas and MacNealy, where there were two types of treatment (oral and written instructions), one might use subscripts with the T, as in T_A equals oral instructions and T_B equals written instructions. (At the school where Douglas and I worked, instruction in word processing

Experimental Group	M_A	T	M_B
Control Group	M_A		M_B

FIGURE 5-2   **Quasi Experimental Design: Non-Equivalent Control Group**

skills was usually given orally to a whole class at a time, so we considered the oral instructions to be the control group. A control group with absolutely no instructions would have been very frustrating to the students involved.)

Although Douglas and I conducted a true experiment in that we randomly assigned students in every class to the two conditions, we could have followed a quasi experimental design and simply used two intact classes for the experimental group and two others for the control group. In that case, our experimental design would have be a nonequivalent control group design as is shown in Figure 5-2. Note the dashed line which represents non-random assignment of subjects. Using this design, of course, would have left us open to the possibility that there was an inherent difference between the groups that was the real cause of any differences in performance.

When educational researchers are forced by circumstances to use a quasi design involving non-equivalent groups, most researchers try to show that any inherent differences are insignificant. In such a case, a researcher might want to do a pre-test to show that the groups were essentially equal in areas that could affect results. The pre-test/post-test design is shown in Figure 5-3, where the first M in each row symbolizes the pre-test, the T symbolizes the treatment, and the second M symbolizes the post-test.

Note that this design can also be problematic if the pre-test and post-test are the same; as you may remember from Chapter 4, subjects tend to do better on the second of two identical tests (testing effect). Thus we might want to use different versions of a test for the pre-test and post-test to avoid testing effects; in that case, we might want to add a subscript number to each M, so M_A would stand for one version of the test, and M_B would stand for a different version (see Figure 5-3). Or if we were doing some sort of educational research such as testing whether taking an aspirin a day would improve students' scores on a test that has only one version, we should use a post-test only design as shown in Figure 5-4 (Campbell & Stanley, 1963).

One major concern with a post-test only design is that there could be some difference in ability between the experimental and the control groups that could affect performance. Campbell and Stanley (1963), whose book on experimental design has come to be an authoritative reference, maintain that randomization will usually take care of this problem if the total number of subjects involved is fairly large. However, researchers using a small sample must still face the problem of a possible difference between experimental and control groups. One answer to this problem is the one used by Wallace and Hayes (1991), who reasoned that their experimental and control groups could have a significant difference in verbal ability even though subjects were assigned randomly to the two groups. To test for this possibility, Wallace and

Experimental Group$_R$	M_A	T	M_B
Control Group$_R$	M_A		M_B

FIGURE 5-3   **True Experiment: Pre-Test/Post-Test Design**

Experimental Group$_R$	T	M
Control Group$_R$		M

FIGURE 5-4   **True Experiment: Post-Test Only Design**

Hayes compared their subjects' verbal ability by comparing their SAT scores (such scores can usually be obtained from the college records office by bona fide experimenters) and found no significant difference. Thus, Wallace and Hayes were able to assume that their subjects' revision performance was not affected by a difference in verbal skills.

Another procedure that is often used when researchers are concerned about a possible inherent difference between groups is known as the Solomon Four-Group Design, shown in Figure 5-5. Note that this design controls two factors by splitting the experimental group into two subgroups and the control group into two subgroups. By giving one subgroup in both the experimental and control conditions a pre-test, the experimenter controls for possible inherent difference between experimental and control groups, and by giving the other subgroup in both conditions no pre-test, the researcher controls for the effect of testing. Some researchers believe that the same test (M) can be used for both the pre- and post-tests in a Solomon Four-Group Design because the design compensates for possible testing effects with the addition of two subgroups having no pre-test (see Figure 5-5).

Whether quasi or true, experimental research always involves comparison, and it frequently involves before-and-after comparisons as well as comparisons between treatment and no-treatment. For example in the aspirin/eyelash study, we would probably want to know the length of all subjects' eyelashes before starting them on the aspirin treatment so that we could assess whether the treatment caused eyelashes to grow longer. This experiment would then involve four measurements, as illustrated in Figure 5-3. In the aspirin/eyelash experiment, we would measure everyone's eyelashes twice: once before and once after. If these measurements were taken at the same time as other body measurements, we would probably not have to worry about the possibility of alerting subjects to the area of interest, although I doubt that

Experimental Group (1/2)$_R$	M	T	M
Control Group (1/2)$_R$	M		M
Experimental Group (1/2)$_R$		T	M
Control Group (1/2)$_R$			M

FIGURE 5-5   **True Experiment: Solomon Four-Group Design**

knowing that we were testing the effects of a pill on eyelash growth would affect how much the subjects' eyelashes grow.

Isolating the Independent Variable

One crucial aspect of experimentation is that all conditions must be equal except for the variable being tested: the independent variable. If there are differences in the treatment of the experimental and control groups, those differences could serve as rival hypotheses in explaining the results. For example, if a researcher gives pills to the experimental group, it is important to give a very similar pill to the control group. The pills given to the control group are often referred to in lay terms as "sugar pills," because in early experiments they were made of sugar. But in modern experimental laboratories, the pills given to the control group are more properly called *placebos,* and they are constructed to be chemically identical to the pills given to the experimental group except for the one ingredient being tested. This principle also applies to research in educational settings so that if one group is given some kind of special treatment or instruction, the other group must also receive treatment or instruction (different) so that there is no effect from special attention being given to one group, i.e., the Hawthorne effect.

For example, in the Wallace and Hayes (1991) experiment on teaching revision, the one group received special treatment in that they were given eight minutes of instruction on revision and the other group received special treatment in that they used eight minutes moving to another classroom. Thus, both the experimental and control group received some special treatment. However, since in both classes, the control group was the one moved out of its usual setting, the question of a possible Hawthorne effect remains: could the moving itself have adversely affected the control group's attitude and therefore the quality of their revisions? (Note that this challenge is very far-fetched because it is unlikely that moving students from one classroom to another could have any effect on revision skills. I mention it only to illustrate the Hawthorne effect and a technique for countering it.) Since Wallace and Hayes used two classes for their experiment, they could have avoided this criticism by moving the control group in one class and the experimental group in the other. In that case, however, they would have had to find some way of filling the eight minute difference between the groups during which the experimental group received special instructions. The original Wallace and Hayes design is illustrated in Figure 5-6. To reduce the possibility of an effect induced by moving, the researchers could have used what is

Class A	Class B	Treatment
1/2 = E Group 1/2 = C Group	1/2 = E Group 1/2 = C Group	Instruction Moved to another room

FIGURE 5-6   **Matrix Illustrating the Original Wallace and Hayes Design**

Class A	Treatment	Class B	Treatment	Location
1/2 = E Group	Instruction	1/2 = C	**	Moved
1/2 = C Group	**	1/2 = E	Instruction	Not moved

FIGURE 5-7   **Matrix Illustrating a Possible Wallace and Hayes Design Counterbalanced for Location Effect**

** Intervening task such as a brief reading assignment.

called counterbalancing—a design illustrated in Figure 5-7. In this design, the groups are counterbalanced for location. When analyzing the data, the experimenter will put all the data from the two halves of the experimental group together in one group and all the data from the two halves of the control group together in one group. Then, the data from the experimental group will be compared to the data from the control group.

Factorial Designs

So far, we have been considering experiments that involve only two variables: an independent variable to be manipulated, such as instruction versus no instruction, and a dependent variable, such as improved revisions (e.g., Wallace & Hayes, 1991). Such experiments are sometimes called "single variable" designs because only one variable is being manipulated. In the aspirin/eyelash experiment, we have planned to investigate only one variable: whether the eyelashes of people taking one aspirin a day will grow longer than the eyelashes of people who don't take any aspirin. Note that in order to assess the effects of aspirin on eyelash growth, we probably should measure the eyelashes before and after treatment or no-treatment. This design is illustrated in Figure 5-3.

However, it is also possible to test several variations of some construct to determine which is most effective. For example, we could ask whether one aspirin a day will make eyelashes grow thicker as well as longer. In this case, we are including two dependent variables, length and thickness, so we have what is called a *factorial* design. Another type of factorial design includes adding a moderator variable such as gender into the mix. For example, in the aspirin/eyelash study, we might wonder if gender is a contributing factor to the effects of aspirin on eyelash length. Now our question is not only whether aspirin makes eyelashes grow longer, but also whether this effect is more pronounced in one gender than in the other. In other words, we are interested in a possible *interaction* between aspirin and gender. Figure 5-8 illustrates the difference in these two designs.

Factorial designs also result from another type of increase in complexity: the number of levels of any one variable. So far, we have discussed variables that are

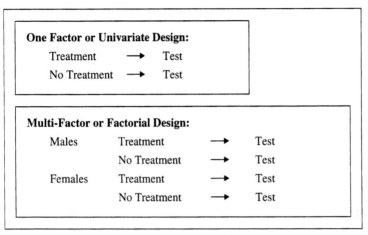

FIGURE 5-8   **A Comparison of a Univariate and Factorial Designs**

dichotomous: either an aspirin was taken daily or it was not; instruction in word processing skills was given in oral or written form. However, a researcher in the aspirin/eyelash experiment could hypothesize that the *amount* of aspirin is the crucial factor in causing eyelashes to grow longer. In such a case, the researcher might have several equal groups: one that took no aspirin, one that took a pill containing 250 grams of aspirin daily, and one that took a pill containing 500 grams of aspirin daily. In this case, there is still just one independent variable, but there are three *levels* of the independent variable. Suppose that the researcher also hypothesized that age is an important factor. For example, one might speculate that as one gets older, a larger amount of aspirin is needed to stimulate eyelashes to increase in length. In other words, there could be an interaction between the amount of aspirin taken and the age of the pill taker. To test for this interaction, we might divide the subjects into three groups: those between 21 and 30; those between 31 and 40; and those between 41 and 50. Now we would have three levels of age in our design and 3 levels of aspirin amount—a 3 × 3 design.

Here, I want to introduce another one of my own research projects to illustrate factorial design (MacNealy and Hedges, 1996). In this case, Katherine Hedges and I wanted to know whether line length had any effect on the concept (reported in prior experiments) that paragraphs have a psychological reality. Thus, we constructed our materials to reflect three different line lengths: 6 inches (the line length of most reports written on 8½" by 11" sheets of paper); 4 inches (the line length in most book pages); and 2½ inches (the line length in most newspaper columns). Thus we had three levels of the line length variable. However, previous research into the psychological reality of the paragraph (Bond & Hayes, 1984; Koen, Becker, & Young, 1969) had focused on the comprehensibility of a text by using two or more versions of the same text—a passage from *Lincoln and His Generals* (Williams, 1952) from which all paragraph markings had been removed—to test the hypothesis that there is a psychological reality of the paragraph. The first line of this text read:

Grant was, judged by modern standards, the greatest general of the Civil War.

Both Koen, Becker, and Young (1969) and Bond and Hayes (1984) also used a second version of the text in which nonsense words were substituted for all except function words and linking verbs, so that the first line read like this:

Blog was, moked by grol nards, the wilest nerg of the Livar Molk.

In these early experiments, subjects were given one of the two texts and asked to insert markers where new paragraphs should begin. Although the second version did remove most of the meaning of the text, the shift in focus from Blog (Grant) to Berond (Lee) at the sixth line of the text still seemed obvious to Hedges and me, so we created a third version based on research by Twyman (1981) in which the capitalization, punctuation, and word length of the original Grant and Lee text were preserved, but all meaning was eliminated because all the letters were converted to x. The first line of that text read like this:

Xxxxx xxx, xxxxxx xx xxxxxx xxxxxxxxx, xxx xxxxxxxx xxxxxxx xx xxx Xxxxx Xxx.

Thus, we had three levels of line length and three levels of text comprehensibility, or nine conditions in all: Original Grant and Lee text in three line lengths; Jabberwocky text in three line lengths; and what we called the "All-X" version in three line lengths (see Figure 5-9).

In factorial designs as in other true experimental designs, randomization is very important. To randomize the subjects who would insert paragraph markings into these nine texts, Hedges and I randomized the texts. First, we created a pile by alternating the nine versions; then we divided the big pile approximately in half and

Text Version	Line Length		
	Newspaper: 2 1/2"	Book: 4"	Report: 6"
Original by Williams			
Jabberwocky			
All X			

FIGURE 5-9   **Matrix Illustrating Design of MacNealy & Hedges, 1996**

stacked what had formerly been the bottom half of the pile on top. Finally, when we visited each of the ten classrooms to perform the experiment, we dealt the versions out like one would deal out cards in a card game, going down each row giving out whatever version was next to whichever student was next. Thus, we achieved random assignment of subjects into the nine conditions. Of course, to analyze the data, we then had to sort all the versions that the students had paragraphed back into stacks according to condition: All X/Newspaper; All X/Book; All X/Report; Jabberwocky/Newspaper; Jabberwocky/Book; and so on.

CHOOSING SUBJECTS

Just as one must take care in choosing materials and methods for an experiment, one must take care in choosing subjects. Considerations when choosing subjects for experiments include finding and recruiting subjects, random assignment of subjects, compensating for non-random assignment, and human subjects' permission.

Finding and Recruiting Subjects

Finding appropriate subjects for experiments is often a challenge in composition and technical writing research. A major concern is to find subjects who are representative of the population of interest. At some universities that emphasize research, some mandatory freshman courses—mostly in psychology, but also in composition in some schools—require students to be a subject in a research project to earn a passing grade for the course. The thinking here is that university students come from various walks of life, and since the requirement is tied to a course that every student in the university has to take, every freshman has an equal chance of participating in a project. This assumption is not totally true because in such courses students also have the option of doing some extra piece of work such as writing a brief paper if they do not wish to be a part of an experiment. Still, the subject pool is as representative as is reasonably possible.

However, at in most universities, freshman composition has no such requirement. Thus, the writing researcher often has to scrounge for subjects. Sometimes a researcher will ask permission from teachers of lower division courses to make a brief appeal for volunteers from a particular class. However, students tend to forget such appeals or they forget that they signed up for an appointment to participate. LaJeunesse (1993) recounts a typical story of frustration in obtaining volunteers in spite of a carefully laid plan. He had to contact 240 students and make follow-up phone calls to about one third of them in order to obtain just 40 subjects. One possible way of motivating students to show up for an experiment is to persuade a colleague to give an A to replace one or two quiz grades to students who bring in a slip from an experimenter certifying that they have participated in an experiment. Or perhaps a researcher in an English department could persuade a person who has access to a subject pool in another department to join a collaborative research team; some good possibilities for finding such a person are Psychology or Education departments.

Practitioners in the workplace who want to do a true experiment will also have to scrounge for subjects, and finding an incentive may be more difficult than offering to replace a quiz with an "A." Obviously a researcher cannot just ask his or her friends to be the subjects because this pool of subjects would not be representative of the population as a whole. One possibility is to circulate via a memo or e-mail a call for volunteers from among one's co-workers, relying on their goodwill toward research or their interest in the topic as motivation. This strategy has the advantage of offering subjects a conveniently located place in which to participate. In such a case, it would be important to tell the potential subjects the general area of research without giving them too many details that might influence their performance. Another possible resource for subjects would be members of a local chapter of the Society for Technical Communication; however, some motivating reward may be needed in order to get technical communicators to set aside time and travel to the place of experimentation. Whether the subjects come from the researcher's workplace or a local professional society, the researcher would have to explain in the final report that the results may not be generalizable because the data were collected from a very localized subject pool.

Random Assignment of Subjects

Do not forget that, because an experiment is based on comparison, the most important tool for a true experiment is random assignment of subjects to at least two groups: experimental (treatment) and control (no-treatment). As was explained in Chapter 4, random assignment of subjects to experimental and control groups helps decrease threats to the validity of your findings. You might want to review suggestions for achieving randomization given in Chapter 4. Even when using whole classes of students, it is sometimes possible to randomly assign the students to two or more groups *within* each class, as I explained in the "Differential Selection" section of Chapter 4. One pair of composition researchers who used a randomization design within whole classes is Wallace and Hayes (1991), whose project on teaching revision was described earlier in this chapter. In their case, students in two classes were randomly assigned to two groups, one of which was led into another classroom for the remainder of the period. The group remaining in the usual classroom had eight extra minutes of instruction on revision, the eight minutes being used up by the other group in travel to their new classroom. On the other hand, in the Hedges and MacNealy experiment on the effects of line length on the psychological reality of the paragraph, we randomized the *materials* in order to randomize the participants.

If, for some reason, it is difficult or impossible to split a class into two groups as did Wallace and Hayes, then the researcher may decide to use a quasi experimental design in which two intact classes are used, one serving as a control group and one as the experimental group. In such cases, the researcher often tries to compensate for the non-random assignment of subjects to the two conditions as is discussed in the next section.

Compensating for Non-Random Assignment

The major threat from non-random assignment is that the two groups differ in some dimension that will affect the results. Suppose, for example, you chose two classes to use, one (meeting at 9:00 A.M. in room 216) as the experimental group and one (meeting at 9:00 A.M. in room 217) as the control group. One might assume that the subjects in these two classes were more or less randomized because in a big school there is usually a wide mix of students in any one class and there is usually no procedure which would cause students with certain abilities to be assigned to specific classes. However, relying on university class assignment procedures does not ensure randomization. In fact, the two classes could be very dissimilar in terms of student ability.

One might also assume that because the two classes met at the same time (9:00 A.M.), neither would contain a majority of sleepy students or unmotivated students or slow-moving students, etc. Thus, one might be tempted to believe that the students in these two classes were more or less equal in the skills that might affect the results—for example, verbal skills. However, because the students weren't truly assigned to the two classes randomly, you could have one class (e.g., the one in room 216) that just happened to have more students with good verbal skills. In fact, at a university whose students tend to come from the surrounding area, classes could differ greatly in quality because students often try to sign up for the same section of a classes that their friends from high school are signing up for. Thus one class could have several students from a high school with a reputation for academic excellence and another class could have a large number of students from a high school with a poor academic record. In such a case, you might find that the experimental group (students in room 216) perform better in the writing test than the control group (students in room 112). However, the better performance of students in room 216 may not have been due to the treatment or instruction they received, but rather the fact that many of the students in room 216 came from Super High School where classes were small and verbal skills heavily emphasized.

Thus, the main concern for a researcher who is using two intact classes as control and experimental groups is to establish that the students in the two classes are essentially equal in skills important to performance on the test. In writing research, one method for assessing equality of verbal skill would be to compare the students' scores on a standardized test such as the SAT. For example, in the Wallace and Hayes (1991) revision study we've been discussing in this chapter, the researchers *did* randomly assign students within each class to the experimental and control groups; however, as added insurance against a possible difference in groups, the researchers examined the students' SAT scores for a significant difference. In this case, the average SAT verbal score for the control group was slightly higher (532.2) than the score for the experimental group (514.4), so one might wonder if the control group wouldn't do a little better than the experimental group on revision which obviously involves some verbal skills. However, Wallace and Hayes ran a statistical test (in this case a *t* test) on the scores and found no significant difference between groups. Thus, they could safely conclude that any difference in the post-test performance was due to the treatment.

Protecting Human Subjects

One possible problem for researchers using human subjects is that the experiment could cause some harm to the subjects. Therefore, federal law requires that no subject be coerced into participation and that a person or persons other than the experimenter examine the design to ensure that no harm could result to the participants. Many colleges and universities have a committee or appointed body that is responsible for reviewing research plans prior to any experiment. These committees usually follow the guidelines set forth in the *Belmont Report,* issued by the National Commission for the Protection of Human Subjects of Biomedical and Behavioral Research (1983). The guidelines primarily call for respect of persons involved, minimal risks, maximum benefits, and justice. Thus, a researcher could not design a treatment which has potential to harm subjects physically or psychologically. Nor can a researcher deprive a particular class or group of students of a treatment that they are entitled to—such as, instruction in some skill that one might reasonably expect students to have learned in that class. For example, in the Douglas and Mac-Nealy (1993) study of instruction in word processing, it would have been unjust to have taken only half of each class to the computer lab and taught them word processing. Thus, we really could not have a control group which received *no* instruction in word processing. In our case, this requirement was no problem because we were interested in two types of instruction, oral versus written, so we designed our experimental and control groups on those terms.

Once researchers receive approval from their university's Human Subjects Oversight Committee, researchers must also present each subject with a form to sign in which the subject gives his or her consent to being included in the experiment. This form must contain enough information about the experiment that the subject can give informed consent. Thus, the form will contain information about objectives, procedures, risks, and benefits. Of course, the researcher does not want the form to give so much information about the experiment that it could influence the subjects' behavior, so these forms require careful preparation.

Sometimes a researcher will want to mislead subjects somewhat about the actual goal of the research in order to keep from influencing subjects' behavior in some way. For example, in the experiment that Douglas and I conducted on using oral versus written instruction to teach elementary word processing skills, subjects were told they could ask questions of novice teachers (teaching assistants, in this case) who were observing the class (Douglas & MacNealy, 1993). Although we didn't explicitly say that the TA's were observing in order to learn to teach in a computerized classroom, we implied that by not being more specific about the TA's actual duties. And in fact, the TA's did learn some things about teaching in a computerized classroom—but that was not the main purpose of their presence in the room. One TA was assigned to each row of subjects, and each TA had a clipboard with paper to take notes on. Each TA recorded the topic of the questions the subjects asked and the time that students finished their tasks. Douglas and I later examined these field notes to determine which tasks were most difficult for the subjects— that is, which tasks elicited the most questions and took the longest time to complete. We were interested in the difficulty of the task, not the ability of individual subjects, and the results of these notes were kept absolutely anonymous. Keeping data anonymous protects the subjects from risks such as actual or perceived damage to their reputations.

The consent forms must also tell the subject that he or she may drop out of the experiment at any time without any penalty, and offer to share the results with the subject after the data have been analyzed. At some universities, researchers are required to debrief their subjects following their participation. In cases in which the consent forms do not reveal the specific question that the experiment is testing, the debriefing usually will. Of course if subjects participate one at a time and are told the true goal in a debriefing following participation, the researcher risks contaminating future subjects through diffusion. In such cases, subjects can be asked to refrain from discussing the experiment with friends and classmates for a certain period of time. For example, in the experiment that Hedges and I conducted on the effects of line length on the psychological reality of the paragraph, we organized a team of researchers so that many classes were visited simultaneously (MacNealy & Hedges, 1996). However, we did visit classes meeting at various times throughout the morning, so we told students that different versions of the text had been used, but we did not say what made them different. Then we asked the students in each class to not discuss the details of their particular version until after lunch. Students usually want to help a researcher, so we believe that our request was honored by enough students that no serious threat from diffusion occurred.

Not all research projects must go through these steps; one exception is research projects conducted as training exercises for student researchers, the results of which will not be circulated beyond the classroom. Another exception is survey research in which confidentiality is sufficiently assured (e.g., mail surveys); in this case, the researcher can assume that a subject returning the survey is agreeing to participate.

MISTAKES AND ERRORS

In discussing the possibility of faulty experimental methods, I am using two terms: "mistakes" and "errors" to differentiate two types of flaws. I will use "mistake" to label faulty research design, and "error" to label faulty interpretation of the results.

Mistakes in Design

Perhaps the major mistake to avoid is choosing the wrong type of design for the problem you want to investigate. If you are testing medicine, or some factor that has life-threatening possibilities, a true experiment is probably a must, at least in the early stages of development of the medicine. At the same time, you must take into account the fact that the activities (and setting, if it is a laboratory) are artificial—such a situation would rarely occur naturally. So once you have used a series of true experiments to prove that the drug is not life-threatening to a significant degree, then you can field test it with humans. In the United States, you must obtain permission from the U.S. Government (Food and Drug Administration) before conducting field tests of medicines with humans.

On the other hand, if you are interested in social or educational questions, you could reasonably choose to use either a true or quasi experiment design, depending on which is the most important to your findings, rigorous control of variables, or a natural setting. Remember, whether you want to do a true or quasi experiment, you will want to plan the design in advance; and the more complex the design, the more important it will be to pilot test it. As you plan an experiment, you need to keep in mind the many ways that validity and reliability of results can be tainted.

Errors in Interpretation

The word "error" in this case refers to setting faulty parameters for evaluating the significance of the results; the most common errors are called Type I and Type II Errors. You may want to refer back to the end of Chapter 4 where I discuss probability and the null hypothesis before reading about these two error types.

Type I Error

In this case, the researcher concludes that there is a significant difference between the experimental and control group when the difference is actually not significant. In technical terms, the researcher rejects the null hypothesis (a statement that there is no significant difference between experimental and control groups after the treatment). If you remember, researchers are supposed to determine in advance of the experiment what level of significance will be used. A Type I Error occurs when the researcher has decided to use a probability setting which is too generous. For example, a researcher may choose a significance level of .05 (the probability is that in 5 instances out of 100, the results happened by chance) and find a significant difference in a case where there truly is no significant difference that would have shown up if the level of significance had been set at .01 (in only 1 case out of 100 would the results have happened by chance). Well, you might say, why not always choose .01 over .05? The answer lies in the risk of a Type II Error.

Type II Error

This type of error occurs when the significance level is too limited (e.g., .01) so that it appears that there is no significant difference between the experimental and control groups (i.e., the null hypothesis is accepted), when in fact there is a significant difference and the null hypothesis should be rejected. Had the significance level been set at .05 instead of .01, the significant difference would have become evident.

These two errors make it sound like setting a significance level is a no-win task, and in fact, it can be somewhat difficult. However, a researcher can reduce the risk of either type of error by carefully considering some aspects of the experiment. One major concern is the possibility of harm to the subjects; it would be better to conclude that a drug is more harmful than a placebo when it actually isn't (e.g., to conclude that there is a significant difference when there is none—Type I). In this case, most researchers choose .01. In writing experiments, there is very little, if any, risk to participants from a particular teaching technique, so researchers often choose .05, believing that if a particular technique can be helpful but not harmful at all, it is preferable to make a Type II Error.

Another aspect to consider is number of subjects involved in the experiment. If the number of subjects is very large (in the thousands), the more generous level of significance (.05) is often acceptable because the large number of subjects reduces the possibility of erroneous conclusions. Note that a researcher should always have enough subjects that the statistics can give a true picture. A rule of thumb is to have no fewer than ten subjects for each variable of interest. Thus a study could have as few as 20 subjects (ten in the experimental group and ten in the control group), but given this low number of subjects, the researcher will probably want to choose the more limited level of significance of .01 or even .001 in order to reduce the risk of a Type I Error.

STATISTICAL ANALYSIS OF DIFFERENCE BETWEEN GROUPS

There are many different statistical tests which can be used to determine if the difference between two or more groups is a significant one. If you have not had a statistics course and you are trying to design an experiment, you would be wise to consult a statistician to help you select the most appropriate test. In this section, I will briefly describe four of the most frequently used tests of difference: Chi Square, one- and two-tailed *t* tests, and ANOVA. To determine which of these is most likely to be appropriate for your study, you first need to understand the different types of measurement variables—nominal, ordinal, interval, and ratio—because the type of data collected determines the type of statistical procedure which can be used to analyze the data. Note that much of the information given in this section can also be applied to quantitative descriptive studies such as discourse analysis and surveys.

Data Types

The type of data you collect will be determined by the questions you want answered and the measurement tools you use. For example, in an experiment you will very likely give the subjects some test to see whether the treatment has had any effect. Test scores are usually interval or ratio variables as you will see from the description below. On the other hand, you could collect some information about the subjects in your experiment in order to put them into sub-groups such as male and female; if so, you would be collecting nominal data. You need to understand these types in order to choose an appropriate statistical procedure for analyzing the data.

Nominal Variables

Nominal variables are usually categories with no numerical value; they cannot be measured in terms of *amount* of the variable. Numbers can only be used to describe the frequency of this type of variable. For example, most people think of themselves as either male or female; hazel, green, blue-, or brown-eyed; European American, African American, Asian, Hispanic, or some other ethnicity. When we use distinct (non-overlapping) categories like these we are using nominal variables. These are easy to count, and we could easily calculate a descriptive statistic such as what percent of the sample in our study belongs to one of these categories (e.g., male) by dividing the number of items or persons in the category by the total number of items or persons in the sample. For example, if our sample contained 33 blue-eyed persons out of a sample of 100 persons we could say that one third of our sample has blue eyes, but we cannot average nominal variables because there is no such thing as a person whose eyes are one third blue.

However, we might design a study in which we want to test whether blue-eyed persons have a more positive attitude toward some action than brown-eyed persons do, so we would include a question about eye color in the survey. Then, to assess the possible relationship of eye color to attitude quickly, it would be helpful to use a computer. Therefore, we would need to assign a number to the eye color categories so that the computer can keep track of them—for example, we might assign the number 1 to brown eyes and number 2 to blue eyes. Using these numbers, the computer can quickly sort the attitude measurements into two categories, blue-eyed and brown-eyed, and calculate the significance of any correlation between the two. If we include green eyes and assigned that category the number 3, then we could look at the list and quickly determine which eye color appears most frequently in a given sample of people. The score which appears most frequently in a list of scores is called the *mode*. For example, in this list of the eye colors of a certain group (1, 1, 1, 2, 2, 2, 2, 3, 3), the mode is 2: blue eyes are the most frequent. Mode is one way to describe central tendency, and it can be used with all four types of variables (see Table 5-1).

On the other hand, you can easily see that we must restrict the use of the numbers 1 and 2 to the function of category labels because otherwise we will make a

TABLE 5-1   **Measures of Central Tendency and the Variables They Can Measure**

Type	Definition	Variables That Can Be Measured
Mode	Most frequently occurring score	nominal, ordinal, interval, ratio
Median	Score that occurs halfway in a ranked list	ordinal, interval, ratio
Mean	The average: the sum of the scores divided by the number of scores	interval, ratio

horrendous mess out of our mathematical calculations. For example, suppose we assigned the 1 to identify the category of female and number 2 to identify the category of male. Then, if we had 33 males in our sample of 100 and multiplied that by 2 (the number we assigned to the category of male) we would get 66, an absolutely meaningless number in this case, especially if we wanted to compare it to the number of females in the sample which would be 67 (100 persons in the sample minus the 33 males equals 67, and then multiply that number by the category number, 1, for females). Such arithmetic would make it seem that we had an almost equal number of males and females in the study—a score of 66 for the male category score and 67 for the female category. If your head is swirling from this funny math, don't worry. Just remember that nominal variables cannot be measured in terms of amount (how much of a given quality is present) or rank (one quality cannot be higher in value than another), the only measurements you can make with nominal variables are how many items or persons are in each category, which category appears most frequently in a group, or what percent of the total number of items or persons belongs in a category. The same is true for eye color, ethnic heritage, dog ownership (yes or no), and other such nominal variables; we may assign numbers to the categories to help us keep track of them on the computer, but the numbers are meaningless in terms of how much of that quality a person may possess or which quality is more highly valued (e.g., using 2 as the numerical label for females and 1 as the numerical label for males does not indicate that females are more valuable than males).

In writing research, nominal variables are often used to categorize types of writing such as memos, letters, reports, etc. Using them, a researcher could determine which type of writing an engineer or a geologist most frequently produces in a given period. In composition studies, nominal variables can also be used to label types of writing such as expressivist (e.g., recording one's feelings or experiences) versus transactional (e.g., attempting to persuade someone to take an action).

Ordinal Variables
Ordinal variables take into account both a quality and a rank ordering of the *amount* of that quality, in general but not specific terms. For example, you could rate memos produced at a business location in terms of probable effectiveness: low, medium, and

high; or you could rate preferences for restaurant types (1 = first choice; 2 = second choice, etc.); or you could ask survey participants to rate the importance of personal characteristics in a co-worker or supervisor (sample question: Using the numbers 1 to 5, with 1 being most important, rate the importance of these characteristics in a co-worker: honesty, charm, education, etc.). In these measures, it is assumed that there is a difference in amount or value, but that difference is not specified in terms of an equal difference between the items. For example, the distance between first and second choice of restaurants is not necessarily equal as would be the difference between 1 and 2 years of college education which is an interval variable. Note that numbers assigned to ordinal variables cannot be used in mathematical procedures such as addition, subtraction, and averaging. For example, you cannot add first and second restaurant choices and get a third choice.

In writing research, ordinal variables are often used to rate the quality of writing or the importance of some characteristic of a piece of writing. For examples, you could ask a group of raters to sort a set of student essays into piles representing excellent, above average, average, below average, and poor. In this type of sorting, rank matters as it did not with nominal variables (blue eyes are not higher in rank than brown eyes), but there is no precise numerical distance between the ranks. Most of the time, letter grades (A, B, C, D, and F) are ordinal variables because the distance between different letters varies. For example, A may be applied to scores between 92 and 100 (a spread of nine points), B to scores of 82–91 (a spread of 10 points), and so on to F equaling scores of 50–61—a spread of 12 points or more since students could conceivably get fewer than 50 points (Connors & Glenn, 1995, p. 95). A useful descriptive statistic for ordinal numbers is the *median,* which is the score that occurs half way in a list of ranked scores (see Table 5-1). For example, in this short list (A, A, B, C, D, D, F) the median score is C. However, if half of the grades on a particular assignment fell below a median of D as in this short list (A, B, C, D, F, F, F), a teacher might want to examine the writing assignment to be sure it was clearly stated.

Interval and Ratio Variables

Interval and ratio variables are different from nominal and ordinal variables in that for these two types of data, it is possible to have a measurement of zero. However, the zeros are not the same for interval and ratio variables, as you will see. One characteristic that interval and ratio variables have in common is that they can be used in mathematical calculations beyond simple counting. Interval variables have equal intervals between the values; therefore, most interval measurements can be used in common mathematical calculations—addition, subtraction, multiplication, division. Thus it is possible to calculate the average or *mean* score (see Table 5-1). Compare this distinction with both nominal and ordinal variables discussed above. You cannot add 1 for brown eyes and 2 for blue eyes (both nominal variables) and divide by 2 to get an average of 1.5 eye color. Likewise you cannot add a 1 to indicate a preference for Chinese restaurants as a first choice and a 2 to indicate a preference for

Korean restaurants as a second choice (both ordinal variables) and get 3 to indicate a preference for Asian restaurants as a third choice. On the other hand, you can add the number of pages in three different books (interval variable), divide the sum by 3, and get an average number of pages for the three books. Some interval variables include age in years, inches in height, and degrees Fahrenheit; note that in all these instances, the zero point is arbitrary. There really is no case of a person with no age at all or no height at all, nor is there a case when there is no temperature outdoors, but there is a zero point on a Fahrenheit scale. On the other hand, it would be possible to get a true zero (meaning absolutely no points) on a test if a person did not answer any question correctly; also, it would be possible to set up a vacuum chamber with zero air pressure. Such measurements are ratio variables. In some areas of research (e.g., the social sciences), ratio variables are rare, so most textbooks refer to both ratio and interval ratios as interval ratios. In describing lists of interval or ratio scores, all the measures of central tendency are appropriate (see Table 5-1).

In writing research, interval variables such as the number of words in a sentence, paragraph, or piece of text are often used to describe pieces of discourse; note that this is not ratio variable because there cannot be zero words in a sentence. Attitude and frequency can also be measured as interval variables if a Likert Scale is used. For example, I'm sure you have answered some questionnaires which asked you to rate your level of agreement with some statement (e.g., The instructor graded the essays fairly) by choosing one of five positions: Strongly Agree, Agree, Undecided, Disagree, Strongly Disagree. Similarly you could ask writing teachers to rate how frequently they use a computer to prepare their lecture notes or lesson plans by choosing one of these positions on a scale: Almost Always, Frequently, Occasionally, Rarely, Almost Never. These points on the scale are assumed to be an equal distance apart, so they are interval variables. Usually the researcher assigns points 1 through 5 to them; in some cases such as Students Instructional Rating forms, Strongly Agree equals 1 and Strongly Disagree equals 5. But there is no rule saying that you couldn't make Strongly Agree equal 5 and Strongly Disagree equal 1. The main thing is to use the same scale for all questions on a questionnaire. Note that there is no zero on these scales.

Scales with a true zero are used to measure ratio variables. Ratio variables could be used to assess grammatical knowledge by giving a test in which students had to mark sentences as either correct or incorrect; in this case, a student might earn a score of zero. The number of spelling errors in an essay would be a ratio variable because it is possible that an essay would have absolutely no spelling errors.

Measures of Central Tendency

In each description of a type of variable above, a measure of central tendency was mentioned as being appropriate for that type of data (i.e., mean, median, mode). However, as you may have noticed in Table 5-1, some measures of central tendency cannot be used with different types of data, so you may be wondering how to determine which to use with a certain set of data. Well, as was mentioned above and is shown in Table 5-1, some measures of central tendency are impossible with certain types of data; for example, you cannot average the numbers you assign to nominal data such as eye color nor ordinal data such as first, second, and third choice of restaurants. However, you can choose whether to use the mode, the median, or the mean with interval and ratio data. In some cases, researchers report all three. Reporting all three would probably be unnecessary in a set of data which fell perfectly along a bell curve because then all three would be the same. However, data sometimes is skewed so that the mean, by itself, does not represent the whole picture. For example, in the set of temperatures in Table 5-2, the mean for both cities is 86.2°, but notice that on more than half the days the temperature in McSouth City was 90° or above, whereas in McEast City only three days were 90° or above. Yet the average temperatures for the two cities is the same. In such a case it would be wise to report both the mean and the median because someone considering whether to retire in McSouth City or McEast City might say, "I can't stand prolonged periods of hot weather, even with a few cool days mixed in."

There are two other statistics that can often be reported along with the measures of central tendency that can help with the interpretation of the data. First is the

TABLE 5-2   **Temperatures for 11 Days in Two Cities**

Day	McEast	McSouth
01	62	70
02	60	81
03	79	89
04	80	90
05	85	91
06	95	91
07	98	91
08	96	91
09	80	91
10	70	80
11	70	77
Mean	86.2	86.2
Median	79	90
Mode	70	91

range—that is the top and bottom score. Note that if we had reported the range of temperatures in Table 5-2, it would be apparent that it is very wide for McEast City (60–98) and fairly small for McSouth City (70–91). Someone trying to decide whether to retire in McEast City or McSouth City might say, "I can take several days of hot weather, but not big temperature swings."

Another statistic that helps with the interpretation of mean scores is the standard deviation. This score describes how all the scores in a list are distributed around the mean—in other words, the standard deviation describes whether scores are clumped around the mean, spread out, or skewed in one direction or the other. To illustrate this concept, let's consider another set of scores—one that teaching assistants often consult me about: scores from student evaluations of their teaching. At my school, the students' evaluations are averaged for each class, and the report shows the mean for the individual class, the mean for all courses in the department, the mean for all courses in the college, and the mean for all courses in the university. These means range from 1 to 5, with 1 being the best score. So a teacher might get the scores shown in Table 5-3 for classes A, B, and C. Notice that this teacher got a perfect mean score for Class A (1.00) with zero for the standard deviation, this means the students were unanimous in their opinion. The teacher also got a pretty good score for Class B (Mean = 1.37, SD = .38), this mean is well below the department, college, and university means. The standard deviation is fairly low, too, meaning that the students' opinions were not too far apart. However, in Class C, the teacher's mean was 1.69 which is higher than the department mean and very close to the college and university mean. In interpreting the score, it is important to note that the students' opinions in Class C are much farther apart (SD = .70) than in the teacher's other two classes, so it is likely that the opinion of one or two students in Class C did not fit in with the majority of the students' opinions. We might expect such a large difference in groups such as all the students in the department or college, but in a small class, a low rating by just one student can adversely affect a teacher's class mean—a fact indicated by the larger standard deviation. One caution in thinking

TABLE 5-3   **Comparison of Means and Standard Deviations**

Source	Mean	SD
Class A	1.00	.00
Class B	1.37	.38
Class C	1.69	.70
Department	1.66	.65
College	1.70	.71
University	1.71	.73

about standard deviations: their range differs according to the possible range of scores. Thus, in some other set of scores, you might find a standard deviation of six which might be low for that particular set of scores.

TYPES OF QUANTITATIVE ANALYSIS

By its very nature, experimental research tries to determine whether there is any significant difference between the control group and the experimental group. If a significant difference is found, then the researcher can infer cause—i.e., the treatment caused the experimental group to behave significantly differently from the control group. The four most frequently used statistical procedures for analyzing difference are chi square, one- and two-tail *t* tests, and ANOVAs. As I discuss each one, I will point out the data types for which it is most appropriate.

Chi Square

This type of analysis is most often used with nominal data—categories. We can use nominal variables to do some analysis of difference between groups when we are primarily interested in the frequency of occurrence of a particular trait or quality. For example, suppose you wanted to try a certain teaching or training technique to see if it would improve a skill in a certain area. You would assign groups so that one received the training, (perhaps instruction on revision) and one did not. Then you would assess the performance on some test such as asking the subjects to revise a piece of text. Finally, you would ask raters to judge whether the text was improved, not changed for the better or the worse, or made worse. In this case you would have three categories of revision quality and two groups of subjects, so your chi square table would look like that shown in Figure 5-10.

The chi square analysis is based on the difference in what is expected to occur and what occurs, so you have to enter the expected or estimated frequency in each cell. Suppose we had 60 students in each condition (instruction vs. no instruction); then we might estimate that by chance, there would be 20 students in each cell (See EF for Estimated frequency of occurrence in Figure 5-11). Next you would enter the *actual* number of subjects in each category, based on the rater judgments (see OF

	Improved	No Change	Made Worse
Instruction			
No Instruction			

FIGURE 5-10   **An Empty Chi Square Table**

	Improved	No Change	Made Worse	Total
Instruction	EF = 20	EF = 20	EF = 20	60
No Instruction	EF = 20	EF = 20	EF = 20	60

FIGURE 5-11   **A Chi Square Table Containing Estimated Frequencies**

for observed frequency of occurrence in Figure 5-12). Now you would use either a computer-statistical package (or formula if you were doing the calculations by hand) to determine whether the actual number of students (OF) in each category is significantly different from the estimated number (EF). Whether you use a computer or do the math by hand, what you learn from the chi square statistic is that a significant difference between groups does or does not exist.

Note also that you would not necessarily assign same estimated frequency (EF) to all cells in a chi square analysis. In most cases, the estimated frequency would be split evenly between cells, but some other conditions in the situation might cause you to assign different estimated frequencies in the various cells. For example, in the case of 200 students voting in a mock national presidential election, you might expect that 50% would vote Republican and 50% would vote Democratic, so you would put the same number (100) in each cell of a chi square analysis. However, if you were studying students in a wealthy suburb, you might want to find out what the distribution between Democratic and Republican parties is in terms of actual voters in the last election in that suburb and use those for your expected frequencies. If the adult population in the suburb is 75% Republican and 25% Democrat, your estimated frequencies in the chi square would be 150 in one cell and 50 in the other. In other instances, prior research may have shown that the expected frequency is probably not 50/50 in a particular population. For example, an uneven expected frequency is often the case with language and math skills in elementary students—there seems to be a gender difference in these areas. Thus, as in all good research projects, you should thoroughly read the literature in a particular area before committing yourself to a particular research design.

	Improved	No Change	Made Worse	Total
Instruction	EF = 20 OF = 30	EF = 20 OF = 25	EF = 20 OF = 05	60 60
No Instruction	EF = 20 OF = 10	EF = 20 OF = 25	EF = 20 OF = 25	60 60

FIGURE 5-12   **A Chi Square Table Containing both Estimated and Observed Frequencies**

One other important thing to remember is that in most cases chi square should not be used for variables other than nominal variables. If, for some reason, you wanted to do a chi square analysis of data from a test that had numerical scores ranging from 0 to 100 (interval data), you would not use the average of all the students' scores in one class or group versus the average from the other class or group. Rather you would set up two categories (nominal variables): passed (those who scored above 70), and failed (those who scored below 70).

t *tests*

These are statistical procedures for analyzing differences between groups when the variables are interval or ratio variables. Both kinds of *t* tests compare group scores against a normal bell curve.

Two-tailed *t* tests.   These tests are used when the scores for the variable of interest can go up or down. For example, you would use a two-tailed *t* test if you wanted to compare scores from a pre-test with scores from a post-test to see if a treatment had caused a difference in weight gain. In this case, some subjects might lose weight, and others might gain weight. This test uses the full bell curve, so it includes scores at both the high and low ends to determine whether two groups are significantly different from each other.

One-tailed *t* tests.   These tests are also based on a comparison with a normal bell curve, but they are used to analyze whether there is a significant difference between two groups on a single variable when the scores can move in just one direction, (i.e., one side of the bell curve). For example, suppose you conducted some kind of test of the effects of a treatment on the growth of third grade children. In this case, some children will grow taller, but none will shrink (at least under normal circumstances). You could use a one-tailed *t* test to make this assessment. A one-tailed *t* test looks at the data on the one side of a bell curve, so it assesses a difference in one direction—in this case, growth.

The advantage of a one-tailed over a two-tailed *t* test (described above) is that the one-tailed *t* test is more sensitive to a significant difference in one direction (e.g., improvement in some skill) than the two-tailed test is. The one-tailed test might show a significant improvement in a case where a two-tailed test would not. The disadvantage is that there may be a significant difference between two groups that the one-tailed test would not identify because the difference was due to a decrement rather than an improvement in performance (e.g., the memos written after the training session were worse in terms of audience awareness). The two-tailed test, on the other hand, would have shown this difference. So why would a researcher choose a one-tailed *t* test over a two-tailed *t* test? Some scientists and statisticians claim you should never use a one-tailed test because that is like cooking the data; however, others say that it is appropriate to use a one-tailed test if, *before you collect the data,* you have good grounds for believing that any difference will be in one direction.

Note that both *t* tests can only be used to compare two groups. If you are using a factorial design, you would have to conduct numerous *t* tests to determine differences between the various factors. For example, in the Hedges and MacNealy study of the psychological reality of the paragraph, we would have had to conduct 18 *t* tests. We would have had to conduct three tests just to compare the All-X versions with each other—the report line length with the book line length, the report line length with the newspaper line length, and the book line length with the newspaper line length. Then we would have had to do three more to compare the Original versions by line length, and three more to compare the Jabberwocky by line length, making a total of nine *t* tests. Next we would have had to do three *t* tests to compare all book line lengths with each other (the Jabberwocky versus the All-X in book length) and so on, making a total of nine more *t* tests. Not only do statisticians advise that multiple *t* tests on a set of data are unwise because they are liable to distortions, but such *t* tests would not have uncovered any interaction between line length and text version. In other words, the *t* tests would have failed to answer whether the subjects paragraphed significantly less accurately with the All-X version in a newspaper line length than with any other combination of text version and line length. When interaction between variables is important, a researcher should use an analysis of variance.

ANOVA (Analysis of Variance)

This procedure can also be used to analyze the difference between two groups, and ANOVAs can be used with interval and ratio variables. Instead of comparing results against a normal bell curve, the ANOVA analyzes how subjects *within* each group (e.g., experimental and control) differ from each other. Then it compares those differences to the differences *between* the groups. An ANOVA should only be used, however, when subjects have been randomly assigned to the experimental and control groups.

One advantage to an ANOVA is that it can analyze differences when more than two groups or more than one independent variable is involved, whereas a *t* test can only analyze the difference between two groups. Also, the results of comparisons between multiple groups are less likely to be distorted using an ANOVA rather than multiple *t* tests. Finally, an ANOVA can provide information (which a *t* test cannot) on any interaction between any of the groups and the independent variable. For example, an ANOVA would indicate whether a treatment significantly increased or decreased participants' weights. And at the same time it could determine whether the difference was more pronounced in males or females.

ANOVAs come in several varieties. A one-way ANOVA is used when there is just one independent and one dependent variable; however, the independent variable can have more than two levels in an ANOVA, but not in a *t* test. Remember, an independent variable with two levels is a kind of either/or variable, e.g., the subjects either receive an aspirin or they don't. However, some independent variables have three or more levels (0 aspirin, 1 gm of aspirin, 2 gms, etc.). A two-way ANOVA is used to analyze the difference between groups when more than one independent variable is used, or when an independent and moderator variable are both used. A three-way ANOVA is also possible for a multifactor analysis, but if you are thinking in terms of a complex design, you should consult a statistician in the early stages of planning. The important thing to keep in mind is that the choice of statistical procedure depends on the type of data and the number of variables in an experiment.

REFERENCES

Bond, S. J., & Hayes, J. R. (1984). Cues people use to paragraph text. *Research in the Teaching of English, 18,* 147–167.

Campbell, D. T., & Stanley, J. C. (1966). *Experimental and quasi-experimental designs for research.* Boston: Houghton Mifflin.

Connors, R., & Glenn, C. (1995). *The St. Martin's guide to teaching writing* (3rd ed.). New York: St. Martin's.

Douglas, R., & MacNealy, M. S. (1993). Effective training techniques: Oral versus written. In *Proceedings of IPCC93—The new face of technical communication: People, processes, products* (pp. 364–368). New York: Institute of Electrical and Electronic Engineers.

Houp, K. W., Pearsall, T. E., & Tebeaux, E. (1995). *Reporting technical information* (9th ed.). Boston: Allyn & Bacon.

Koen, F., Becker, A., & Young, R. (1969). The psychological reality of the paragraph. *Journal of Verbal Learning and Verbal Behavior, 8,* 49–53.

LaJeunesse, T. (1993). Stalking the student research volunteer. *Interchange, 12,* 6–7.

MacNealy, M. S., & Hedges, K. (1996). Effects of line length on the psychological reality of the paragraph. In R. J. Kreuz and M. S. MacNealy (Eds.), *Empirical approaches to literature and aesthetics* (pp. 99–124). Norwood, NJ: Ablex.

National Commission for the Protection of Human Subjects of Biomedical and Behavioral Research. (1983). *Belmont Report: Ethical Principles and Guidelines for the Protection of Human Subjects of Research.* (DHEW Publication No. 0578-0012). Washington, DC: U.S. Government Printing Office.

Soderston, C., & German, C. (1985). An empirical study of analogy and person in computer documentation. In *Proceedings of the 32nd International Technical Communications Conference* (pp. RET:13-RET:16). Arlington, VA: Society for Technical Communication.

Twyman, M. (1981). Typography without words. *Visible Language, 15,* 5–12.

Wallace, D. L., & Hayes, J. R. (1991). Redefining revision for freshmen. *Research in the Teaching of English, 25,* 54–66.

Williams, T. H. (1952). *Lincoln and his generals.* New York: Knopf.

▶ 6

Meta Analysis

In this chapter, I want to introduce a research methodology that hasn't yet been used very frequently in research on writing; however, I expect more and more writing researchers to use meta analysis as the field grows. Because many principles of meta analysis are similar to principles in experiments, I am putting the two chapters side by side although, in some respects, a meta analysis is a type of literature review—one that is conducted empirically and analyzed statistically.[1] To introduce you to meta analysis, I am going to start with a new fictional problem (no eyelashes in this chapter) and explain how a meta analysis can help solve that problem.

A FICTIONAL PROBLEM

Suppose you became interested in the application of the "you attitude" (Houp, Pearsall, & Tebeaux, 1995, pp. 235–236) to the design of user manuals, so you searched the literature for empirical projects which could tell you whether or not the use of the "you attitude" in computer manuals is an effective rhetorical strategy. Much to your surprise, you find that several studies have been done to evaluate the use of "you" in formal writing. Researchers in most of these studies prepared two versions of a text—one which used "you" frequently and the other which used first or third person pronouns frequently—and then asked subjects to say which version was more

---

[1]Note that I am restricting the term meta analysis to an integration of *quantitative* findings. Thus, I exclude from this discussion the article by Smeltzer and Thomas (1994) which is labeled a meta analysis. The authors, themselves, explain that they could not carry out the statistical analysis because the articles they examined did not include necessary data. Instead, Smeltzer and Thomas grouped the articles they studied into three categories and then reviewed them much as one would do in a literature review. However, Smeltzer and Thomas' article differs from a literature review in that they did use meta analysis procedures to select the articles they included in their study.

effective. Other researchers used tests to measure comprehension after subjects had read one of two versions of a text. Still other studies timed subjects who were asked to perform a task by following the directions in one of two versions of a user's manual. Table 6-1 contains a list of some of these imaginary studies.

Examining Table 6-1, we can see that some researchers studied the use of "you" in memos (e.g., Adams; Davis); others studied business letters (e.g., Ellis; Insler). Three projects studied the use of "you" in computer manuals (Carter; Fox; Gerrig). However, the results of all these studies are mixed: some found that using "you" in formal writing was in bad taste (Brown); others found that using "you" helped to promote a cooperative attitude in the recipient of the memos (Ellis); still others found that using "you" in job application letters created a favorable attitude in interviewers (Lane). Note that since we are particularly interested in computer manuals, we have a problem because Gerrig found negative results while Carter and Fox found positive ones. So who should we believe?

One poor strategy would be to simply count to see if more of the studies found a positive result for the "you attitude" because six of the studies had positive results and six negative (see Table 6-2). But even if there had been more studies that found

TABLE 6-1   **Fictional Studies Showing Reactions to Materials with a "You Attitude"**

	Form		Subjects		Material	Findings
Author	**Type**	**Time**	**Num**	**Pool**		
Adams	True	3 wks	10	students	Memos	Negative
Brown	True	3 wks	20	relatives	Letters of Complaint	Negative
Carter	True	1 wk	30	students	Manuals	Positive
Davis	True	4 wks	40	phone list	Memos	Positive
Ellis	True	2 wks	50	students	Letters of Adjustment	Positive
Fox	Quasi	5 wks	60	senior cit.	Manuals	Positive
Gerrig	Quasi	10 wks	70	employees[a]	Manuals	Negative
Hahn	True	7 wks	80	students	Letters of Complaint	Negative
Insler	True	1 wk	90	students	Letters of Adjustment	Negative
Jones	True	5 wks	100	students	Job Application Letters	Negative
Kepler	True	9 wks	110	students	Oral Conversation	Positive
Lane	True	2 wks	20	managers[b]	Job Application Letters	Positive

a = employee list from personnel office at ABC Company
b = personnel managers from Memphis firms employing more than 1,000 persons

TABLE 6-2 **Fictional Studies Showing Significance of Reactions to Materials with a "You Attitude"**

Author	Form Type	Subjects	Material	Findings	Probability
Adams	True	10	Memos	Negative	.05
Brown	True	20	Letters of Complaint	Negative	.04
Carter	True	30	Manuals	Positive	.02
Davis	True	40	Memos	Positive	.025*
Ellis	True	50	Letters of Adjustment	Positive	.01**
Fox	Quasi	60	Manuals	Positive	.03*
Gerrig	Quasi	70	Manuals	Negative	.06
Hahn	True	80	Letters of Complaint	Negative	.001**
Insler	True	90	Letters of Adjustment	Negative	.03
Jones	True	100	Job Application Letters	Negative	.04*
Kepler	True	110	Oral Conversation	Positive	.02
Lane	True	20	Job Application Letters	Positive	.02*

*significant at $p < .05$
**significant at $p < .01$

positive results, counting the studies by this system doesn't take into account whether the findings were statistically significant. Moreover, if we counted up the studies in Table 6-2, we would end up with six studies which found a significant difference between writings with a "you attitude" and those without; and our count would produce six studies that didn't find a significant difference between the two versions. Does that mean there is no significant difference? No, because studies with a small number of subjects often don't find a significant difference when one really exists—a problem we will look at more closely in a few minutes. The major difficulty in deciding to compare the number of studies that found a significant difference with those that didn't is that we have not taken into account whether the findings were significantly positive or negative. If we restrict our count to only those studies that found a significant difference, we end up with four studies that found significantly positive results (Table 6-2: Davis, Ellis, Fox, and Lane) and two studies that found significantly negative results (Table 6-2: Hahn, and Jones), but what does that tell us? Thus, finding a way to really integrate a number of studies, each with different findings, could help sort out this jumble and show the true state of any difference.

META ANALYSIS: AN INTEGRATION TOOL

What is needed to resolve the problem described above is a way of integrating the findings from the various studies. Such an integration also has the potential to balance out the strengths and weaknesses of the various studies. In this situation, a meta analysis can be very helpful.

Another problem where meta analyses have proven very useful is the proliferation of research in an area. The number of scientific journals has multiplied so rapidly that many scientists now claim that they simply haven't the time to read every published report of research in a particular area, let alone reports of projects completed, but not published, as is the case with most dissertations and theses (Cooper, 1982; Glass, McGaw, & Smith, 1981; Hunter, Schmidt, & Jackson, 1982). In such a situation, many researchers rely on literature reviews, but these can be problematic also for several reasons. First, no literature review can hope to cover all the reports produced in some areas; for example, in 1981 Glass et al. estimated that well over 5,000 projects had investigated gender differences. Even if the number of articles in a particular area is only 1,000, how can a reviewer deal with all of these in one review article other than by presenting a list of brief annotations?

Another reason that literature reviews are limiting is that the author picks and chooses which reports to include based on the author's perception of relevance to his or her topic; or worse, the reviewer picks those studies which agree with his or her own opinions. And finally, literature reviews are subject to bias in that authors of reviews make judgments about the results or quality of the research methods. These judgments are sometimes idiosyncratic. For example, Glass, et al (1981) describe a study which compared evaluations between a group who did a qualitative review and a group who did a quantitative review of just seven research reports, totaling some 50 journal pages. The conclusions the two groups reached were vastly different. On the other hand, because a meta analysis relies to a great extent on statistical measures, the resulting integration of research findings is less problematic.

However, a meta analysis is really not feasible until a discipline has developed to the state in which several studies have been completed. To do an effective meta analysis, you probably need to find at least six studies which meet all your criteria for inclusion. Because technical communication is a relatively new discipline, there may not be a sufficient number of studies in any one area to make a meta analysis feasible. Smelzer and Thomas (1994) did attempt a meta analysis of research on managers as writers. Although they found a sufficient number of studies on this topic, they were unable to complete the meta analysis because some of the research reports lacked the necessary data. On the other hand, composition studies have a longer history than professional writing studies, so a few meta analyses of issues in composition have been completed: for example, Atkinson's (1993) study comparing the effects of three modern methods of teaching writing—workshopping, teaching inquiry skills, and computer assisted instruction. Another meta analysis (Schramm

1989) looked at studies on the effects of using a word processor on revision—an area in which the results of one study are often contradicted by the results of another (see, for example, Hawisher, 1988; McAllister & Louth, 1988; Schriner, 1988).

The granddaddy of meta analysis in composition studies is that conducted by George Hillocks in the early 1980's. Over the years a great many composition research projects had tried to determine the effects of teaching grammar and mechanics on students' writing ability, but the results didn't mesh because some findings suggested one thing and some another. Therefore Hillocks designed a careful meta analysis to integrate these findings. As we explore facets of meta analysis in this chapter, I will refer both to the Hillocks (1986) study and to the fictional problem described above (the effectiveness of the "you attitude") as illustrative examples.

What is a meta analysis? Briefly, it can be described as a kind of experiment in which prior experiments are the subjects. For example, in an experiment, after a treatment has been given to the experimental group, we measure the performance of the subjects in both groups and enter a score for *each subject* separately into an analysis package. In a meta analysis, we consider that the treatment has been given and the results measured in each study, and we enter a score from *each study,* one-by-one, into an analysis package. Thus, many of the same issues and constraints of experimental research are present in a meta analysis; perhaps the major question is how to select the subjects (i.e., specific research reports) from among the prior research projects in a particular area. Then the matter of integrating a variety of scoring techniques has to be solved—but more about that later. Selecting subjects for a meta analysis involves two steps: a broad search for everything that is available (published and unpublished, as you will see) on the topic of interest, and choosing a purposeful sample of available reports to include in the analysis.

SELECTING SUBJECTS: THE BROAD SEARCH

First, of course, you have to identify all possible candidates for use in the study. This step is more complex than you might think. Of course, there are the usual sources including computer searches of data bases such as Dissertation Abstracts International and journals in the field. However, the power of a meta analysis depends on doing a really broad search for possibly relevant research reports. Thus, a thorough researcher will use three other strategies as well: ancestry, descendancy, and invisible colleges (Cooper, 1982).

You will be familiar with at least two of these strategies from Chapter 2 on library research: *ancestry,* which refers to scanning reference lists for prior research mentioned in the text of an article or book; and *descendancy* which refers to searching citation indices for research reports published subsequently to the ones you've read. For a descendancy search, most authorities suggest using electronic searches such as ERIC, as well as searches in paper indices such as *Humanities and Social Sciences.*

The third source of possible studies, *invisible colleges,* was also briefly described in the second chapter when I advised you to ask your professor for suggestions. In many disciplines, professors know something about projects their friends and colleagues are currently engaged in or have previously investigated. Often professors send preliminary reports about their work to their colleagues. One reason invisible colleges are an important source is that the results of some projects may never be published. For example, scholarly journals often don't publish reports of research in which no significant difference was found; however, these reports could make an important contribution to a meta analysis. Also, as was discussed in Chapter 2, some research doesn't get published because it isn't on a topic that is currently "hot." When you approach a professor for help in finding invisible college resources, you can make the professor's task much easier if you provide him or her with a list of all studies you have already found (Hunter, et al., 1982).

Your goal, then, in stage one of a meta analysis is to do a broad search for research on the topic. This task involves a tremendous amount of time, such that a meta analysis is rarely undertaken by just one person unless that person is working on a dissertation. In Hillocks' (1986) case, he obtained a grant to fund a research team of several graduate students. The team located more than 500 studies which at least partially involved testing the effectiveness of teaching grammar and mechanics. For the imaginary study on the "you attitude," we will consider that we found 13 studies on pronoun effects—those listed in Tables 6-1 and 6-2, plus one other (Morris) which I discuss later.

SELECTING SUBJECTS: CHOOSING A SAMPLE

This step really involves two subprocesses: setting criteria for inclusion and then evaluating each candidate in terms of those criteria. As you know, Hillocks (1986) found over 500 candidates for his meta analysis. He could have included all of them, but if his original search was truly broad (and it was), then some of the candidates, on closer inspection, would prove to be inappropriate. The key to making this decision is similar to that in any empirical project: you have to define the construct or concept you want to investigate and define the criteria for selection. In defining the criteria, you will want to consider what constitutes effective and ineffective criteria. For example, in the case of our "you attitude" project, we did a broad search for projects involving *pronouns* and located 13 studies. At this stage, we will want to carefully define our topic of interest (the construct) as the effects of the use of "you" on a reader. With this definition, we will drop out one study (Morris) which investigated only first versus third person pronouns, leaving us with the 12 studies in Tables 6-1 and 6-2. Also, we should drop the Kepler study because it involves *listening,* not *reading.*

However, we don't want to make our definition too restrictive. For a meta analysis to have some teeth, it probably needs to have at least ten projects to use as subjects. Hillocks (1986) selected 60 out of the more than 500 studies he found, but the low number was not the result of a desire to select a small random sample. Instead, Hillocks set some criteria for inclusion and eliminated all studies which didn't fit. This procedure would be similar to selecting a purposeful sample or population of interest for an experiment; for example, we might only be interested in eyelash growth in males (how did eyelashes get in here?), so we would define the population as male and eliminate any studies which used only females from the group of possible subjects. But we could include studies which used both male and female subjects if measurements were reported according to gender.

Thus, in a meta analysis, the most important step in selecting the studies we will include as subjects is to define the criteria for selection. Of course these criteria differ according to the researchers' goals, but in any case, decisions will have to be made about such issues as whether to use only true experiments or to include quasi ones as well. In order to point out the issues involved in setting criteria for evaluating studies from the broad search, I will first point out some ineffective criteria and then some effective ones.

Ineffective Criteria for Selection

As I mentioned above, one important issue to settle is whether to include quasi as well as true experiments. On this question alone, you will want to do some careful thinking. As I pointed out in the last chapter, the results of a quasi experiment may be considered a little less precise than those in a true experiment because the subjects are not randomly assigned to conditions. However, a quasi experiment has the advantage of being conducted in a more natural environment, and it is often the only type experiment available to researchers in educational settings.

Glass (1978) recommends not dropping candidates because they seem "poor" or "weak" (e.g., perhaps the methods used were not very rigorous). He explains that studies have shown that poor studies do not adversely affect the results unless there is a major bias in assigning subjects to conditions. On the other hand, because weak studies increase the size of the data base, they can help the analysis add up to a strong conclusion. A large data base in a meta analysis also means that the analysis can be subdivided to look at several issues more or less simultaneously. For example, Atkinson's (1993) study compared three teaching methods: work-shopping, inquiry skills, and computer-assisted instruction. If sorting your broad sample according to a specified construct leaves you with a huge database, you could subdivide the studies along some variable to assess the effect of a moderator variable. For example if we had turned up a large number of studies about the "you attitude," we could have subdivided the studies into genres, so we would analyze the effects of the attitude on memos, on job application letters, on manuals, and so forth. But we would want to be cautious about setting up sub-categories for analysis because the smaller the number of subjects in an analysis, the less likely one is to find a significant difference. Hillocks (1986) decided to include both true and quasi experiments if they met other criteria. So let's do the same for our meta analysis of the "you attitude."

Having decided to include both true and quasi experiments, we have set up a possible problem of bias in subject selection because, if you remember, quasi experiments do not include random assignment of subjects to the various conditions. How can we be sure that the subjects were all equal before the treatment? Well, many quasi experiments include some measurement to show that there is no significant difference between subjects in the experimental and control groups. Such measurements include a pre-test, a matching design, or some relevant measure such as a test of verbal ability for an experiment in writing. Hillocks (1986) decided to include only those quasi experiments which used a pre-test or matching procedure. However, we should ask whether a pre-test or other strategy to insure that the subjects are equivalent is necessary in our "you" study. Remember, that some of the studies on our list tested the effects of two or more versions of the *same* texts, and each version was considered to be a treatment or condition—so we don't have to establish that the conditions were equal before the treatment in those studies. On the other hand, we should carefully examine two studies from our list—those by Fox and Gerrig—in order to determine if any bias was present in the assignment of subjects to the two conditions or if any measurements were used to show that the subjects in the two conditions were essentially the same before treatment.

Next, I think it goes without saying that we are *not* going to leave out a study whose results don't fit our pre-conceived notion of what they should have been. Another possible, but ineffective, approach would be to include only those studies which found a significant effect, whether in favor of "you" or opposed. This is an ineffective strategy because it rules out studies whose results were marginally significant. In fact, some of these results may have been significant except that the researcher made a Type II Error (you may want to review error types in the previous chapter) and concluded that the results were not significant, when in fact their significance would have shown up if the researcher had used a .05 level of probability instead of a .01. For example, look at the study by Davis in Table 6-2 in which 40 subjects were recruited by phone and then randomly assigned to experimental and control conditions. If Davis had set his probability level at .01 and the results were .025, he would have to conclude that the difference was insignificant, although it is easy to see that the results are significant when the *p* value is .05. Similarly, the results in the studies by Adams, Brown, and Carter would all be considered significant if the *p* value had been .05. This point is especially important when the number of subjects is small: remember that Type II Errors (the *p* value is too low: .01 instead of .05) can be affected by the number of subjects. Thus, we will include studies with both positive and negative findings and studies whose results were significant or not because the subjects from these studies will increase the size of our subject pool (Adams by 10; Brown by 20; and Carter by 30, to name but a few). Thus, the sample size in our meta analysis will be larger and less susceptible to error.

A fourth ineffective criterion for eliminating studies from a meta analysis is to set an arbitrary number of subjects that a study must have. Studies with larger numbers of subjects are more reliable; however, selecting studies to be used as subjects in our meta analysis on an arbitrary basis of at least 50 subjects in the study would be foolish. For example, we know that the number of subjects in an experiment ought to be no less than ten per condition, and since an experiment has two conditions (experimental group and control group) a good study should have at least 20 subjects. Therefore, we have some grounds for dropping Adams from our meta analysis. However, consider that the small number of subjects in Adams' study is going to be balanced out when those numbers are added to the number of subjects in the other studies. Thus, dropping a study just on the basis of number of subjects is not wise.

A fifth ineffective criterion for selecting research reports to be included in the analysis is source of publication. For example, Glass, et al. (1981) caution against using only journal articles and excluding book chapters, theses, dissertations, and so forth. As I pointed out earlier, journals tend to be a biased set because most do not accept reports on research that failed to find a significant difference between groups. Remember, however, that although unpublished studies tend to have smaller effect sizes (Hunter, et al., 1982), they will still add power to the meta analysis by increasing the total number of subjects. Moreover, we don't want to restrict our sources to professional journals because such journals often don't accept research reports on topics considered not current or important.

Sixth, note that Table 6-1 gives the duration of the period of data collection. The duration of the treatment in many experiments could be an important criterion for selection. Hillocks (1986), for example, did not include any study which was so short that it evaluated only one piece of writing. This criterion makes a lot of sense for Hillocks' study because one of the factors he was examining was mode of instruction, and a mode of instruction can hardly be assessed unless the instruction is given over a period of time. In fact, some experts suggest that in cases where length of time, or some similar variable, might have affected the results, the meta analysis researcher could assign weights to various studies based on some specific criterion (Rosenthal, 1984). If you decide you need to assign weights, however, you must get at least two judges to make independent decisions about which studies should be more heavily weighted. In contrast to Hillocks, the time involved in the treatment for our investigation into the effectiveness of the "you attitude" is not important: the time needed to write a memo or a manual is not the focus of our study. What we are interested in is the reaction of readers to the presence or absence of the "you attitude" in the piece of writing.

Finally, the question arises about what to do with a study whose results are so different from the results of the other studies, that one may suspect an anomaly. Some years ago, a good meta analysis excluded studies which were outliers. An *outlier* is a subject whose performance is so very different from the other subjects, that including that subject will skew the results. Today, statisticians have devised formulas to adjust the outliers (see, for example, Hunter, et al., 1982). However, to get a grip on the concept of outliers, let's look at a similar instance that you are probably very familiar with: grading on the curve. Most students don't like grading on the curve because it limits the number of A's that can be earned; grading on the curve is based on the assumption that the grades in a class should follow the pattern of the bell curve with some students in each letter-grade category, and with most students' grades clustered around the average (those would receive a C). Let's look at a case in which grading on the curve might be beneficial to students. Imagine that on a test, the grades looked like this: 65, 65, 66, 66, 67, 70, 70, 71, 71, 71, 72, 72, 73, 74, 75, 75, 76, 76, 77, 99. Using a grading scale of 94–100 = A; 85–93 = B; 76–84 = C; 68–75 = D; and 0–67 = F, only one student would get an A, no one would get a B, three would get a C, eleven would get a D, and five would get an F. If we graded on the curve and used the same spread between letter grades, students within four points of either side of the average (73) would get a C and so on. Then no one would get an F, five would get a D, fourteen would get a C, and one would get an A, but there would still be no B's—a skewed distribution because something is still out of kilter. However, if we drop the 99 when we calculate the average and use the same spread between letter grades, students scoring four points on either side of 71 would get a C, so there would be no F's, four D's, twelve C's, three B's, and one A—a much more even distribution. The fact is that the score of 99 is some kind of fluke—in statistical terms, an outlier.

Meta analysis researchers who want to avoid the skewed results of including an outlier usually run a statistical test of homogeneity to ensure that none of the studies under consideration has produced results which would make it an anomaly. Following a test of homogeneity, Hillocks dropped three studies from his sample because the test showed them to be true outliers. In the sample of studies we have assembled on the "you attitude," we may spot one that looks like an outlier, or we may conclude than none look like outliers. But we should not rely on our hunches to determine the homogeneity of the studies. We need to consult a statistician to help us do a test we can use as the basis for our decision and possibly bring the outlier into a closer relationship with the other studies by use of statistical procedures that will measure the deficiency and correct for it.

Effective Criteria for Selection

Effective criteria should help us exclude studies whose focus does not match our area of interest or whose methodology casts some question on the reliability and validity of the results.

First, the focus of the studies in the broad pool must be examined carefully to be sure that the construct studied is the one we are interested in. For example, in our fictional study, we are concerned with effects of the "you attitude" on *writing*, so we dropped Kepler's study of the effects of the "you attitude" in oral conversation (see Table 6-1). Similarly, Hillocks included only those studies that measured a *written product* after the treatment, so he excluded any studies which used only tests such as multiple choice to determine whether students had control of grammar.

Second, we want to be sure that any study we include is not flawed in a major way by some threat to validity. Remember, we don't want to exclude weak studies (those, for example, in which just one class of students meeting in the evening was asked to evaluate two versions of a piece of writing) because such findings can help develop the overall picture. Thus we must determine what constitutes a major methodological inadequacy, given our topic of interest. According to Hunter, et al. (1982), all studies are inadequate in some way. However, we will want to determine some basic criteria to eliminate major threats, such as researcher bias, that occur in educational research when there is only one researcher and he or she is the teacher. For example, Hillocks excluded any studies that did not have minimal control over the possibility of teacher bias. He specified that each condition, experimental and control, had to be taught by at least two teachers, so either a study had to have a minimum of four teachers, or if only two teachers were used, each one would have had to teach both an experimental and a control class. Hillocks was also concerned about a possible bias in the judges of the writings. He eliminated any study in which judges might have had some grounds for guessing whether a piece of writing was produced by a student in the control condition or the experimental condition. We, too, should be concerned about bias, and thus, we should eliminate Brown's study from our sample since Brown used her relatives as her subjects (see Table 6-1).

ANALYZING THE RESULTS

As with the other quantitative studies described in this book, meta analysis requires statistical tests to determine whether the results of the studies included are significant in some way. One poor strategy is to add up all the probability scores and average them to see if the average p (probability) score indicates a significant difference. If we summed the scores in Table 6-2, we would come up with a total of .335. Dividing .335 by the number of studies (11) would give us a p value of .03. However, this value is meaningless for several reasons. Foremost, we cannot interpret the significance of a p value unless we have stated in advance which level of probability we will consider significant. (You may want to review the information on probability in Chapters 4 and 5).

However, let's suppose for a moment that we did select .01 as the level of probability that we would consider significant (i.e., in only one chance in 100 projects like ours could the results have happened by chance). Since our average p is .03, we would have to conclude that the results of all the experiments in Table 6-2 are insignificant—no doubt a Type II Error (see Chapter 5). On the other hand, we could have selected .05 as the level of probability we would consider significant. In this case, our average p of .03 would seem to indicate that the results of all the studies in Table 6-2 are significant. But we would then have to say in what way they are significant—an impossible task because we have added results from experiments that found a positive effect with those which found a negative effect (e.g., the subjects in Insler liked the versions with "you" less than they liked the versions without "you," but the findings from Lane are exactly the opposite). Remember that the p value doesn't say whether something is worse or better; it only states the probability that the results happened by chance.

What to do, then? Remember that a meta analysis is rather like an experiment in which each study is a subject, and the data from each study are entered into a statistical analysis procedure just as the measurements of each subject's eyelashes are entered into a statistical analysis at the end of our aspirin and eyelash study. Note, however, that whereas we measured all our subjects' eyelashes with the same instrument, the studies included in a meta analysis may have used very different sets of measurements. In measuring the quality of essays, one researcher may have decided to use a five point scale (e.g., 5 = excellent, 4 = good, 3 = average, 2 = poor, 1 = failure). In a different study, a researcher may have used a four point scale with 1 meaning excellent. Obviously you cannot add such scores together to get an average score for all the essays. Therefore, researchers often convert the raw scores to *z* scores, using a mathematical formula based on the average score. A statistician can help you with this task as well as the other statistical procedures mentioned earlier. In fact, it would be wise to set up a data matrix of the studies you want to analyze. In the matrix, you could list the various statistics given in the study such as the number of subjects in each group, the Chi Square value or the *F* score from an ANOVA, the degrees of freedom, the mean for each group, the standard deviation, and so forth. With this data, a statistician can help you correct for sampling errors, errors in measurement, and range variation as Hunter, et al. (1982) recommend. A statistician can also help you calculate some of the statistics (for example, degrees of freedom) that the authors of the study failed to provide.

Finally, researchers conducting a meta analysis often use a statistic called *effect size* to evaluate the results. When researchers calculate effect size, they need only four pieces of information: the mean scores and the standard deviations for both the experimental and control groups. The effect size is calculated by subtracting the mean score of the control group from the mean score of the experimental group and dividing that number by the pooled standard deviation. This procedure is complex enough that you will probably want to consult a statistician for help and advice if you plan to conduct a meta analysis. However, if you simply want to evaluate a report of a meta analysis conducted by someone else, then it is helpful to know that effect size scores typically range from –3 to +3. A score of .20 to .50 indicates an important effect; a score of .50 or above indicates a major difference (Lauer & Asher, 1988). Note that effect size scores can be either positive or negative. Thus, Hillocks found that the teaching method he labeled as "inquiry skills" had a substantially positive effect on students' learning (ES = +.56); in contrast, the teaching method he labeled as "grammar/mechanics" also had an important effect size, but in the opposite direction (ES = –.29) so that one could reasonably conclude that this teaching method is harmful to students who are trying to learn to write well.

Note that the information we have collected in Tables 6-1 and 6-2 does not contain the means or standard deviations from the eleven studies we plan to include, so we cannot complete our meta analysis of the effects of the "you attitude" on readers. Unfortunately, a very similar problem occurred in the only meta analysis of a technical communication issue that I know of (Smeltzer & Thomas, 1994). Although these researchers did a very broad search and set good criteria for selection of studies, in the end they had to resort to doing a literature review rather than a statistical meta analysis because the original research reports did not contain the data needed to calculate effect size.

However, the question of whether using the "you attitude" has a positive effect on readers deserves some further attention. Soderston and German (1985) reported positive effects from the use of the "you attitude" on readers of manuals, but as far as I know, there aren't enough other studies on this issue for anyone to do a meta analysis. So if you are looking for a good topic for a research project, you might want to think about exploring this question and thus helping build a sufficient body of studies so that a meta analysis on the "you attitude" in writing can someday be done.

REFERENCES

Atkinson, D. L. (1993). A meta-analysis of recent research in the teaching of writing: Workshops, computer applications, and inquiry (Doctoral dissertation, Purdue University, 1989). *Dissertation Abstracts International, A 54:09,* 3354.

Cooper, H. (1982). Scientific guidelines for conducting integrative research reviews. *Review of Educational Research, 52,* 291–302.

Glass, G. V. (1978). Integrating findings: The meta analysis of research. In L. S. Shulman (Ed.), *Review of research in education* (Vol. 5). Itasca, IL: F. E. Peacock.

Glass, G. V., McGaw, B., & Smith, M. L. (1981). *Meta analysis in social research.* Beverly Hills, CA: Sage.

Hawisher, G. (1988). Research update: Writing and word processing. *Computers and Composition, 5,* 7–23.

Hillocks, G., Jr. (1986). *Research on written composition: New directions for teaching.* Urbana, IL: ERIC and the National Clearinghouse on Reading and Communication Skills.

Houp, K. W., Pearsall, T. E., & Tebeaux, E. (1995). *Reporting technical information* (9th ed.). Boston: Allyn and Bacon.

Hunter, J. E., Schmidt, F. L., & Jackson, G. B. (1982). *Meta-analysis: Cumulative research findings across studies.* Beverly Hills, CA: Sage.

Lauer, J. M., & Asher, L. W. (1988). *Composition research: Empirical designs.* New York: Oxford University Press.

McAllister, C., & Louth, R. (1988). The effect of word processing on the quality of basic writers' revisions. *Research in the Teaching of English, 22,* 417–427.

Rosenthal, R. (1984). *Meta-analysis procedures for social research.* London: Sage.

Schramm, R. M. (1989). The effects of using word processing equipment in writing instruction: A meta analysis (Doctoral dissertation, Northern Illinois University, 1989). *Dissertation Abstracts International, A 50:08,* 2463.

Schriner, D. K. (1988). Risk taking, revising, and word processing. *Computers and Composition, 5,* 43–54.

Smeltzer, L. R., & Thomas, G. F. (1994). Managers as writers: A metanalysis of research in context. *Journal of Business and Technical Communication, 8,* 186–211.

Soderston, C., & German, C. (1985). An empirical study of analogy and person in computer documentation. In *Proceedings of the 32nd International Technical Communication Conference* (pp. RET:13–RET:16). Arlington, VA: Society for Technical Communication.

ADDITIONAL RESOURCES

Hedges, L. V. (1982). Estimating effect size for a series of independent experiments. *Psychological Bulletin, 92,* 490–499.

Hedges, L. V., & Olkin, I. (1985). *Statistical methods for meta analysis.* Orlando, FL: Academic Press.

Shulman, L. S. (Ed.). (1979). *Review of research in education* (Vol. 5). Itasca, IL: F. E. Peacock.

▶ 7

Discourse or
Text Analysis

WHAT ARE DISCOURSE AND TEXT ANALYSIS?

One window into a better understanding of practices in writing and teaching writing is an examination of actual discourse produced on the job, in the classroom, in meetings, and so forth. The term, *discourse analysis,* is most often associated with scholarship in linguistics, where discourse is taken to mean use of language. In its early history, linguistics focused on formal properties of language such as morphology, syntax, and phonology (Asher, 1994; Brown & Yule, 1983). However, today the field of linguistics is much more inclusive, even to the point of considering fashion and food systems as forms of communication worthy of scholarly interest (Asher, 1994). Analysis of written texts flourished in the middle 1700s as a tool for biblical scholars (Carney, 1972). In the early 1900s, communications scholars began using similar methods to analyze newspapers, although this type of research was and is referred to as "content analysis." Even though the method is called *content* analysis in communications research, characteristics of surface appearance (i.e., location on the page, number of inches used, and size of headline) interest researchers fully as much as the semantic content (Carney, 1972; Krippendorff, 1980; Weber, 1990). This type of research grew in importance during World War II because of the role of propaganda in military planning, and one result was an expansion in the types of discourse studied from written text to speeches, radio broadcasts, and TV programs and commercials. For example, TV commercials have been analyzed in terms of length, setting, promises made, presence of entertainment such as singing and dancing, and even photographic techniques such as pan and zoom (Thorson, 1989). Most of this sort of research continues to be carried out by scholars in communications; however, other disciplines are also beginning to emphasize systematic analysis of discourse as I will explain in the next sections.

At this point, it seems appropriate to give a more detailed definition of how the terms "discourse" and "text analysis" are used in this book. First, I use *discourse* and *text* to mean oral, written, and graphic materials that have been produced in *natural* situations for a particular audience and purpose (e.g., conversations, classroom discussions, speeches, reports, letters, and memos), as well as communicative materials produced for other reasons such as entertainment (e.g., novels, short stories, and magazine articles), and even pieces of text produced by students for a grade. Although "discourse" is commonly assumed to refer to a chunk of related words larger than a sentence (Asher, 1994; Brown & Yule, 1983), I use "discourse" and "text" to refer to chunks of related words, ranging from one-word commands to three or four-word fragmentary sentences to much longer pieces of text such as proposals and even textbooks. Second, *analysis* in this chapter means the use of systematic methods of study, including empirical techniques such as carefully defined populations of interests (e.g., essays written by grade school children or articles reporting on research in technical communication), carefully selected representative samples, and clearly defined procedures for collection and interpretation of data. In short, discourse analysis is a quantitative descriptive type of research, and, like the other empirical methods described in this book, discourse analysis relies on a well-designed, systematic method of investigation.

WHY STUDY DISCOURSE?

Studying discourse enables scholars to add to a body of knowledge in a particular discipline by making data-based inferences about the person[s] who created the discourse, the audience for the discourse, and the social and political context for the discourse, even when the persons involved have been long dead. Furthermore, studying current pieces of written discourse allows scholars to make similar inferences about people unobtrusively to avoid the possibility that the researcher's presence during a conversation might affect that conversation. On the other hand, it should be noted that a study of any set of texts is never entirely free of bias because very few pieces of discourse produced by marginalized elements of society are preserved, and thus available for analysis.

Scholars in different fields analyze discourse for a wide variety of reasons. For example, linguistics scholars, psychologists, literary scholars, and writing researchers often have very different purposes for analyzing discourse; and these purposes determine the methods used. However, in most cases, scholars use discourse analysis to provide data for making inferences about people, events, and objects that cannot be directly observed. For example, we cannot directly observe the people of classical Greece, but we can learn a lot about their beliefs and behavior by analyzing their extant discourse. To illustrate the way researchers from different disciplines use discourse analysis in their work, let's look at some specific examples.

Linguistic Scholars

Linguistic scholars study discourse to learn more about language itself and the ways it is used. Most linguistics scholars are interested in conversational discourse generated in natural settings; they study such phenomena as turn-taking, code switching, intonation patterns, small talk, apologies, politeness, and so on. However, recently some linguistics scholars have begun to study aspects of literature as well. For example, Kreuz, Roberts, Johnson, and Bertus (1996) wondered whether various types of figurative language tend to occur together. These researchers were not trying to uncover information for others to use for a pragmatic purpose such as improving the teaching of writing; instead, Kreuz and his colleagues wanted to know more about metaphors. This project is only one of many that examine metaphors. In fact, empirical research on metaphor often appears in non-literary scholarly journals (see, for example, Pollio, Smith, & Pollio, 1990; Smith, Pollio, & Pitts, 1981). Furthermore, one scholarly journal (*Metaphor and Symbolic Activity*) is devoted to publishing studies on metaphor.

Anthropologists

Anthropologists, on the other hand, use discourse analysis to provide data for making inferences about aspects of human beliefs and behaviors that cannot be directly observed. Like linguistics scholars, they may not have a practical goal in mind. Instead, some anthropologists want to learn more about how a group's cultural or religious beliefs influence behavior, so they study folktales, myths, and riddles. Sometimes they find commonalities in structure or motif across cultures. For example, Frazer (1978) found a number of motifs (e.g., the Magician King, human scapegoats, and worship of trees) common to early civilizations in a variety of places. Insights from these studies are sometimes picked up and used by researchers in other areas. For example, Roy Freedle (1996) investigated the effects of folktale characteristics such as common motif (e.g., greed), redundancy, and triadic structure on students' ability to recall the story of *Goldilocks and the Three Bears* after ten years.

Psychologists

Psychologists (in particular, clinical psychologists) have long used discourse analysis procedures to identify personality traits and group behavior patterns (Krippendorff, 1980). On the other hand, cognitive psychologists often analyze discourse to help them understand human memory and cognitive aspects of reading and writing. Freedle's (1996) study is one example. Another is Bourg's (1996) analysis of the coherence (in terms of causal structure) of two short stories; she counted the number of causal connections and clauses in the two stories. Her study was prompted by an earlier study of reading comprehension in which she found a difference in comprehension between sixth grade students who were taught strategies for empathy building and those who were not taught these strategies when the students read one short story, but no difference between the groups when they read a different story. In trying to explain the results of her earlier study, Bourg wondered whether the structure of the two texts used in the first study was a contributing factor. Thus, in her second study, Bourg analyzed the structure of the two texts and found that, indeed, they were different in amount of cohesion and that this difference affected comprehension.

Communications and Marketing Researchers

Communications and marketing researchers also often study the effects of text structure and content on audience emotions and beliefs. Much communications research has focused on newspapers, especially the editorials in newspapers. Several researchers in this area have attempted to identify characteristics of propaganda and the effects of propaganda on the citizens of countries engaged in war (for a summary of some of this work, see Krippendorff, 1980). More recently, communications researchers have been interested in rating violence in television shows and its possible effects on children's behavior (see, for example, Reglin, 1996). Marketing researchers are, of course, mostly interested in the effects of various advertising strategies such as brand names on audiences. However, recently a pair of marketing professors studied the occurrences of brand names in the six "Rabbit" novels of John Updike in an attempt to learn more about how consumer culture is embedded in the literature of a period (Cornwell & Keillor, 1996).

Literary Scholars

Literary Scholars have often used discourse analysis procedures to construct concordances (i.e., an index of the principal words in a book) and to settle questions of authorship and date of composition. For example, in a recent issue of *PMLA: Publications of the Modern Language Association of America*, Donald W. Foster (1996) bases much of his argument that Shakespeare is the W. S. who wrote *A Funeral Elegy* on a comparison of rare words used in that poem compared with words used 12 times or less in the complete body of Shakespeare's plays. Foster's claim aroused a flurry of letters from scholars who pointed out various problems with this type of analysis in the *Forum* section of a later issue (May 1997) of *PMLA*. Additionally, some literary scholars have become interested in how students read literature. For example, Gibbs and Nacimento (1996) asked students to read love poetry aloud and to comment on the meaning. Transcripts of these verbal protocols were analyzed for evidence of the presence of conceptual metaphors about love (e.g., LOVE IS A JOURNEY) in order to determine whether readers make use of previously identified conceptual metaphors of love in their attempts to understand a poem.

Writing Researchers

Writing researchers, like most of the non-linguistics researchers described in this list, are usually not so much interested in language itself as they are interested in what they can learn about something else through studying the language used in a particular situation. For example, I'm also currently involved in a project studying the use of metaphor, but what I want to know is whether metaphor is a useful strategy for technical communicators. Right now, I want to find out how frequently (if at all) metaphors appear in various types of published articles in technical writing journals because that will tell me whether technical writers find metaphors useful. Later, I may investigate the effects of metaphors on readers of technical writing.

As with other methods of empirical research, discourse analysis was first used in writing research by scholars interested in improving education in writing. Thus, some writing researchers compared texts produced by children in various grade levels in order to learn more about the development of writing skills; for example, Bereiter and Scardamalia (1987) compared texts written by students in the fourth grade with texts written by students in the eleventh grade. Both groups were given the same task: to write a set of instructions for a game they had learned by watching a videotape. An analysis of the students' written instructions showed that the students in the eleventh grade included an average of 20 out of a possible 23 relevant ideas, whereas the students in the fourth grade included an average of only eight out of the 23 relevant ideas. This disparity is not surprising in itself, given that one might expect a difference in memory capacity related to age. What is surprising is that follow-up interviews found that children in the fourth grade remembered the rules of the game quite well. Thus, the researchers were able to postulate some difference in writing ability rather than memory capacity.

Other researchers in writing have compared texts produced by novices and experts to learn what skills novices need to learn in order to become more expert writers (e.g., Flower & Hayes, 1980; Hayes & Flower, 1988). Still others have studied pieces of discourse to determine the truth of popular writing maxims. For example, Meade and Ellis (1970) examined 300 paragraphs from three sources (a literary magazine, a scholarly journal, and a newspaper's letters to the editor). They found that over half (56%) of the paragraphs were not developed according to patterns (e.g., comparison and contrast) advocated in textbooks for writers.

More recently, writing researchers have studied the discourses of certain communities, both modern and historical, to learn more about writing practices in those particular communities. For example, Bazerman (1988) has studied the rhetoric of the scientific article, as have Hyland (1996) and Vande Kopple (1994), and Walters (1993) has studied the rhetoric of the Royal Society in the 17th century, to give you but a few examples.

Additionally, technical communication researchers have studied texts in order to learn more about the development of their discipline. For example, I examined 20 years of the proceedings of the International Conference of the Society for Technical Communication in order to see how empirical research in the field has developed over time (MacNealy, 1992). One of my goals was to evaluate the amount and type of empirical research carried out by technical communicators and to identify those areas needing more empirical study. Another technical communication researcher, Elizabeth Tebeaux (1997), studied "how-to" books produced during the English Renaissance in order to better understand the development of principles now used by technical writers.

These examples are intended to show the many different purposes researchers in writing have for doing discourse analysis. In the rest of this chapter, I will describe various techniques for analyzing texts and point out areas where such techniques would be particularly suited to helping writing researchers learn more about writing and writers—both academic and non-academic—and teaching writing—both composition and technical communication.

CHOOSING TEXTS TO ANALYZE

When undertaking a discourse analysis project, a researcher will want to use many of the same principles described in Chapters 3 and 4 to ensure the reliability and validity of their findings. The purpose of the research project, of course, determines which texts a researcher will want to analyze. As I have mentioned previously, good research projects often arise from some kind of dissonance, such as a clash in beliefs, a lack of important information in some area, or expectations that are violated in some way. Sometimes, a researcher will want to analyze certain texts as part of a case study or ethnographic study of some community (e.g., Sperling, 1994). Other times, a researcher may devote his or her entire research effort to the analysis of certain texts as a way of answering a particular question, such as whether a certain teaching strategy helps students revise their writing (e.g., Wallace & Hayes, 1991). The scope of the project often determines how many pieces of discourse a researcher will examine and the method of examination. When a large body of possible texts for analysis exists, a researcher will want to use random sampling techniques to select the portions for analysis. Note that, in some instances, a stratified random sample may be called for because the researcher is interested in a particular subgroup of texts.

To illustrate my point, let me share a bit of personal history. Some years ago, I was surprised when I attended my first conference of a professional organization devoted to writing because so few of the presentations reported empirical research. Instead, I found paper after paper dealing with "How to do X" or "How my school/company does X." Later, I began to wonder if this state of affairs was limited to that particular conference and what areas of writing are particularly lacking in empirical research. After mulling over these questions, I decided to look at the *proceedings* of the STC's (Society for Technical Communication) annual conference over a 20 year period to answer some of my questions, at least in the area of professional communication (1992). Note that I selected a subgroup (*STC Proceedings*) from the larger topic of published articles reporting research in technical communication. Because I was interested in any changes in the amount of empirical research being done, I decided to look at each article in every STC proceedings over the 20 year period so that I could chart very precisely just what percent of the articles each year were based on empirical projects, and I could look to see if the situation showed improvement over time.

However, I knew that some recent proceedings included brief abstracts or introductions to stems (a sub-group devoted to a particular area of interest such as visuals) and panel discussions, as well as full-size articles in the tables of contents. So I planned to conduct a stratified sample of the 3,479 table of contents entries in that 20 year period: I decided to examine only those articles that were one page or longer. Sorting possible texts for analysis in this way produced a sample of 2,640 articles which I examined to determine whether or not they reported on empirical research (i.e., did the author use a standard empirical research methodology such as survey, case study, or experiment). Then I used a comparison of the number of articles reporting on empirical research versus the number that didn't to evaluate how much attention was placed on empirical research and how that attention increased as the discipline developed. My next step focused on an even smaller stratified sample: I categorized all the reports on empirical research that I found (only 148) by type of methodology, and I examined the description of the methodology in each report to assess its quality. Had I found a really large number of articles reporting on empirical research in these proceedings, I would probably have taken a random sample rather than examined the total set.

To give you an example of a project where a random sample is appropriate, let me describe a project I am currently working on with Kim Lindsey, a graduate student. Kim came to me questioning what to believe because she was reading in some textbooks that one should not use metaphors in technical writing because, by its nature, technical writing should be free of literary embellishments. However, other technical communicators were claiming that metaphors can help a reader better understand a piece of technical prose. So Kim and I decided to try to learn whether technical writers themselves use metaphors when they publish in the top five professional writing journals. Although we are limiting our study to one year (again a stratified sample), that is still a great deal of text to examine, so we are using a random number table to help us choose three pages from each published article. Those pages will be the chunks of discourse we will examine in detail. In some other project, researchers may decide to examine a certain number of sentences or paragraphs chosen at random, depending on the purpose of their research project.

DETERMINING APPROPRIATE SEGMENTS FOR ANALYSIS

Purpose determines the size of the segments of a text that are appropriate for a particular research project. In some instances, researchers decide to use the whole of a text. In composition studies, in particular, experts claim that evaluation of writing ability should never be based on anything less than a whole text such as an essay or a letter or a report. In fact, many teachers believe that writing ability is best assessed by examining portfolios. On the other hand, Elliot, Kilduff, and Lynch (1994) have developed a system for scoring "clusters" of student writing—that is a portion of a portfolio. These researchers have found that evaluating whole portfolios takes more time than most writing teachers have to devote to evaluating student writing. To evaluate student writing ability, researchers in writing most frequently use holistic scoring of student essays; these scores are then often used to measure the results of some teaching technique (see Chapter 5 for a description of holistic scoring methods; see also Cooper & Odell, 1977, for a description of other methods of evaluating student writing).

In research in technical writing, whole texts are also the choice of many researchers. For example, if one wants to determine the characteristics of a particular genre, then one would examine several examples of that genre, much as Bazerman did when he analyzed the characteristics of scientific articles (1988) and as Walters did when he investigated the scientific method and prose style of the Royal Society in the 17th century (1993). Some researchers choose even larger pieces of discourse such as whole textbooks; for example, Teresa Kynell (1994) examined five editions, ranging from 1971 to 1991, of one author's technical writing textbook as a way of learning about the development of technical writing as a discipline.

On the other hand, a researcher may only be interested in specific segments of some texts. For example, some one could decide to look only at specific portions of a scientific article, such as its list of references. Eugene Garfield has done extensive work with reference lists, trying to identify superstars—those authors whose work is referenced over and over in a given field (1986). Similarly, Elizabeth Smith (1996) examined the reference lists in articles published in the five major technical journals from 1971 to 1992 in order to learn from the frequency of citations which authors have had a significant impact on the development of the discipline of technical writing. Reference lists were also used by Phillips, Greenberg, and Gibson (1993) to trace the development of composition studies as a discipline.

In spoken discourse, segments for analysis are often tape-recorded conversations of various lengths (see, for example, Tannen's 1994 work on how the verbal interactions in naturally occurring conversations between men and women contribute to or construct their relationship in terms of power). A writing researcher interested in analyzing a teacher's typical response pattern in a classroom might tape-record student/teacher discourse and then break the recorded discourse into units of student-question-plus-teacher-response. Another writing researcher interested in turn-taking strategies might want to examine a longer piece of recorded conversation such as that taking place in student peer-group evaluations.

Still smaller segments of text have been used by some writing researchers. For example, Dallin D. Oaks (1995) looked at advertising slogans to determine what strategies help create structural ambiguities which capture the reader's interest. The units Oaks examined range from tags such as "Pepper with Personality" to complete sentences such as "Cheese can make you a hero this weekend" (p. 372). Another researcher who used very small segments of text is Zhu (1995) who examined the quantity and quality of written and oral peer feedback on student writing.

A different type of discourse segment studied by technical writing researchers is the graphics used in an article or book. For example, Jansen and Lentz (1996) examined the illustrations used in Dutch product instructional materials published between 1880 and 1990 to determine the prevalence of realistic pictures of human beings using the equipment. Gregory Wickliff (1996), on the other hand, selected 23 photographic images from 40 illustrated texts published between 1854 and 1900 to examine the rhetorical roles photographs filled in that period.

By now, you can see that the portion of text used for discourse analysis varies according to the purpose of the researcher. For those researchers using graphics, it is easy to identify where the graphic segment begins and where it ends. Similarly, researchers can rely on other visual cues in the text to identify segments of interest. For example, it is usually obvious where a numbered list begins and ends or where an abstract begins and ends. Paragraph indentations are visual cues for the beginning and ending of paragraphs. One caution about using paragraphs as a unit of analysis: if you are studying paragraph structure, then the indentations are useful markers of segments for analysis. However, if you are studying content, you should be aware that the topic of a segment of discourse could be carried on for three or more consecutive paragraphs. In such a case, textual cues are very important. For example, if you were studying the use of extended analogies, you might be able to identify the beginning of a segment of interest by looking for words and phrases commonly used to introduce hypothetical situations, such as "When a person…", or subjunctive verbs, such as "If a man were to…". In such cases, researchers have to look closely at the content of a piece of text to determine where segments of interest begin and end. In other cases, it is fairly easy to identify the boundaries of a segment of interest. For example, those scholars examining conversational patterns such as student-question-plus-teacher-response have little trouble identifying where the segments begin and end. Other textual markers used by researchers are verbal cues such as "for example" for those studying development of ideas by means of examples, and "in those days" or "in my class" which are used to identify the beginning of an illustrative narrative. Whatever boundary markers you decide to use, you should clearly identify them in your description of your methodology.

TOOLS FOR ANALYSIS

As experts have pointed out, there is no single correct way of analyzing discourse (Carney, 1972; Weber, 1990). Each researcher must choose the tools that will best suit his or her purpose. However, most tools for discourse analysis are based on one principle: categorization. In some studies, it is also important to count the number of items in each category, and in other studies it is important to register omissions of expected material. But more about these concerns later. First let's consider some principles for developing effective categorization schemes. Then I will describe methods appropriate for analysis of different types of discourse features such as style, structure, rhetorical strategies, and semantic information.

Defining the Construct of Interest

The first step in developing a plan for doing discourse analysis is to carefully define the construct. Then the categories are developed by considering the ways that the construct can be divided up. The validity of classification schemes is based on the extent to which the categories accurately represent the facets of the construct of interest. Perhaps you recall the discussion of constructs from an earlier chapter and the care that should be taken in defining them. For example, the construct of "dog owner" could be variously defined as (1) the person who provides for the physical needs of the dog—i.e., food, water, shelter; (2) the person who buys the license for the dog; or (3) the person who most frequently plays with the dog. In a typical family, definitions 1 and 2 probably fit parents better than children, but definition 3 could fit a child better than a parent.

In discourse analysis, the range of possible constructs is very large. Writing researchers are often interested in assessing the quality of a piece of writing. In student essays, quality has been found to correlate with length, so many researchers measure the length of the piece of writing. Other researchers have based assessment of quality on the number of ideas an essay contains.

Researchers in composition most frequently use holistic scoring of student essays to assess the quality of student writings. Holistic scoring can be accomplished fairly quickly if raters are well-trained, and these scores are usually used to measure the results of some teaching technique. In holistic scoring, usually at least three persons read each paper and give it a score (between 1 and 4) based on their overall impression. Then the scores are summed, or, in some cases, averaged. (See Odell and Cooper, 1980, for a succinct description of holistic scoring and other methods for evaluating student writing). Thus, holistic scoring assumes that the qualities which characterize good writing cannot be separately assessed.

In professional writing, accuracy of description, concern for audience needs, and conciseness are often associated with good quality. However, researchers in writing often turn their attention to descriptive tasks rather than evaluative ones. For example, a researcher may be interested in learning what features are characteristic of a particular genre or of the writings of a particular community, past or present. How you define the construct you want to investigate will determine what procedures you will use to examine the texts.

Choosing Recording Units

Once you have defined the construct of interest, you will need to specify what features of the discourse you want to count or categorize. If you are interested in length, you could count words. However, in research with newspaper articles, researchers often measure length in column inches. If you are interested in grammatical features, you may decide to count parts of speech, linking verbs, passive voice, and so on. On the other hand, if you are focusing on semantic properties, you will have to decide whether to count synonyms and pronouns in the same group with their referent or count them separately. Later, in the section where I describe types of discourse analysis, you will see a great variety of recording units chosen by those who have used discourse analysis procedures to study writing.

Creating Categories

When considering possible categories, you will probably be pulled in at least two directions. First, you need a sufficient number of categories so that you can make meaningful distinctions between the data. If, for example, you find that the category labeled "other" contains a really large part of the data, you will need to develop some additional categories. Also, the categories you select should be so carefully defined that a piece of data can logically be placed in only one of them. If you find you have overlapping categories, then you may need to create additional ones to help reduce this confusion. Or you may need to rewrite the category definitions to narrow their boundaries or to make the boundaries more specific. On the other hand, a set of categories should not be so large that managing them becomes unwieldy. After all, the purpose of categorization is to reduce data by systematically grouping them into units that enable a researcher to make inferences about the construct of interest. For example, look at the text in Figure 7-1 and think about various possibilities for categorizing portions of it.

One way to categorize the data in Figure 7-1 is to group all words according to the letter of the alphabet that they begin with (26 categories), but what would be the point? On the other hand, we could look for instances of alliteration (a series of words beginning with the same sound). In this case, we would be interested in *style*—especially literary style—so it would make sense to have other categories of literary devices such as simile, metaphor, and so on in our categorization scheme. As an alternative, we could analyze the *structure* of the sentence in Figure 7-1 by counting the number of introductory subordinate clauses set off by the conjunctive adverb "when" at the beginning and a semicolon at the end. Or, analyzing the sentence in Figure 7-1 in a fourth way, we could develop categories based on the *rhetorical strategies* used, for example, appeals to emotion, reason, or authority. Yet another way to analyze the sentence in Figure 7-1 would be to develop categories to assess specific *information* in the text such as the number of segments describing physical violence versus the number of segments describing psychological damage. From this last set of data, we might infer that at the time of King's imprisonment, African Americans suffered more physical violence from incidents of racial intolerance than they do today, or vice versa. Of course to make this inference, we would have to use more than the single sentence in Figure 7-1 as the discourse we analyze; we would have to use other writings and speeches by civil rights leaders of that period and writings and speeches by civil rights leaders today.

But when you have seen vicious mobs lynch your mothers and fathers at will and drown your sisters and brothers at whim; when you have seen hate-filled policemen curse, kick, and even kill your black brothers and sisters; when you see the vast majority of your twenty million Negro brothers smothering in an airtight cage of poverty in the midst of an affluent society; when you suddenly find your tongue twisted and your speech stammering as you seek to explain to your six-year-old daughter why she can't go to the public amusement park that has just been advertised on television, and see tears welling up in her eyes when she is told that Funtown is closed to colored children, and see the depressing clouds of inferiority beginning to form in her little mental sky, and see her begin to distort her little personality by unconsciously developing a bitterness toward white people; when you have to concoct an answer for a five-year-old son asking in agonizing pathos: "Daddy, why do white people treat colored people so mean?"; when you take a cross-country drive and find it necessary to sleep night after night in the uncomfortable corners of your automobile because no motel will accept you; when you are humiliated day in and day out by nagging signs reading "white" and "colored"; when your first name becomes "nigger," your middle name becomes "boy" (however old you are) and your last name becomes "John," and when your wife and mother are never given the respected title, "Mrs"; when you are harried by day and haunted by night by the fact that you are a Negro, living constantly at tiptoe stance never quite knowing what to expect next, and plagued with inner fears and outer resentments; when you are forever fighting a degenerating sense of "nobodiness"; then you will understand why we find it difficult to wait.

FIGURE 7-1   **Periodic Sentence of 313 Words by Martin Luther King, Jr. from "Letter from Birmingham Jail" (1963)**

Generally speaking, it is better to have at least two people sort the data into categories. However, sometimes just one person conducts a research project involving discourse analysis. In this case, the researcher should ask a colleague to sort at least 10% of the data selected at random, and then the results of the two sortings should be compared. If you intend to use statistical methods to determine the significance of differences between two groups, then you should also use statistical methods to assess inter-rater reliability (i.e., how closely the two sortings match). If, on the other hand, you are describing the data but not making inferences about significance, then you could report the level of agreement in terms of percent of items sorted in the same way by you and the other researcher. In either case, this assessment should be made before holding discussions to resolve differences in the sorting (Krippendorff, 1980; Weber, 1990).

Counting the Data

You all know how to count, so you may wonder why I am including a section on counting data. However, in discourse analysis, counting can proceed in two ways: straight numerical counts that include zero, and scales which record comparative amounts. First let's consider straight counts. I'm sure I don't have to tell you how to count the number of segments you put into any one category, and I've already mentioned that segments of discourse should fit well into only one category in a taxonomy. However, I want to caution you about dropping any category that ends up with zero items in it. An empty category may provide an important insight precisely because it lacks what one might reasonably expect to be there. It is just as important to notice what's absent as it is to count what is present. For example, suppose all the examples I used in this book referred to research done by men. In terms of information presented, one would have to conclude either that women haven't done any research in writing or that this book presents a very biased view. Or suppose you were examining a piece of text which presented all the widely known information about some historical event except one fact. Such an omission should cause you to wonder why the author omitted it. Could it be that the author truly didn't know about that fact? Is there any evidence that the author was present when the fact was discussed by others? Was that fact reported in sources the author was known to read faithfully? As you can see, omissions should send you to other sources to account for the missing piece of information. If, in fact, you can show that the author could be presumed to be aware of the omitted fact, then you would be justified in asking whether the omission was deliberate—whether including that bit of information would have contradicted the point the author was trying to make.

However, sometimes researchers group data into categories that fall along a scale. For example, one could categorize segments of the sentence in Figure 7-1 according to the degree of law-breaking in the examples. If there were no laws at that time that forbade people to curse others, then the segment about kicking, cursing and killing could be divided up into three degrees of law-breaking: cursing (no law-breaking); kicking (minor law-breaking as kicking is not usually associated with great bodily harm unless the victim is already severely injured); and killing (major law-breaking, of course). Having devised this categorization scheme, we would probably need to add a category to cover incidents which are more serious than kicking but less severe than murder. Next, we would use these categories to sort out the other activities described in the texts being examined.

Using Context in Interpreting Data

Note that in both examples of counting above, I base part of the decision on the context: what information was available to the author who omitted the one important fact, and what actions were against the law in Birmingham, Alabama, in 1963. It is absolutely essential that you are familiar with the context of the discourse you analyze if that context will make a difference in the way you count data or interpret your findings. For example, Connor and Connor (1992) criticize Jo Allen for claiming that William Harvey, a 17th century scientist, used Copernican theory when he described the circulation of the blood. According to Connor and Connor, there are at least three pieces of evidence that Harvey followed a Ptolemaic model. For example, in one of his published works, he refers to the "circular movement" of the sun (p. 196). In the same issue of the journal, however, Allen (1992) explains that if one defines the Copernican view of the universe as a set of bodies with the sun at the center, then this view was known to scientists 200 years before Copernicus because it was set forth in 1440 in works by Nicholas of Cusa.

A similar pitfall can occur when one is using individual words as counting or recording units because many words do not have rigidly prescribed meanings. In fact, words rarely occur alone, and the accompanying words affect the meaning. For example, in *Webster's Third International English Dictionary,* four general definitions are listed for the noun, "pit," and the first of these definitions has two subcategories (a and b); the 1-a category has nine variations on the meaning and category 1-b has ten variations. To put it another way, you would create one mental image upon hearing the word "pit" if I were talking about peaches, but quite another mental image if I were talking about gravel.

Even in the few instances when a word is used alone, it is not without a context that influences our interpretation of it. For example, a driver's interpretation of the word "STOP" on a street sign is influenced by the fact that it appears in all caps, that the background is red, that the shape of the sign is octagonal, and that the sign is located on a street corner. However, it is also the case that the audience brings a particular purpose and prior experience to encounters with words that strongly influence how they are interpreted. For example, linguistics professors reading the name of this chapter may expect it to be concerned only with the type of discourse analysis done in their discipline; and communications professors might think the chapter doesn't have anything to do with the kind of research they do because they prefer the term "content analysis." This interactive construction of meaning is important to keep in mind as you carry out discourse analysis research because you, too, will be bringing prior experiences to your constructions of a classification scheme and to interpretations of the data.

TYPES OF DISCOURSE ANALYSIS STUDIES

In classifying types of discourse analysis studies, we could use any one of at least four constructs: style, structure, rhetorical strategies, and semantic information. Note that style could be an artifact of structure. In this taxonomy, style and structure could be defined as surface features in contrast to semantic content because often the same basic information can be presented in different structures (e.g., lists versus paragraphs) and styles (formal versus informal). On the other hand, style and structure can also contribute to semantic information: as McLuhan has famously said, "The medium is the message" (1964, pp. 7–21). However, for the sake of ease in describing tools for discourse analysis, I'm going to demonstrate these tools under the constructs of style, structure, rhetorical strategies, and semantic information. To illustrate each construct, I will briefly describe some research using these tools.

Stylistic Analysis

Stylistic analysis of texts has usually focused on countable features such as word length and sentence length. Although these measures are problematic in terms of assessing readability, as I explain below, they are still sometimes used by researchers to describe and evaluate texts (see, for example, Roy & Roy, 1992). On the other hand, some researchers in writing have turned their attention to more sophisticated stylistic analysis techniques such as comparison of the number of elaborative elements (e.g., metaphor, simile, anecdote, personification, etc.) in newspaper articles on science and technology in two communities (Ramsey, 1995). The author of this study was interested in whether the amount of elaboration in such texts is related to economic development and technological growth of a community. In the next three sections, I discuss some different types of stylistic analysis of texts—and their strengths and weaknesses.

Readability Tests

Readability tests were one of the earliest discourse analysis procedures to have a major impact in educational practice and in technical writing, especially Rudolph Flesch's formula for determining how easy a piece of text is to read (1948). Over time, a variety of other formulas for testing the readability of text have been developed. All follow some basic principles, namely that sentence and word length can be used to assess readability. Because these formulas were seen as objective (i.e., scientific) ways of evaluating texts, school boards and other educational institutions such as military training units, began to use readability scores as part of the criteria when ordering textbooks or training materials (Duffy, 1985). However, a number of scholars have raised serious objections to readability formulas (e.g., Duffy, 1985; Huckin, 1983; Selzer, 1983). To help you understand the issues, let's look at Flesch's formula for determining reading ease. To calculate Flesch's reading ease score, you can use this simplified procedure:

1. Select a passage of 100 words.
2. Count the number of syllables in the passage and multiply that number by .846.
3. Subtract the results of Step 2 from 206.835.
4. Count the number of sentences and divide 100 by that number to get the average number of words per sentence. Then multiply this number by 1.015.
5. Subtract the results of Step 4 from Step 3.

The resulting number should be between zero and 100; and according to Flesch, the closer to 100 the score is, the easier the text is to read. The problem with this formula (and others like it) is that it is based on the assumption that reading ease is achieved by using short words and short sentences. You can see for yourself how faulty this assumption is by calculating the reading ease score of a text you think of as difficult (say, a passage from James Joyce's *Ulysses*) and the score of a text you think of as relatively easy to comprehend. For example, if we calculated the score of the first 100 words of the nonsense poem *Jabberwocky*, by Lewis Carroll, (about a "tove" that is "slithy," some "borogroves" that are "all mimsy," etc.) we would get a score of 87.565, which indicates the poem is easy to read. On the other hand, if we calculated a reading ease score for the first 100 words in the first paragraph of this chapter, we would get a score of 28.355, which indicates the text is very difficult to read. Two other comparisons might help you see the value of readability formulas: the score for the first 100 words of Lincoln's Gettysburg Address is 42.91 (fairly difficult), and the score for the 313-word sentence by Martin Luther King, Jr. shown in Figure 7-1 is –7.85. I don't think Flesch ever imagined that a text could so completely fail an assessment of reading ease using his formula. Interestingly, the King text fails because of one factor: sentence length. Yet, the sentence is a model of clarity and emotional power.

What is worse, some practitioners and teachers of writing advise writers to revise their prose to achieve a better readability score. In other words, good scores from such readability formulas such as Gunning's Fog Index and the improved version of Flesch's formula have been suggested as goals for writers. Since these scores put a premium on short words and sentences, writers can improve their scores by increasing the number of short words in a text and by cutting sentences up to make them shorter. Yet it is ridiculous to suggest to a technical writer that he can improve the readability of his text by substituting a shorter word for "angioplasty" or "electromagnetic" or some other technical term for which there is no synonym. Thus, if a writer cannot avoid using a multi-syllabic word in his text and he wanted to achieve a better readability score, he would have to add a number of very short words, whether they are needed to convey the meaning or not, to lower the average number of syllables per word in his text—a ridiculous strategy. Of course, some writers should be encouraged to use plain English rather than pompposities such as "utilize"; however, using readability formulas to set goals for writers is not only foolish, but harmful.

Computer Style Analyzers

Computer style analyzers are a kind of spin-off from readability formulas. Most of them calculate word and sentence length. Some use the number of characters to calculate word length (thus "bought" would be 8), and others use syllables to calculate word length (thus "bought" would be 1). Some of these programs calculate the Flesch Reading Ease Score and/or the Gunning Fog Index; others give readability scores in grade level. One even claims that "standard writing averages seventh to eight grade" (Microsoft Corporation's *User's Guide to Microsoft Word*, (1994) p. 101). As I have explained above, such scores are not really useful. So it is surprising to see an article such as that by Roy and Roy (1992) which relies heavily on a computer style analyzer, in this case, *Rightwriter 4.0*. The authors of this study found a correlation between successful sales letters and readability scores that suggests that readers don't respond well if the text is too easy or too hard to read. However, this finding was based on an analysis of just 14 letters, and it is not clear from the authors' description of how the letters were selected whether statistical data were used by the person who ranked the level of success of the letters or whether that person selected the letters because he or she thought they were good examples. What is most troubling is the authors' claim that "the audience for these letters prefers brief simple words and sentences" (Roy & Roy, 1992, p. 230) because a correlation does not establish cause and effect. You can read more about correlations in Chapter 8.

However, some computer style analyzers can be very helpful to a writer because they also point out instances of sexist language, such as the use of "fireman" or "mailman," and suggest alternatives such as "fire fighter" and "letter carrier." Some recent word processing programs also include "grammar checkers" which can point out problems in subject-verb agreement, wordiness, and use of clichés.

Also, many computer style analyzers point out instances of passive voice. I have mixed feelings about this use of a style analyzer because the implication is that using passive voice is bad, and I think that such blanket caveats are often wrongheaded. Although many teachers of writing believe that writers should avoid the use of the passive, in some instances such as the methodology sections of research reports, using the passive voice enables a writer to keep attention focused on the process rather than the person carrying out the steps of the process. Passive voice is also useful in maintaining focus on the topic of a paragraph. As Coleman (1997) points out, the passive voice can achieve a variety of goals such as promoting paragraph unity and coherence, avoiding sexist language, and creating an objective tone.

On the other hand, computer style analyzers have the potential to be very helpful. One example is Hart's (1997) *Diction* which has a 10,000 word corpus designed to help researchers analyze the tone of a passage. Brochures describing *Diction* say that it counts words indicating such aspects of tone as certainty, optimism, and commonality. Another possibility would be to customize a program such as *Diction* so that it could be used to analyze the number of first, second, and third person pronouns. This type of analysis could help a researcher investigate the effect of the "you attitude" described by Houp, Pearsall, and Tebeaux (1995, pp. 325–327). For example, such an analysis would no doubt rate the King passage in Figure 7-1 as heavily "you" in focus because it contains only one first person pronoun, only six third person pronouns (interestingly, all are feminine), and 26 second person pronouns. Furthermore, an analyzer programmed to count subordinating conjunctions (often considered markers of sentence sophistication) would disclose that King's sentence uses "when" 12 times, and that in 11 of those instances, the "when" is followed by a second person pronoun.

Language as a Social or Professional Marker

Language as a social or professional marker is a more sophisticated method of stylistic analysis that focuses on the ways that certain types of language use mark the attitudes, culture, or social status of the user. Words can be strongly associated with certain professions. For example, Henry and Roseberry (1996) examined travel brochures to identify the most frequently used words. Hyland (1996) examined 26 articles from molecular biology journals to identify the hedges that scientists commonly use, such as "probable," "might," and "suggest." He then grouped these into grammatical categories such as adverbs, verbs, and so forth. This study will help persons interested in the rhetoric of science better understand how scientists achieve credibility with their audience.

Structural Analysis

Structural analysis is used by still other writing researchers, very often with a view to describing genres. In some cases, researchers look at the overall structure of a piece of discourse to identify its organizational pattern, but in other cases, researchers may look at words and phrases to see how the elements in the discourse are connected to each other. Structural units such as topic strings, given/new organization, and point-making are some of the traditional aspects of texts that scholars have looked at (see, for example, Colomb & Williams, 1985; Huckin, 1983). Still other researchers have begun looking at texts in terms of how the information is arranged to be helpful to readers.

One project which illustrates the organizational changes that have occurred in document design is Jansen and Lentz's examination of a 1926 set of instructions in Dutch for a Singer sewing machine (1996). The authors found that these instructions buried the individual steps in one long paragraph, broken only by punctuation and parentheses. They contrast this organizational layout with a bulleted list of the same steps that a modern reader would expect to find.

On a more local level, Loges (1994) examined a 15th century treatise on fishing, trying to identify, among other things, how the writer tried to make his text accessible to the reader. Loges found that all 51 paragraphs in the treatise have topic sentences, and in 49 of these paragraphs, the first sentence in the paragraph is a topic sentence. The author of the treatise also used headings and forecasting statements to give an overview of material to come.

In a completely different context, Chapman (1995) attempted to identify genres used by first graders in their writing at school. Chapman sorted the children's writings into two major categories: action/event oriented and object oriented. Then, using these classifications (and some sub-categories) she drew conclusions about the children's development over the school year.

Structural analysis can also take place on the sentence level. For example, Vande Kopple (1994) investigated the length, in number of words, of the subjects of sentences in scientific writing. He found that in four articles in prestigious journals in the sciences (physics, chemistry, ecology, and medicine) the authors tended to use long grammatical subjects with an average of 6.011 words. Next he examined the structure of the sentence subjects to determine what factors contributed to their length, and found rather extensive pre- and post-modification of a single head word—a practice he attributes to the scientists' strong desire to be precise.

Rhetorical Analysis

Rhetorical analysis is often used to investigate persuasive techniques. For example, Ferris (1994) examined rhetorical strategies in 60 student compositions categorizing them in terms of the Toulmin argument theory of claims, data, and warrants (Toulmin, 1958). Ferris also noted instances of counterargument and audience adaptation. Using these features, he then described the differences between the frequency of their use by native and non-native speakers of English. Another study which looked at rhetorical practices in persuasion is Faber's (1996) analysis of proposals submitted to the Conference on College Composition and Communication in the years 1989, 1990, and 1992. He identified several features of the more successful proposals including genre characteristics (e.g., problem statements, methodology, product, and clearly stated objective), as well as indications of the insider status of the author, and a tendency of the proposals to expand into other disciplinary areas.

Wickliff (1996), on the other hand, examined 23 photographs and their accompanying text from a review of 40 illustrated 19th century scientific and technical texts in order to begin to create a definition of photographic rhetoric. He noted that authors seemed to use these photographs to communicate truth and a sense of realism, or to stimulate reader interest. Although the authors of the 40 texts often presented the photographs as evidence of truth, in many cases, the authors admitted to staging the photographs.

Semantic Analysis

Semantic analysis is often carried out to measure the writing ability of students. For example, Mathison (1996) examined the writings of 32 students in a sociology class. The students were assigned to write critiques of texts they had read for class. Mathison wanted to determine what features characterized those critiques which were given good grades. She used a construct of topic-comment as the recording unit and categorized the comments as positive, negative, or neutral. She also categorized the comments according to their source: i.e., whether the students used material from class discussion, the source text, outside reading, or their own personal experience. She found, as have others (e.g., Thury & Friedlander, 1996), that in spite of the assignment, students tended to write summaries of the material rather than critiques. The student writings contained an average of 9.88 topics and 28 topic-comment units per paper. When Mathison compared the features of the texts with the quality ratings given by four professors, she concluded that this assignment was difficult for the students because the professors had expectations for the writings that the students were unable to meet.

Note that Mathison used a construct of topic-plus-comment to asses the quality of the content of the student writings. This construct is one of several that have been used for this purpose. Another similar system is the T-unit, which is a minimal terminal unit containing one main clause and all its modifiers, including subordinate clauses. The idea is that the longer a T-unit is, the more information it contains. Therefore, if one calculates the number of T-units in a piece of text and the average T-unit length, one should have a fairly accurate measurement of the amount of information a text contains. However, this measurement does not discriminate when students repeat their ideas as a means of development, and I often find the novice writers tend to repeat ideas. For example, a student might write "It was a very good movie," and two sentences later write "I liked the movie because it was so interesting." These would count as two T-units even though the second sentence does not add any real support to the first sentence.

Another system for measuring semantic content is assertions (Carney, 1972). An assertion is basically a topic plus some attribute of the topic. For example, "The movie is a romance" is one assertion; "The movie is a historical romance" constitutes two assertions. Still other discourse analysts have proposed very complex schemes for recording content. For example, propositions can be recorded in this formula

predicate (argument 1, argument 2)

Applying this formula to the sentence "The movie was interesting," we would have

was (movie, interesting)

Thus, in order to count propositions in a text, the researcher has to rewrite the text and the longer the sentence, the more complicated the formula gets. (For a further explanation of propositions, see Brown and Yule, 1983.)

On the other hand, semantic analysis can be used to compare certain texts as in Hagge's 1994 study of 14 disciplinary style manuals (e.g., MLA, APA, etc.). In this study, Hagge counted the number of pages devoted to formal conventions (e.g., bibliographic style and design of graphics) and informal conventions (e.g., audience concerns and techniques for invention). He interpreted the number of pages on a topic as an indicator of the importance of the topic. Based on page counts, he concluded that compositionists may need to rethink the focus of the freshman writing course so that more attention is paid to formal conventions because of their importance in all disciplines. Note, however, that his assumption about what factors are of major importance in a discipline may be inaccurate. The name "style manual" itself implies those features which Hagge labels "formal conventions," so it is not surprising that most of the pages in the manuals are devoted to these matters. The purpose of a style manual is to help writers present their ideas in the style expected by members of the discipline, especially journal editors. Certainly, manuscripts which violate expected formal conventions face a harder time being accepted for publication but a manuscript that is stylistically perfect but which has nothing of importance to say to the journal's audience has absolutely no chance of being accepted for publication. Yet it is the content of the article that is most likely to be affected by the informal conventions (e.g., invention) which don't receive a lot of attention in style manuals.

Semantic analysis can also be used for measuring change or development in a discipline. For example, Kynell (1994) found that from the first edition of John Lannon's textbook, *Technical Writing,* to the most recent, there has been a shift in the discipline to include more attention to persuasion and audience analysis. Smith has also helped portray the development of the discipline by describing the electronic databases where bibliographic information from the five technical writing journals can be found (1996). The semantic content of reference lists was also used by Harmon (1992) who wanted to identify superstar authors in the scientific literature.

ADVANTAGES AND DISADVANTAGES OF DISCOURSE ANALYSIS STUDIES

From going through the recent literature in writing research, I have gained the impression that discourse analysis is a very frequently used method of research. Of course, to substantiate this impression, someone should do a study of the literature from the past several years to see whether, in fact, discourse analysis makes up a large part of the research effort in writing. If, in fact, there has been an increase, or the method is used much more frequently than other research methods, we might want to consider possible reasons.

One advantage to doing discourse analysis is that, in most cases, the researcher can work wherever and whenever she wants as long as she has access to the texts she wants to analyze. In contrast to experiments, case studies, and ethnographies, discourse analysis can take place wherever there is light enough to read and equipment (even paper and pencil) to record the assignment of recording units into categories. Discourse analysis is also relatively free of contamination and threats to validity and reliability such as diffusion, mortality, and bias, as long as the researcher carefully defines the categories and the recording units and tries to ensure the reliability of the sorting by training additional persons to sort the data. Additionally, discourse analysis procedures and results are usually convincing to readers because they convey the image of a scientific (systematic and objective) research method. Finally, discourse analysis can often help a researcher carry out another type of empirical design. For example, suppose you wanted to evaluate a teaching or training technique. One possible way to measure the results of the technique is to analyze some discourse produced by subjects in the experimental and control conditions and compare them.

However, discourse analysis has two major disadvantages that a prospective user needs to consider. First, the method is labor intensive. Defining categories, dividing texts up into recording units, and sorting the recording units into the categories consume large amounts of time. Also the individual tasks are not so easy. For example, defining categories can be a very frustrating task because, even though you think you have set up enough categories and defined them so carefully that another researcher can use them and achieve the same results you did, you will soon learn that you overlooked something. That is why user-testing your categories with a piece of similar text is essential.

Perhaps one reason so many researchers in writing use discourse analysis procedures is that these techniques enable researchers to examine, in a systematic way, actual writings. Whether the researcher wants to learn something about the writings themselves (e.g., genre characteristics) or something about the producers or consumers of the writings, discourse analysis strategies are valuable tools.

REFERENCES

Allen, J. (1992). Commentary: A response to J. T. H. Connor and Jennifer J. Connors's analysis. *Journal of Technical Writing and Communication, 22,* 203–209.

Asher, R. E. (Ed.). (1994). *The encyclopedia of language and linguistics.* Oxford: Pergamo Press.

Bazerman, C. (1988). *Shaping written knowledge: The genre and activity of the experimenta article in science.* Madison: The University of Wisconsin Press.

Bereiter, C., & Scardamalia, M. (1987). *The psychology of written composition.* Hillsdale, N. Erlbaum.

Bourg, T. (1996). The role of emotion, empathy and text structure in children's and adults text comprehension. In R. J. Kreuz & M. S. MacNealy (Eds.), *Empirical approaches literature and aesthetics* (pp. 241–260). Norwood, NJ: Ablex.

Brown, G., & Yule, G. (1983). *Discourse analysis.* Cambridge: Cambridge University Press

Carney, T. F. (1972). *Content analysis: A technique for systematic inference from commun cations.* Winnipeg: University of Manitoba Press.

Chapman, M. L. (1995). The sociocognitive construction of written genres in first grad *Research in the Teaching of English, 29,* 164–192.

Coleman, B. (1997). In defense of the passive voice in legal writing. *Journal of Technic Writing and Communication, 27, 191–203.*

Colomb, G. G., & Williams, J. M. (1985). Perceiving structure in professional prose: A mu tiply determined experience. In L. Odell & D. Goswami (Eds.), *Writing in nonacadem settings* (pp. 87–128). New York: Guilford Press.

Connor, J. T. H., & Connor, J. J. (1992). Commentary on rhetorical analysis of William Ha vey's De Motu Cordis (1628). *Journal of Technical Writing and Communication, 2* 195–201.

Cooper, C. R., & Odell, L. (1977). *Evaluating writing: Describing, measuring, judgin* Urbana, IL: National Council of Teachers of English.

Cornwell, B., & Keillor, B. (1996). Contemporary literature and the embedded consumer cu ture: The case of Updike's Rabbit. In R. J. Kreuz & M. S. MacNealy (Eds.), *Empiric approaches to literature and aesthetics* (pp. 559–572). Norwood, NJ: Ablex.

Duffy, T. M. (1985). Readability formulas: What's the use? In T. M. Duffy & R. Waller (Eds *Designing usable texts* (pp. 113–143). Orlando, FL: Academic Press.

Elliot, N., Kilduff, M., & Lynch, R. (1994). The assessment of technical writing: A case stu *Journal of Technical Writing and Communication, 24,* 19–36.

Faber, B. (1996). Rhetoric in competition: The formation of organizational discourse in Conference on College Composition and Communication abstracts. *Written Communication, 13,* 355–384.

Ferris, D. R. (1994). Rhetorical strategies in student persuasive writing: Differences between native and non-native English speakers. *Research in the Teaching of English, 28,* 45–65.

Flesch, R. (1948). A new readability yardstick. *Journal of Applied Psychology, 32,* 221–233.

Flower, L., & Hayes, J. R. (1980). The dynamics of composing: Making plans and juggling constraints. In L. W. Gregg & E. R. Steinberg (Eds.), *Cognitive processes in writing* (pp. 31–50). Hillsdale, NJ: Erlbaum.

Foster, D. W. (1996). *A Funeral Elegy:* W[illiam] S[hakespeare]'s best-speaking witnesses. *PMLA: Publications of the Modern Language Association of America, 111,* 1080–1105.

Frazer, J. G. (1978). *The illustrated Golden Bough, an abridged edition,* M. Douglas, (Ed.). London: George Rainbird.

Freedle, R. O. (1996). Recalling the *Three Bears* after 10 years: Exploring new vistas for discourse and text-processing models through the study of folktales. In R. J. Kreuz & M. S. MacNealy (Eds.), *Empirical approaches to literature and aesthetics* (pp. 157–177). Norwood, NJ: Ablex.

Garfield, E. (1981). *Essays of an information scientist, 4,* 1979–1980. Philadelphia: ISI Press.

Gibbs, R. W., Jr., & Nacimento, S. (1996). How we talk when we talk about love: Metaphorical concepts and understanding love poetry. In R. J. Kreuz & M. S. MacNealy (Eds.), *Empirical approaches to literature and aesthetics* (pp. 291–307). Norwood, NJ: Ablex.

Hagge, J. (1994). The value of formal conventions in disciplinary writing: An axiological analysis of professional style manuals. *Journal of Business and Technical Writing, 8,* 408–461.

Harmon, J. E. (1992). An analysis of fifty citation superstars from the scientific literature. *Journal of Technical Writing and Communication, 22,* 17–37.

Hart, R. P. (1997). *Diction* (Version 4.0) [Computer Software]. Thousand Oaks, CA: Scolari.

Hayes, J. R., & Flower, L. (1988). The writing process and the writer. In J. K. Tarvers (Ed.), *Teaching writing: Theories and practices* (pp. 125–139). Boston: Scott, Foresman.

Henry, A., & Roseberry, R. L. (1996). A corpus-based investigation of the language and linguistic patterns of one genre and the implications for language teaching. *Research in the Teaching of English, 30,* 472–489.

Houp, K. W., Pearsall, T. E., & Tebeaux, E. (1995). *Reporting Technical Information* (9th ed.). Boston: Allyn & Bacon.

Huckin, T. (1983). A cognitive approach to readability. In P. V. Anderson, R. J. Brockmann, & C. R. Miller (Eds.), *New essays in technical and scientific communication: Research, theory, practice* (pp. 90–108). Farmingdale, NY: Baywood.

Hyland, K. (1996). Talking to the academy: Forms of hedging in science research articles. *Written Communication, 13,* 251–281.

Jansen, F., & Lentz, L. (1996). Changing standards in technical communication. *Journal of Technical Writing and Communication, 26,* 357–370.

Kreuz, R. J., Roberts, R. M., Johnson, B. K., & Bertus, E. L. (1996). Figurative language occurrence and co-occurence in contemporary literature. In R. J. Kreuz & M. S. MacNealy (Eds.), *Empirical approaches to literature and aesthetics* (pp. 83–97). Norwood, NJ: Ablex.

Krippendorff, K. (1980). *Content analysis: An introduction to its methodology.* Beverly Hills, CA: Sage.

Kynell, T. (1994). Considering our pedagogical past through textbooks: A conversation with John M. Lannon. *Journal of Technical Writing and Communication, 24,* 49–55.

Loges, M. (1994). The treatise of Fishing with an Angle: A study of a fifteenth-century technical manual. *Journal of Technical Writing and Communication, 24,* 37–48.

MacNealy, M. S. (1992). Research in technical communication: A view of the past and a challenge for the future. *Technical Communication, 39,* 533–551.

Mathison, M. A. (1996). Writing the critique, a text about a text. *Written Communication, 13,* 314–354.

McLuhan, M. (1964). *Understanding media: The extensions of man.* New York: McGraw Hill.

Meade, R. A., & Ellis, W. G. (1970). Paragraph development in the modern age of rhetoric. *English Journal, 59,* 219–226.

Microsoft Corporation. (1994). *User's guide to Microsoft Word.*

Oaks, D. D. (1995). Structural ambiguities and written advertisements: An inventory of tools for more resourceful advertisements in English. *Technical Writing and Communication, 25,* 371–392.

Odell, L., & Cooper, C. R. (1980). Procedures for evaluating writing: Assumptions and needed research. *College English, 42,* 35–43.

Phillips, D. B., Greenberg, R., & Gibson, S. (1993). *College Composition and Communication:* Chronicling a discipline's genesis. *College Composition and Communication, 44,* 443–465.

Pollio, H. R., Smith, M. K., & Pollio, M. R. (1990). Figurative language and cognitive psychology. *Language and Cognitive Processes, 5,* 141–167.

Ramsey, S. (1995). Elaboration in text as breadth and depth. *Journal of Technical Writing and Communication, 25,* 11–25.

Reglin, G. (1996). *Television and violent classroom behaviors: Implications for the training of elementary school teachers.* Paper presented at the European Conference on Educational Research, Bath, England, September 1995. ERIC: ED394687.

Roy, S., & Roy, E. (1992). Direct-mail letters: A computerized linkage between style and success. *Journal of Business and Technical Communication, 6,* 224–234.

Selzer, J. (1983). What constitutes a "readable" technical style? In P. V. Anderson, R. J. Brockmann, & C. R. Miller (Eds.), *New essays in technical and scientific communication: Research, theory, practice* (pp. 71–89). Farmingdale, NY: Baywood.

Smith, E. O. (1996). Electronic databases for technical and professional communication research. *Technical Communication Quarterly, 5,* 365–383.

Smith, M. K., Pollio, H. R., & Pitts, M. K. (1981). Metaphor as intellectual history: Conceptual categories underlying figurative usage in American English from 1675–1975. *Linguistics, 19,* 911–935.

Sperling, M. (1994). Constructing the perspective of teacher-as-researcher: A framework for studying response to student writing. *Research in the Teaching of English, 28,* 175–207.

Tannen, D. (1994). *Gender and discourse.* New York: Oxford.

Tebeaux, E. (1997). *The emergence of a tradition: Technical writing in the English Renaissance, 1475–1640.* Amityville, NY: Baywood.

Thorson, E. (1989). Television commercials as mass media messages. In J. J. Bradac (Ed.), *Message effects in communication science* (pp. 195–230). Newbury Park, CA: Sage.

Thury, E. M., & Friedlander, A. (1996). Factors in transactions with literature: An analysis of student response journals. In R. J. Kreuz & M. S. MacNealy (Eds.), *Empirical approaches to literature and aesthetics* (pp. 419–443). Norwood, NJ: Ablex.

Toulmin, S. (1958). *The uses of argument.* Cambridge: Cambridge University Press.

Vande Kopple, W. J. (1994). Some characteristics and functions of grammatical subjects in scientific discourse. *Written Communication, 11,* 534–564.

Wallace, D. L., & Hayes, J. R. (1991). Redefining revision for freshmen. *Research in the Teaching of English, 25,* 54–66.

Walters, F. D. (1993). Scientific method and prose style in the early Royal Society. *Journal of Technical Writing and Communication, 23,* 239–258.

Weber, R. P. (1990). *Basic content analysis* (2nd ed.). Newbury Park, CA: Sage.

Wickliff, G. A. (1996). Toward a photographic rhetoric of nineteenth-century scientific and technical texts. *Journal of Technical Writing and Communication, 63,* 231–271.

Zhu, W. (1995). Effects of training for peer response on students' comments and interaction. *Written Communication, 12,* 492–528.

▶ 8

Surveys

All of you, I'm sure, have been asked to participate in at least one survey. We get them in the mail, we get them via the telephone (especially at dinnertime), we get them on pull-out cards in magazines and journals, and sometimes we are even stopped near voting places and in malls, supermarkets, and street corners by persons wanting us to answer "just a few questions." Why are surveys so ubiquitous? The main answer is that they are the only research tool available to obtain certain kinds of information, namely opinions, preferences, beliefs, feelings, and other personal information. Surveys provide a way to describe a population in quantitative terms.

No matter what type of survey is being considered, the researcher should first establish a clear purpose because the purpose determines, or at least influences, the answers to many of the other concerns a survey researcher must deal with. A second important issue is selecting a sample that will be representative of the population of interest. A third issue is the design of the survey instrument, itself. Before I address each of these issues, I will briefly describe three types of surveys, discussing some advantages and disadvantages of survey research. At the end of the chapter, I will discuss some statistics that are commonly used to analyze the results in survey research.

TYPES OF SURVEYS

Surveys are often thought of in terms of paper questionnaires, which may be the most prevalent type. However, surveys are sometimes conducted online, over the telephone, and in person. In all of these types, the subjects or participants are usually people. However, one can also survey texts as I will discuss later in this chapter. But first, let's begin with the paper questionnaire.

Paper Questionnaires

Paper questionnaires are a relatively easy and inexpensive way to gather data. Sometimes, questionnaires are passed out at meetings to learn member preferences, as in preferences for programs in a particular organization. These surveys are usually rather informal, and the designers don't worry very much about whether the design of the questions will affect the validity of the results. In other situations, paper questionnaires serve a vital information-gathering purpose and represent a sizable investment, so designers think carefully about how various features of the questionnaire might influence the findings.

Paper questionnaires have certain advantages over other types of questionnaires. Because the questions on a paper questionnaire have no intonation, as is the case with phone or person-to-person surveys, they may be less subject to questioner bias. Second, paper questionnaires are less limited geographically because it costs a lot less to mail a survey than it does to send an interviewer to distant locations. Also, paper questionnaires involve a lot less work than phone or person-to-person surveys, and since paper questionnaires can be addressed, stamped, and mailed by untrained personnel, they are less expensive to administer than person-to-person interviews that require trained interviewers. Many paper questionnaires are even constructed so that the answers can be scanned electronically instead of tabulated by hand. Moreover, paper questionnaires provide more of a sense of anonymity for the participants than does a personal interview. Finally, paper questionnaires allow the respondent time to think over answers and choice of time and place for filling out the questionnaire.

On the other hand, if paper questionnaires are sent by mail, some expense is involved: the postage on the original mailing as well as the postage on the self-addressed envelope, enclosed to encourage respondents to answer. Mailed paper questionnaires also have the disadvantage of a low return rate—20–40%, according to Frankfort-Nachmias and Nachmias (1992). Because response rate was typically low in the past, researchers tended to accept responses as useable even though the rate was below 50% (Dillman, 1978); however, now many researchers seek strategies to improve response rates. (For a review of empirical research in this area, see Bradburn, 1983.) Other disadvantages to paper questionnaires are the limited amount of information that can be elicited because follow-up and clarification questions are not possible, as they would be in a personal interview. Also, mailing paper questionnaires may not produce a set of respondents that are truly representative of the population of interest. For one thing, a researcher cannot tell whether the returned questionnaire was filled out by the person it was addressed to or someone else. Furthermore, poor readers and busy persons may simply throw the questionnaire away.

Computer Networks

One way of cutting the expense of mailing the survey and tabulating the returned data is to use computer networks as survey research instruments. Computer-delivered surveys have a number of other benefits according to Chou (1997). For example, computer-delivered surveys arrive faster as e-mail can be sent to anyplace in the world in just a few seconds, and the sender knows immediately whether the message arrived at the address intended. Further, computer-delivered surveys allow researchers to send the survey, receive replies, and read the data at their own convenience rather than having to get up in the middle of the night to phone someone in a different time zone.

However, two current and major disadvantages to computer-delivered surveys are the limited number of people who can be reached via a computer network, and the skill needed to set up a computerized delivery system (Chou, 1997). Also, I wonder whether persons with Web accounts want their mail filled with surveys. I know how irritated I get when I find a bunch of ads on my account when I log in: it takes too long to go through the list to see what I want to read. Furthermore, I know of instances when newsgroup postings overloaded an account to the extent that the sender could not get through. Perhaps some of the new mail-sorting software will help alleviate this problem, but then I suppose potential respondents could also use the mail-sorter to keep out surveys along with junk mail.

Person-to-Person

Person-to-person surveys can be conducted over the phone, in homes or places of work, or in public locations such as shopping malls. Such surveys often use a paper questionnaire for recording answers, but more and more telephone researchers are recording responses on computers, which certainly facilitates analyzing the data. In the interview-type survey, answers are often tape recorded for future analysis. Of course, participants must be asked if they are willing to have their answers tape-recorded.

Person-to-person surveys, whether personal interviews or telephone surveys have the advantage of allowing flexibility in question wording and order, as well as allowing follow-up questions and probes that can provide a richer depth of information. Such surveys can take advantage of the open-ended interview-type questions typical of exploratory research; and unexpected useful information can pop up during a personal interview or telephone survey. Moreover, person-to-person surveys allow more control over the order in which respondents answer questions—a factor which could be important to the results since some research shows that question order affects response (Balson, 1996). For example, Carpenter and Blackwood (1979) found that in questions using scales for answers, the first and last questions on the questionnaire received the highest and lowest scores on the scale. Additionally, some research indicates that person-to-person surveys have higher participation rates than telephone or mail questionnaires (Yu & Cooper, 1983)—person-to-person surveys certainly have the potential to include people for whom reading is a problem. A final advantage to person-to-person surveys is the speediness of collecting a response. Many times people procrastinate answering mail surveys or even hand-delivered surveys which require writing.

However, person-to-person surveys have numerous disadvantages, not the least of which is cost. Obviously, person-to-person surveys are expensive because they are labor intensive—a trained researcher must personally contact prospective participants and then personally collect the data from each one. If the surveying involves going to people's homes, the interviewer's safety is also an issue, especially in some urban areas.

One variation on the face-to-face technique takes advantage of the higher participation rate gained from the personal touch but involves less time for the researcher. In this combination technique, the researcher contacts potential participants personally at their front door, leaves a copy of the questionnaire, and makes arrangements to return later to pick it up (Babbie, 1990). However, with the rise in crime, many people are now reluctant to open their doors to strangers. One adaptation would be to contact potential participants over the phone or in a public place such as a shopping mall and then give or send them a paper questionnaire to mail back. One of my students is using a combination of paper and a face-to-face approach to collect data from persons in local hair salons. His research interest has nothing to do with hair care—in fact, it concerns preferences for geometric shapes. However, he selected hair salons because both men and women use them, people from most economic and age levels use them, and people using hair salons often have time to kill while waiting their turn. In this case, Harold introduces himself as a student working on a master's thesis and asks potential participants if they would take a few minutes to fill out a questionnaire on design preferences. Of course, Harold obtained permission from the hair salon owners before approaching their customers.

An often mentioned disadvantage of person-to-person surveys is the possible effect of bias of the question-asker, either through posture or through intonation. Also, such surveys do not provide much assurance of anonymity for the participant. In fact, some participants in telephone surveys will hang up in the middle of the survey if a particular question bothers them—something that rarely happens in a face-to-face interview.

Telephone surveys used to be considered quite biased because many poor people didn't have phones, so the sample relied heavily on responses from the middle class or the rich. However, about 98% of U.S. households now have telephones, so telephone surveys are gaining in respect. One problem, however, is those persons who have unlisted numbers. To avoid omitting this section of the population from the sample, researchers now often use a digital dialing system. The basic idea is to use the first three digits common in an area and then choose the last four digits randomly from numbers 0001 to 9999. For example, in my neighborhood of Memphis, many phone numbers begin with 754, 755, and 756, so a researcher could use one of these numbers and then add four more numbers at random. Randomized dialing is accomplished quite easily with a computer-generated dialing program; however, some states have begun to regulate computerized dialing. An additional benefit of telephone surveys is that the data collectors can be monitored to reduce deviations from the script and thus reduce possible bias whereas face-to-face data collections cannot unless a supervisor accompanies interviewers—a very expensive arrangement and one that would probably intimidate both interviewer and interviewee. Although participation rates are high for telephone surveys versus mail surveys, this trend could reverse as people get more and more fed up with telephone sales pitches intruding on their dinner hour or a favorite TV program. I was once told-off for phoning during a big football game. Finally, telephone surveys may involve several attempts to make contact at a particular number because of modern lifestyles in which both spouses work or are frequently away from home because of leisure activities.

Text Surveys

Text surveys do not involve living participants. Instead various texts (i.e., letters, manuals, novels, etc.) are examined in a systematic way with the data recorded on paper questionnaires. See Chapter 7 for a fuller discussion.

PURPOSE

Consideration of purpose plays an important role in the design of a survey. Sometimes surveys seem like the answer to an organization's problems; the reasoning is that an organization can better serve its members if the organization knows something about members' likes and dislikes. However, such surveys can bring unexpected problems to an organization, particularly churches and volunteer service organizations. Let me explain. Sometimes churches decide that they could get members more actively involved in the activities of the church if they knew what kind of activities the members were interested in. In such cases, members are urged to fill out a questionnaire which asks them what their talents are and what particular activities (choir, ushers, Sunday School teachers, etc.) they would most like to be a part of. Such a questionnaire implies that the church leaders will then ask the respondent to join the group he or she indicated. However, all too often the respondent is not contacted again for many months, if ever. One reason might be that the church choir is not really open to all volunteers but asks prospective members to audition for membership. Or maybe the ushers group is open only to male, long-time members of the church. In such cases, a survey does more harm than good. So if you are approached about designing an informal survey for an organization, you should discuss this problem with the organization's leaders and help them determine exactly what their purpose is and whether a survey will do more harm than good to their organization.

Purpose also determines the selection of the sample to be surveyed. In the case of informal surveys for clubs and volunteer groups, it is probably best to try to query the entire group of interest. Thus, techniques for obtaining a representative and random sample are not an issue. However, if the purpose of a survey is to determine product satisfaction, then obtaining a sample representative of product users is vital. If the total population of users of a particular product is small, then choice of participants will probably be based on completeness rather than randomization. On the other hand, when the population of interest is large enough to make a complete survey unfeasible, then researchers must be concerned about random selection of participants. I briefly discuss some procedures for random selection later in this chapter.

Not surprisingly, purpose affects question content and design. I often notice a tendency on the part of students designing a questionnaire to include a question asking the respondent's gender (and often age) although neither have any relevance to the real topic of the questionnaire. I think this tendency arises from the fact that all of us see a lot of marketing surveys, and they always ask for such information, so we tend to assume such questions are just part of survey methodology. However, marketing experts ask questions about gender, age, income, and so forth in order to construct a buyer profile in order for them to design more effective advertising. On other projects, the researcher needs to ask whether such information is really pertinent to the main purpose of the survey. Leaving out such questions will not only shorten the questionnaire (and shorter questionnaires are more likely to be returned than longer ones), but it also avoids turning off a potential respondent who dislikes personal questions.

Additionally, purpose affects the layout of the questionnaire and the design of individual questions. Notice that marketing surveys almost always put sensitive questions last. If people encounter questions they don't like, they are more apt to give such information if they have already taken the time to fill out the rest of the survey. If your purpose is such that you really need sensitive information, you can often design the questions to be less formidable. For example, asking people to check a box next to a range of salary figures is less apt to irritate respondents than asking for the respondent's salary outright. The same principle applies to questions about age.

Another way that purpose affects question design is in the area of open-ended versus close-ended or check-off questions. Check-off questions are much easier to tabulate, but they are inappropriate for exploratory surveys that are often carried out in an area about which little is known. In such cases, it is better to use many open-ended questions rather than multiple choice questions because multiple choice limits possible answers to those that the researcher thinks are likely. Open-ended questions, on the other hand, can elicit information that the researcher may not anticipate, so they are especially appropriate for surveys of an area about which little is known. In designing open-ended questions, though, the researcher should take care to provide enough room for answers. I find that almost no one leaves enough room on forms for me to sign my name, and I don't write in a large script. One way to test the space you plan to allot is to ask people with different sizes of handwriting to actually try to answer your question. However, you should be aware that check-off boxes are easier for a respondent to complete, and so the response rate is apt to be higher when checking off boxes is all that is required.

Finally, research purpose affects the actual word choice. Question wording needs to be carefully examined for subtle bias and offense. Later in this chapter, we will consider question wording in some detail. For now, consider the effects of asking members of a local chapter of the Society for Technical Communication which they prefer: an upscale restaurant that caters to professional people or a neighborhood "ma and pa eatery." Of course, this question is slanted in favor of the classier restaurant by the reference to "professional people." The second choice is also slanted (negatively) by the word choice "ma and pa eatery" instead of "family owned restaurant." When I encounter such poorly designed questions, I usually stop filling out the survey and throw it away in disgust. Most importantly, however, the question does not really find out much about the members' major concerns in regard to a meeting place. For example, it is possible that for many members, the main concern is safety i.e., is the restaurant located in a safe neighborhood with well-lighted parking? Here, either multiple choice or open-ended questions may give more information about members' concerns.

SAMPLING

Sampling techniques depend on the researcher's purpose, of course, so in the discussion of the various types of sampling, I do not intend to imply that any one method is superior to the others. Still, it is helpful in understanding the types of sampling if we first divide them into two categories: probability and non-probability sampling. The main difference is that random selection is used in probability studies; that means that every member of the population of interest has an equal chance of being selected (you may want to review the discussion of the importance of random selection in Chapter 4). Probability sampling does have one advantage over non-probability sampling in that the researcher can calculate the level of confidence in the findings. Level of confidence is a statistical term which is similar in meaning to level of significance; a level of confidence of .05 means that only five times out of 100 would identical surveys produce different results. However, it is not always necessary to calculate a level of confidence, especially in an exploratory study. Because some purists don't grant the same validity to non-probability types of sampling, you must be careful to state just how you selected your sample.

Before reviewing the four types of probability sampling and three types of non-probability sampling, I want to first remind you of the difference between a sample and a population. Researchers usually select a sample when the population of interest is too large to question every single member. Instead, researchers use various techniques to select a smaller sample of the population of interest, being careful that the sub-group or sample is truly representative of the total population. For example, if you were doing research about characteristics of technical communicators, it would be impossible to find a list that contains the name and address of every technical communicator in the world. Even if you defined your population as technical communicators in the United States, you still wouldn't be able to find a comprehensive list because the largest list of technical communicators in the United States is probably the membership list of the Society for Technical Communication (STC) which would be only a partial list because not every technical communicator joins the STC. Therefore, researchers always have to settle for available lists. Even so, researchers must be careful about how they decide to use a particular list. For example, the membership list of STC, although it contained 18,423 names as of July 1996 (personal communication), also contains names of members from other countries. If the researcher is interested only in technical communicators in the United States, he or she will have to weed out the names of those whose address is outside the United States.

In other cases, deciding on a good source is not so easy. For example, suppose your population of interest is the American public. You can't rely on voter registration lists because many Americans don't ever vote; you can't rely on telephone books because some Americans don't have phones—or have unlisted numbers. I could give more examples, but I think you see the problem. Most researchers, then, try to define their population of interest in terms of an available source of participants. In the list that follows, I give a brief definition of sampling methods.

Probability Sampling Techniques

These techniques are the most stringent types of random sampling. They should definitely be used if a certain level of confidence is important to the research project.

Straight random sampling.   This technique is no different from the random sampling discussed in earlier chapters. The main goal is to avoid bias in selecting participants so that every member of the target population has an equal chance of being selected. One method for obtaining a random sample is to assign a number to every name on the list, and then use a random number table to draw out the members of the sample. (For an example of a random number table, see Chapter 4.) If the population is not too large, you could put slips of paper containing names of people in the population into a hat, shake them up, and then draw out the number you need for your sample. But if the population is this small, you might be better off to try to do a complete survey.

Systematic random sampling.   This technique is somewhat easier than straight random sampling because you don't have to use a random number table. Instead, you decide what percent of the population of interest you want to sample (e.g., 10% of a population of 100), then choose a beginning location at random (e.g., the third name on the list), and then choose every nth (in this case, tenth) name. Before deciding to use a systematic random sampling strategy, you need to be sure that your source list isn't organized in some way that will result in a biased sample. Babbie (1973) describes the case of a researcher using a military roster. Because the people on these rosters are listed by rank within units, it would be possible that your nth number corresponds to a certain rank. For example, if each unit contained ten soldiers with the unit sergeant in the first slot and the unit corporal in the second slot and you take every tenth name beginning with the second, your sample will be all corporals. Even if you begin with the fifth name, your sample will still be biased because it will include no sergeants or corporals.

Stratified random sampling.   This technique is another type of probability sampling which tries to control for sampling error by arranging the original list into categories so that the distribution of a particular group in the population of interest will be closely replicated in the sample. For example, suppose your population of interest is a university campus which is 60% male. To make sure that your sample is 60% male, you would need to list the students by gender, then select every nth male from the list of males until you reached 60% of the sample size you want; then you would use the same techniques to select a 40% sample of participants from the list of females.

Cluster sampling.   This technique is often used when no master list of the population is available, but lists do exist for various groups. For example, if you wanted to survey technical writing students in the United States, you would not be able to find one list that includes them all. However, you might be able to ask colleges and universities that have technical writing programs for lists of students in those programs. Then you might find that you have a huge list of names. To reduce the work involved, you would be better off to first select randomly a certain number of colleges and universities from the list of those having technical writing programs. Then, you could randomly select names from the lists provided by those colleges and universities.

Non-Probability Sampling

These sampling techniques are used in circumstances where probability samples cannot be obtained or where levels of confidence are not that important. A researcher should choose one of these types when it better suits his or her research goals. At the same time, the researcher must be very careful about generalizing beyond the sample.

Convenience sampling.   This technique is sometimes called accidental sampling. A researcher will often choose convenience sampling when he or she has no way to obtain a list of members of a certain population. As I explained earlier, there is no list of people who could be labeled "general public." So convenience sampling surveys are often conducted at convenient locations such as a shopping mall, a certain busy intersection, or a laundromat because the researcher hypothesizes that these locations will be used by the general public. To do a convenience sample, a researcher goes to one of these locations and asks passers-by to participate.

Purposeful sampling.   A researcher will often choose purposeful sampling to select a sample that has the characteristics (usually experience, but it could also be gender, age, education, etc.) necessary to answer questions about a certain matter or product. For example, a manufacturer may want to know how customers have reacted to a change of design in equipment, but there may be no list of purchasers available. In such a case, researchers might go to a store selling the equipment and ask customers who come in whether they own the equipment in question. The researchers then might ask the first ten who claim to own the equipment if they would mind answering a few questions about it. Similarly in educational settings, students are often surveyed about programs, facilities, and product preferences. If the researcher wants to know students' attitudes about the library's online search system, the logical group to ask is those students who try to use the system. These opinions would be representative only of the students at a particular library.

Snowball sampling.   A researcher will often use snowball sampling in those rare cases when the population of interest cannot be identified other than by someone who knows that a certain person has the necessary experience or characteristics to be included. For example, it would be really hard to find a list of writing students with dyslexia or a list of technical communicators who have lost their job through downsizing. However, if the researcher knows one such person, that person may be able to suggest another person with a similar problem or experience, and thus one participant leads to another.

DESIGN ISSUES

In designing survey instruments, three issues must be considered: the format or layout of the instrument, the types and wording of the questions, and the scales used for the answers. In each of these areas, the survey designer must keep in mind the potential participant because these three areas will heavily influence whether a questionnaire recipient will take the time to answer the questions and return the questionnaire. Some research indicates that certain types of people are more apt to participate than others. For example, the more education a person has, the more likely he or she is to fill out a questionnaire. One obvious reason is that, for well-educated people, reading survey questions is an easy task. For other potential participants, the reading task may seem onerous. Thus, one basic principle of the design is to keep the survey attractive, with an easy-to-read and easy-to-do appearance (LaGarce & Washburn, 1995).

Format

First impressions are extremely important whether it is a job interview or the format of a questionnaire. For example, research has shown that the use of color or unusual covers may increase response rate (LaGarce & Washburn, 1995; Matteson, 1974; Nederhof, 1988). Further, potential participants are busy people who will hesitate to take on a task that looks like it will take a lot of time. Therefore, some questionnaire designers try to keep the questionnaire short—even just one page if possible—thus, they need to consider carefully whether a particular question is critical to the research purpose. On the other hand, Dillman claims that if the questionnaire is less than 12 pages, the length will not affect the response rate (1978).

White space makes a document look easy to read, whereas dense paragraphing makes the task look difficult. Leaving sufficient white space further reduces the number of questions that can be asked, so designers have to work to achieve a balance between the amount of text and the amount of white space. One way to provide space for both content and white space is to edit questions to make them as succinct as possible. On the other hand, question brevity must not be achieved at the expense of question clarity.

The ease of response is often a critical factor in survey design because potential participants will throw away the questionnaire or procrastinate if the survey looks as if it will take very much time to fill out. Writing even a couple of words takes longer than putting a check mark in a box, so one way to make a questionnaire look easy-to-do is to use check boxes where possible, especially near the beginning of the questionnaire. Check boxes are better than blank lines because when participants mark a choice in a vertical list of blank lines, it is often not clear which line they mean to mark. Certainly the questionnaire designer can do much to help participants mark their answers in the correct place if grouping and dividing design principles are used. For example, the check box or line should be placed very close to the related answer and separated by white space from other possible related answers. Note that in Figure 8-1, a respondent may choose the wrong space because the possible answers run together. A better arrangement would be to place the possible answers in a vertical list with a box placed very close to its answer.

Whichever check-off or circling design you choose, the design will have the advantage of looking easy to use. If short answers are required, it is better to put them at the bottom or on the second page so that the initial impression is that little effort will be needed to participate. If the system for answering the questions is obvious, then fewer instructions will be needed, so more white space will be available.

To summarize, design of questions and the layout of the questionnaire can affect the willingness of participants to fill out the questionnaire. Therefore, you might want to use the checklists in Figure 8-2 to evaluate and revise a draft questionnaire.

Question Order

Most experts advise putting an interesting question first to capture attention. In fact, Sheatsley (1983) claims that some questionnaire designers begin with a throw-away question for this very purpose. Certainly the first question must be non-threatening,

```
A. Which is your highest degree?
   _____BA; ____MA; _____PhD


B. Which is your highest degree?
       ___BA

       ___MA

       ___PhD

C. Which is your highest degree?
       BA

       MA

       PhD
```

FIGURE 8-1   **Possible Designs for Multiple Choice Questions**

easy to understand, and easy to answer. Subsequent questions should be grouped so that one question leads logically to the next. The respondent's task is made easier if several questions in a row use the same question design, for example a Likert Scale. However, if all the questions are of the same design or on the same topic, respondents tend to get bored and less careful with their answers. Perhaps a useful rule of thumb is Miller's "Magical number seven, plus or minus two" (1956). Although Miller was exploring the limits of short-term or working memory, his findings may also apply to the line where interest shifts to boredom (this issue, itself, is worth studying!). Sheatsley (1983) suggests using transition statements to indicate a shift in topic if the questionnaire is long and includes several topics.

Another rule of thumb for question order has already been mentioned: put sensitive or difficult-to-answer questions near the end so that a level of trust has been built with the respondent through the easy earlier questions.

Finally a questionnaire designer usually arranges questions so that the more general questions come before the more specific ones. This arrangement keeps the specific questions from influencing the answer to the more general question, and when a broader question precedes a question asking for specific details, the broader question gives the respondent a context for considering the more particular question (Dillman, 1978; Sheatsley, 1983). However, the reverse may be preferable if the researcher wants the respondent to have more opportunity for considering a complex issue and its various parts before making a decision on a more general level.

Checklist for Designing Questions

1. Be sure that the reader knows how the questions are to be answered. For example, if the reader should use a number 2 lead pencil, say so up front.

2. Use plain English. For example, don't say "consume" if you can use "eat" or "drink." Don't use double negatives.

3. Avoid acronyms unless you are sure they are part of your reader's usual vocabulary or the context makes them clear. For example, using NASA in questions about space exploration may be OK, but using NASA in relationship to population trends in Houston could cause confusion.

4. Avoid emotionally charged words and leading questions. For example, "Does the writing exhibit ignorance of commonly accepted grammatical conventions?" There is no need for the word "ignorance"—some errors could be accidents due to haste.

5. Step carefully between concreteness and vagueness. A question such as "How many hours a day do you use a word processor?" could cause a difficulty if the respondent doesn't use a word processor very often. You might be better off to ask respondents to indicate level of use on a scale between "very infrequently" and "very frequently."

6. Limit each question to just one issue. Avoid double-barrelled questions such as "Is your office equipment up-to-date and easily accessible?"

7. Avoid direct questions about sensitive or personal issues. Instead offer answers with a choice of ranges for questions about age, salary, and personal spending habits.

8. Take advantage of pattern recognition by using the same pattern for similar questions. For example, if in one question you use a rating scale with "very frequently" on the left and "very infrequently" on the right, in a subsequent question keep the higher amount on the left and the lower on the right, as in: highly satisfied......highly unsatisfied.

Check List for Question Order

1. Make your first question one that obviously relates to the purpose of the survey.

2. Put easy-to-answer questions before hard-to-answer questions.

3. Put general questions before specific questions.

4. Put questions about famililar topics before those about unfamiliar topics.

5. Put sensitive questions last.

FIGURE 8-2   **Checklist for Designing and Ordering Questions**

QUESTION TYPES

A researcher has many question types to choose from: bipolar (e.g., yes or no), multiple choice, rank order, fill-in-the-blank, essay, and so on. In general, survey questions can be divided into two categories: open- and closed-ended questions. The primary concern should be to choose the kind of question which will most likely obtain the information you want and which will create the least work for the respondent.

Closed-Ended Questions

Closed-ended questions are advantageous to both the researcher and to the respondent. Respondents tend to like close-ended questions because they can be answered quickly and easily. Researchers tend to like them because they are easy to tabulate. Closed-ended questions include bipolar, contingency, and multiple choice.

Bipolar questions provide the respondent with just two choices, such as "yes" or "no," "male" or "female," and so forth. However, one must be careful when deciding to use a bipolar question: are there really only two possible answers? For example, members of Congress sometimes want to know how the voters in their district feel about various budget items such as defense spending and welfare. When the survey asks the voters which of two items it would be better to cut, defense spending or welfare, the question puts the respondents in an unfair position because maybe they believe neither should be cut. So, in selecting question design, a researcher should be sure that bipolar questions are used only for truly dichotomous issues such as gender, home ownership, and the like.

Another problem with bipolar questions is that they may not elicit the really important information on a particular issue. A good example is a question about owning a computer. You may really want to know whether a technical communicator owns a computer or not; however, that question tells you nothing about whether the technical communicator uses his or her computer for word processing or what tasks the respondent uses a word processor for.

Contingency questions are often used following bipolar questions to pursue an issue beyond its obvious level. A contingency question consists of a filter or sorting question and a follow-up question. For example, for the filter question, a researcher could use a bipolar question about calculator ownership, and then a follow-up question about calculator usage:

Do you own a calculator?　　☐ Yes　　☐ No

Which of these tasks do you use your calculator for? (Check all that apply)

When contingency questions are presented on a computer, there is little chance for the respondent to get lost because the computer will display the follow-up question only when a respondent has indicated "yes" for the sorting question. On a paper questionnaire, however, the designer will have to tell the respondent which question to answer next. Some designers use text (e.g., "If you answered yes, please go to question 9"), and others use visual cues as illustrated in Figure 8-3.

Multiple choice questions help a researcher in two ways: first they are easy to tabulate, and second, they can stimulate a respondent to consider some possible choices that he or she might otherwise not have thought of. And multiple choice questions are usually easy for respondents. A good way to discover good possible choices when designing multiple choice questions is to brainstorm for possible concerns, choose the most likely, rank order them, and then select a reasonable number

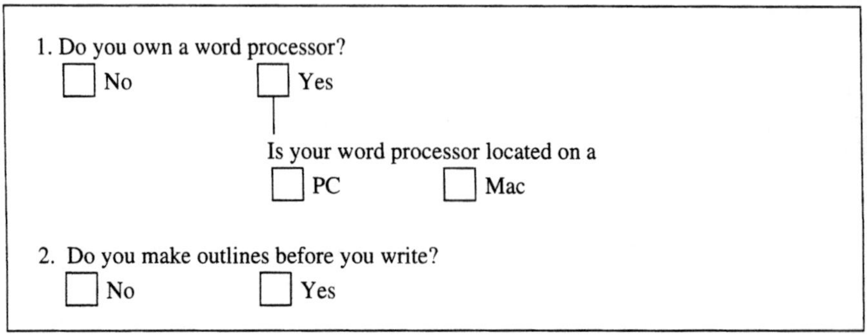

FIGURE 8-3 **Using Visual Cues to Direct the Reader**

of the most important ones to use as choices in the question. Questionnaire designers can save themselves some work in the analysis phase if answers in a multiple choice list are designed so that the respondent circles the number accompanying his or her choice because these numbers can easily be entered into a computer analysis program. However, the questionnaire designer must make sure that only one number will be perceived as relating to a possible choice by placing the number very close to the answer it pertains to. Another problem with numbering choices in a list is that the arrangement of choices in a numbered list may imply that the number one answer is better or more important than the number four answer. Some designers try to avoid this problem by changing the order in the list of possible answers so that in some questionnaires an answer, "memos," for example, is first on the list in 20 questionnaires, second on the list in 20 other questionnaires, third on 20 more, and so on. Although this system does avoid placing memos in a prominent position that could bias answers, it also, of course, defeats one of the main purposes of numbering answer choices: making the answers easy to tabulate.

Open-Ended Questions

These questions can be either fill-in the blank or long-answer. Because they require respondents to actually write something down, some respondents will not participate, usually because open-ended questions appear to take more effort, but also sometimes respondents will not participate because they feel insecure about their handwriting. Open-ended questions also create problems for researchers because they are frequently hard to tabulate. Their main advantage is that they do not limit the possible answers that may be given. However, open-ended questions are not questions designed so broadly that they try to catch any and all information on any possible topic. Instead, good open-ended questions are based on what is known and unknown; in other words, they are grounded in theory (Strauss & Corbin, 1990) or based on what has been learned from prior research. The two main types of open-ended questions are fill-in-the-blank and essay questions; however, these options are the extremes of a continuum ranging from one-word to brief phrases, to complete sentences, to even longer, more carefully constructed answers.

Fill-in-the-blank questions are as not as intimidating to most respondents as long-answer questions are, and they are often fairly easy to tabulate. The major problem is designing the amount of space needed for respondents to write in their answers. For example, I often get membership renewal forms that ask for my home phone, my office phone, my FAX number, and my e-mail address. Often these questions are all put on one line with the same amount of blank space for each. However, I need space for only ten numbers and two dashes (total = 12) for the phone and FAX numbers, but I need space for eight characters for my last name alone in my e-mail address, plus another 10 letters and one period for the address string after my name (total = 19). Design mistakes like this sometimes happen when a researcher uses a template which is set up to divide the space on a line equally rather than proportionately according to what might be written in the space.

Essay or long-answer questions are a good choice when the researcher is doing an exploratory study because they limit responses only by the amount of white space allotted for the answer. Again, it is a good idea to user-test the questionnaire design. You may find that one question tends to elicit much longer responses than another and therefore needs more space for respondents to write in. On the other hand, too much white space can make the questionnaire look as if it will take a lot of work to fill out, so respondents may procrastinate or throw it away.

When exploring a new area with a survey, you will probably want to use the grounded theory approach and rely on numerous open-ended questions (Strauss & Corbin, 1990). Much as explorers of new geographical territories use theories to guide their work (following a river upstream will lead you to its source or to its tributaries), researchers exploring new frontiers in composition or technical writing use theory as a guide to question content. For example, Leon Heaton and I recently investigated possible answers to Charles Sides' (1994) question about where technical communication is going as a discipline. One of the issues Sides raises is where technical communication programs should be located in the university structure in order to maximize their potential. To learn more about the preferences and experiences of teachers of technical communication, Heaton and I surveyed technical communication professors, using both rating questions to gather information on perceptions about current locations, and open-ended follow-up questions to probe the depth of feelings involved and possible reasons for them. For example, one question asked how much respect professional communication professors are given by colleagues in other areas in the department. This question provided a rating scale for answers. The next question asked respondents to comment on or explain their answer. By using the second open-ended question, we hoped to learn more about circumstances contributing to negative and positive attitudes of colleagues. Understanding the underlying circumstance could help program planners create environments where technical communication programs could flourish, either in their current locations or in new locations. However, we did not directly ask respondents "why?" because sometimes people haven't given very much attention to why they do things—perhaps they do something out of habit. Asking "why" directly forces respondents to come up with an answer even if they don't really know why they said or did something, so respondents may offer the first reason that pops into their mind and it may not have any real connection to their true motive. On the other hand, providing space for "comment" on an answer gives the respondents a chance to give reasons, or tell a story as an illustration, or even comment on the wording of the question. Such responses can provide a wealth of information not otherwise available to a researcher.

One problem with open-ended questions is that the data are often hard to tabulate. The discourse analysis procedures described in Chapter 7 can help with this task, the main objective being to create and use categories to sort the answers given by the respondents. For example, in the survey Heaton and I conducted of technical communication professors, we followed almost every ranking question with an open-ended invitation for respondents to write their comments. To categorize the answers to one of the questions, first Heaton and I decided to use a very simple procedure with only three categories: mainly a positive attitude, mainly a negative attitude, and attitude neither mainly positive nor negative. We could then assign a number to each of our categories and statistically compare the answer with that given in the rating question to test the validity of responses.

To verify the coding, I coded 10% of the replies chosen at random and then compared my coding with his. Even with this careful procedure, we found ourselves confronted by some quandaries. For example, how would you code this response: "Some of the department views us with benign neglect, and some see us as vocational, but the younger faculty respect our contributions and envy our placement record"? On the one hand, Heaton and I could say that this statement contains one negative ("see us as vocational") and two positives ("benign neglect" and "the younger faculty respect...and envy [us]"). Thus, we could code this response as mainly positive. However, is "benign neglect" really a positive? Furthermore, if there are only two younger faculty out of 15 faculty in this department, how positive is the remark about younger faculty?

Another problem with open-ended questions is how to choose which answers to use to illustrate trends when writing up the results of the research. For example, Heaton and I plan to use the responses to our open-ended questions as sources of explanatory quotations when we discuss our findings. Thus, we hope to make our findings more alive to our readers. So should we choose the most typical response even though it is dull and formulaic, or should we choose a response that is a bit atypical, but more vivid? There are no easy answers. As I explain in Chapter 12, researchers must stay as true to the data as possible, but they also need to use quotations that will help their readers see the point.

INFORMATION TYPES

When trying to determine which question type is most suitable, it is helpful to consider what type of information you really want to collect. For example, do you really want to know whether a person owns a computer or how the person uses a computer? Some question types are better suited to some information types than others; I will point out possible matches between question and information type as I discuss each of four information types below.

Characteristics

Sometimes a survey researcher is looking for characteristics or attributes of a person, thing, or event. Some examples are personal characteristics such as gender, age, and level of education. Other examples are academic program characteristics such as semesters or quarters and graduate or undergraduate; location characteristics such as urban, suburban, or rural; and job characteristics such as temporary or full-time. Check-off boxes for bipolar or multiple choice questions work very efficiently for this type of information when you already know which characteristics are important for your purpose. Even if you already know most of the characteristics associated with your research topic, you may want to use an occasional open-ended question to flush out characteristics not yet identified by other researchers or your own reasoning.

Whether you use open- or closed-ended questions, you can usually count on the answers to the questions about personal characteristics to be accurate. However, when respondents are asked for characteristics of a program, a policy, or some construct a bit distant from personal experience, their answers may vary in accuracy depending on how much they really know about the construct. In this case, answers from several marginally knowledgeable respondents can still paint a fairly good picture of the area under investigation.

Practices or Behaviors

Sometimes survey researchers want information about those activities that the respondents take part in, but questions could be asked about behaviors that respondents have heard about. Of course the more closely related the respondent is to actual participation in the area of interest, the more accurate the answers are likely to be. Sometimes researchers include questions that will help them evaluate the accuracy of answers to other questions. For example, if the respondent is a new member of an organization, he or she cannot be expected to know as much about typical behaviors in the history of the organization as those who have been long-time members. Therefore, the researcher will include a question about how long respondents have been a part of some group. I believe that if accuracy of the answer is important, then an open-ended question is best; however, sometimes multiple choice questions using ranges of years are adequate for the researcher's purpose.

Some examples of behaviors and practices in the field of writing include the classes that professors teach, the types of writing that a technical communicator works on, the types of research the respondent has carried out, the number of hours worked per week, the frequency of attendance at professional conferences, and so on. When typical activities are already known (e.g., types of writing produced would probably include memos, letters, reports, proposals, etc.), a multiple choice question would work well to learn which activities the respondent participates in. However, if the question is how much time is spent in the various activities, then you might want to consider whether a fill-in-the-blank question with a space beside each activity would work better than individual questions with a rating scale for each possible activity. If little is known of the typical activities, then a very open-ended request such as "Describe a typical day's activities" would be best.

Beliefs

This kind of information is almost impossible to obtain by any research method except interviews and surveys because the researcher is looking for a respondent's perception of reality; in other words, questions probing for this type of information are probing for facts, not opinions and attitudes. Perhaps the distinction will be clearer if we consider some examples. For example, students could be asked a question like this:

Is your teacher knowledgeable about writing practices in engineering?

Yes___ No___

This question does not ask for an opinion as to the teacher's ability to teach; nor could the researcher use the answers to this question to claim that the teacher is or is not knowledgeable about writing practices in engineering. What is learned from this question is what the student believes to be a fact about the teacher's knowledge.

You may wonder why this distinction is important, so let's consider some uses of the information obtained from such a question. For one thing, if your respondents are engineering students and if they have expressed dissatisfaction with the course, this question could help locate a possible source of dissatisfaction. It might be the case that the teacher has actually studied a good bit of engineering writing, but that she has not communicated this fact to her students. Therefore, one way to increase student satisfaction with the course would be to disseminate information about the teacher's knowledge of engineering writing. Or let's consider another imaginary case in which the management at a firm was making plans to hold a one-day writing seminar for employees. If the planners want to know which day and time would least interfere with work, they could survey the employees asking questions like this:

Circle the day of the week when a seminar in writing for engineers would least interfere with your work: M   T   W   TH   F

Attitudes

This kind of information is also hard to elicit with any research method except interviews, surveys, and focus groups, although one can sometimes make inferences about opinions by collecting information about behaviors. For example, if you have some way of keeping track of which movies a person has attended over a period of time, you might make some inferences about kinds of movies that person likes. However, if you can ask a person directly about his or her likes and dislikes, you might have a more accurate picture. Information about attitudes and opinions can be explored with a wide variety of question types. For example, you could ask a respondent to compare two products in various ways: its ease of use, its relative cost, the results obtained from its use, and so on. Or you could ask respondents to rate a product on those features. A Likert Scale is very useful when probing attitudes and opinions, as in this example:

My college coursework adequately prepared me for the work I'm doing now.

strongly agree____   agree____   disagree____   strongly disagree____

Attitudes and opinions are often elicited with scale-type questions because the intensity of the respondents' attitudes is important. For example, a researcher could want to know how a respondent feels about the issue of non-sexist language. In this case a researcher could design a question with a Likert Scale of level of agreement for response to a statement such as "The use of sexist language offends me." Or a researcher could ask technical communicators to rank order a list (including sexist language) of the most serious breaches of etiquette in the field. Yet another way to determine attitudes is to create a set of cards, each containing a quotation (invented or real) which typifies an attitude or a circumstance (e.g., "We don't need a secretary—all secretaries do is sit around giving themselves manicures"). Respondents are asked to sort these cards into categories such as sexist versus non-sexist attitude, or offensive versus inoffensive remark. Some scales that other researchers have found useful are given in Figure 8-4. You might also want to review the information on scales in Chapter 5.

* always . . . . frequently . . . . seldom . . . . never
* excellent . . . . . . good . . . . fair . . . . poor

* too much/many . . . . too little/few . . . . about right
* better . . . . worse . . . . about the same

FIGURE 8-4   **Some Scales for Measuring Attitude**

MOTIVATING RESPONDENTS

Probably the biggest problem facing survey researchers is the response rate. For example, in 1985 Paul Anderson reported that the response rates in most surveys of writing in the workplace ranged below 50% (Anderson, 1985). On the other hand, Dillman (1978) reported an average response rate of 74% on surveys using his "total design method," with none of the 48 surveys achieving lower than 50%. These surveys were on a range of different topics from attitudes toward Native Americans to characteristics of truckers; however, the majority were sent to residents in one state—Washington, and the research was undertaken 20 years ago before people became fed-up with surveys.

Much research has been conducted to learn the factors which influence response rates. For a good review of some of this research, see Yu and Cooper (1983). Response rates seem closely tied to motivation, so survey designers need to consider ways to increase the motivation of potential participants. The following list gives some suggestions for motivating potential participants.

Create a Credible Image

As I said earlier, the proliferation of junk mail and scams by telephone or mail has sorely tested potential participants' willingness to believe that a survey is what it claims to be. For example, I often receive a telephone call from someone claiming to be conducting a survey only to learn as the conversation progresses that the person on the phone wants to sell me magazines. I have also received mail questionnaires purporting to be doing research in some medical problem such as cancer; then at the end of the survey is a statement along the lines of, "Please consider enclosing a check to help us continue to find ways to cure cancer."

Thus, a survey researcher must be concerned to present evidence of legitimacy and credibility. One strategy is to write a cover letter on letterhead from a reputable organization associated with the research such as a department in a university or a government agency. Then, the questionnaire must present a professional appearance; a good desk-top publishing software package can often help a designer develop a questionnaire that meets this standard. Finally, the design of the questions can create the appearance of professionalism. For example, compare the first and second versions in Figure 8-1: version B looks more professional than does version A.

Appeal to Altruism

Without question, surveys impose on participants' busy lives. Therefore a survey designer has to convince a potential participant that the survey is worth the time it will take. Most people want to help a good cause, so a survey designer has to clearly point out (probably in the initial moments of a conversation on the phone or in person, or in a cover letter, but maybe also briefly at the top of the questionnaire) the purpose of the survey and the good cause that will be aided by the participant's response. Dillman (1978) suggests that pointing out a problem in an area of interest to the respondents is a good way to enlist their participation. I find that most people are willing to help students, so I encourage my students to include in their statement of purpose the fact that they are a student. However, Dillman cautions that the general public may perceive dissertation research as esoteric, and of little practical use (1978). Most importantly, as Sheatsley (1983) suggests, you should tell the truth about the purpose of the survey. Those survey designers who are not students can explain how the results will help in making something better: a program, a public policy, a product, and so forth. Finally, you could say something to convince the potential respondents that their participation is very important to the project. Dillman (1978) recommends that the cover letter should explain that the respondent is one of a very small number of people who were selected to represent a specific population, such as taxpayers or the people of a particular community. If the researcher wants only a certain segment of the population, e.g., adult females, to fill out the questionnaire, the restriction should be clearly stated and a reason given.

Design an Easy-To-Do Appearance

As I explained above, most people are busy. If the survey appears easy-to-do, potential respondents are more likely to participate. Earlier in this chapter, I explained how question design and layout can make the questionnaire look easy-to-do. Another way to convince potential participants that the survey is easy-to-do is to tell them how long it has taken others to do it. Of course, you will need to test the questionnaire or interview procedure with at least three persons to estimate the amount of time that participation will take.

Providing a self-addressed, stamped envelope, of course, is essential for mail surveys. No one wants to take the time to find an envelope, address it, and hunt a stamp for it. For a telephone survey, the interviewer could possibly state just how many questions (if fewer than ten or so) will be asked. In the case of a questionnaire which has to be filled out with a number 2 lead pencil, the researchers might be wise to include tiny pencils that the respondent can use.

Promise (and Deliver) Anonymity

Even if the issue is not a touchy one, some potential respondents don't want to go on record with personal information, behaviors, beliefs, and attitudes. Sometimes students ask me if they can't code the questionnaires or return envelopes in some way so that they will know which potential participants responded. The students aren't proposing to distribute the information they receive so that it can be connected to the person who gave it; rather they want to know who to send follow-up materials to, or they want to know whether all their responses came from one segment of their intended sample. While both motives seem good, I believe that if you promise that the respondent will be anonymous, then you must deliver on that promise. Other researchers try to avoid the issue by promising "confidentiality." In a legalistic sense, a promise of confidentiality may allow the researchers to use a method of identifying the respondent; however, I still believe that no researcher should use a hidden method of identifying the respondent when promising "confidentiality" or "anonymity." On the other hand, Dillman (1978) claims that identification numbers can be used if the system is clearly explained in the cover letter, along with an assurance that the respondent's name will never be attached to the questionnaire.

Adopt a Personal Tone

One way to create a personal tone is to use a personal address for the envelope and cover letter: "Dear Angela Smith" versus "Dear Writing Teacher." Word processors make this step fairly easy with Mail Merge features. Putting the name and address directly on the envelope instead of on address labels also creates a more personal tone—but at some additional cost if your printer cannot handle envelopes. Another way to achieve a personal touch is by using the word "you" in the cover letter where possible (for more on the "you attitude" in letters see Houp, Pearsall, & Tebeaux, 1995, pp. 325–327). A more personal note can also sometimes be achieved when the researcher explains how the respondent's name was selected.

Offer a Reward

Some researchers have found that offering a small reward can motivate potential participants to respond (Denton, Tsai, & Chevrette, 1988; see also Yu & Cooper, 1983). I remember once receiving a dollar bill with a survey—an expensive reward if the survey is being sent to very many people. Of course, one dollar is not really adequate pay for the time the respondent will have to use, but one dollar is large enough to make many respondents feel guilty if they use the dollar without filling out the survey. I suppose guilt also plays some role in enclosed rewards such as a magnet for the refrigerator or a coupon for a discount at a store, but not much.

Some academic researchers offer to share their findings with respondents, and this strategy often works when the respondents are academics who are interested in the production of new knowledge. However, sending reports of all the data to those respondents who indicate an interest can be expensive if many pages are involved. Also, this type of reward means that respondents who wish to receive a copy of the findings will have to relinquish their anonymity and provide a return address.

Do a Follow-up

Sending out a follow-up postcard has been shown to almost double the response to mail questionnaires (Dillman, 1978). Furthermore, follow-up postcards can be sent without compromising anonymity. In this case, the researcher sends the same postcard to everyone on the original mailing list. The postcard thanks those who have already responded and pleads with those who haven't. Where anonymity is not an issue, some researchers send a follow-up postcard only to those who have not yet responded and also send a later follow-up mailing with another copy of the questionnaire. Dillman (1978) recommends sending a follow-up postcard within a week of the first mailing, a letter after three weeks, and even a third follow-up after seven weeks, if needed. The postcard and letters jog the memory of a recipient who intends to respond but who has laid the questionnaire aside for the moment.

TEST THE QUESTIONNAIRE

Even though I've now written almost a whole chapter about designing questionnaires, let me assure you that I would never send one out without testing it in two or three ways. First, I would ask a colleague who is knowledgeable about research methods to look over a draft for clarity and ease of use. If the subject of the questionnaire is complex, I might also ask a subject matter expert to look it over for clarity. Finally, I would actually test the questionnaire by asking persons typical of the population of interest to either fill out the questionnaire while I watched or to participate in a trial interview. I would have a copy of the questionnaire or interview guidelines with me so that I could make notes on it if my test participant hesitated someplace or asked me a question. Also I would note the time my test participants needed to fill out the questionnaire. Knowing the average length of time needed means that the researcher can be specific in the cover letter when she or he tries to assure potential participants that filling out the questionnaire won't take too much time.

QUANTITATIVE ANALYSIS OF THE DATA

Most survey researchers use quantitative procedures for analyzing the data they have collected. These procedures are fairly straightforward for data collected with check-off boxes or circle-the-number answers. However, even when researchers have used open-ended questions, they will often want to convert the answers into quantifiable data by categorizing the answers so that data can be described succinctly, and so that comparisons and predictions can be made. In this section, I will first discuss the presentation of frequency data; then I will briefly review measures of central tendency and their presentation. Finally, I will describe a type of statistical analysis often used with survey data: Pearson product-moment correlation.

Frequency Data

Frequency data, the type most often collected by surveys, simply means how many respondents chose a particular answer or fit a particular category. These data are often presented in tables because tables of raw data take up much less space than sentences containing raw data. Tables also help readers interpret the data; readers can quickly compare amounts in one cell with amounts in another. To help in the interpretation of frequency data, researchers often present the percentages along side the raw data. In a table of frequency data, the larger set of categories is often arranged down the left side and the smaller set across the top, no doubt due to the fact that book and journal pages are longer than they are wide. For example, if you collected data about types of cars owned by men and women, it would make sense to list the types of cars (a long list) down the left side and the gender categories across the top.

Researchers often order these categories from that with the largest number of respondents at the top to that with the smallest number of respondents at the bottom, but there really is no rule specifying order for categories not related by rank. For example, if your categories were regions of the United States, it would not matter whether you put Northeast or Northwest at the top of the list. On the other hand, if you were listing educational level, you would not put B.A. first, Ph.D. second, and M.A. third.

Measures of Central Tendency

Survey researchers often report their results using measures of central tendency. These were described in Chapter 5, so a brief definition of each will probably suffice at this point. The mean is the average. In a survey, for example, you could determine the mean salary of technical communicators by adding up the salaries reported by the respondents and dividing that number by the number of respondents. The median is the half-way point on that list of salaries: 50% of the salaries would be above the median and 50% below. The mode is the number that appears most frequently on the list. These data are usually presented in sentences in the text, but they could also be presented in tables if tables would be more concise.

Analysis of Correlation

This statistical procedure is used to determine the degree of relationship between two variables—e.g., if the amount of one variable goes up, does the amount of the other variable go up to a similar degree? For example, a survey researcher might want to know whether people who drink beer also tend to mow their own grass (at least, this isn't an eyelash example). In this case, one question on the survey would ask respondents to estimate the number of 12 ounce cans or bottles of beer they drink each week. Another question later in the questionnaire could ask respondents to check one of three answers:

_____ I pay someone else to cut my grass

_____ I cut my own grass

_____ Not applicable

To learn if there is any correlation between the two behaviors, the researcher would use only those questionnaires in which respondents chose one of the first two grass cutting options. Then the researcher would assign a numerical value to the two options—perhaps assigning the digit 1 to the first option and digit 2 to the second. An analysis of correlation would then show whether the two sets of data match: high (number of beers) with high (option 2); and low (number of beers) with low (option 1) to a degree that wouldn't happen by chance. Note that even if we found a high correlation between these two sets of data, we could not infer that one caused the other—i.e., drinking beer does not cause a person to cut his own grass. Causal inferencing gets tricky though when we consider that if a person who likes beer cuts his grass on a hot day, that person might drink more beer that day. You can read more about causal analysis in Chapters 5 and 6.

Correlation as an Indicator of Internal Validity

Quantitative researchers are often concerned about the validity of their findings, as was explained in Chapter 3. Survey researchers often test the validity of the questionnaire by analyzing the degree of correlation between two questions. To illustrate, let's suppose that in an early question, respondents were asked to indicate their level of satisfaction about working conditions and in a later question respondents were asked to rate their level of satisfaction with office machinery provided. In a way, these two questions are asking much the same thing, only one is more specific than the other. Therefore if respondents' answers were quite different for these two questions, the reliability of the survey is questionable. On the other hand, if the answers are correlated (respondents who indicated satisfaction with working conditions also tended to indicate satisfaction with office machinery provided), then one could assume that the survey is uncovering reliable information about the satisfaction of workers.

Correlation as a Predictor of Performance

Educational researchers often use a correlation analysis to determine if a relationship between two variables is strong enough to predict performance in one variable based on the amount of another variable. One example is standardized tests such as the SAT and ACT. High scores on these have been shown to correlate significantly with performance in college classes. In writing research, analyses of correlation are sometimes used to help assess how well a certain test will predict behavior in a certain class. For example, we ought to find a positive correlation between the results of tests of verbal skills and grades in a writing course, but we may not because other causal factors, such as motivation, maturity, teacher effectiveness, and so forth, are also involved.

Thus, analysis of correlation can be used to indicate areas where follow-up research to isolate causes would be appropriate. Just because two variables are highly correlated does not mean that one causes the other. No doubt a statistical analysis of the relationship between shoe size and height would show a positive correlation;

however, that does not mean that large feet cause one to grow taller. A positive correlation (+1) simply means that respondents who have a high score in one factor are very likely to have a high score in a related factor, and vice versa. A negative correlation (−1) means that respondents who have a high score in one factor are apt to have a low score in another factor. Zero correlation means just that—there is no relationship between the factors. To determine causal relationships, researchers often use a Chi Square, ANOVA, or *t* tests—procedures discussed in Chapter 5.

REFERENCES

Anderson, P. (1985). Survey methodology. In L. Odell & D. Goswami (Eds.), *Writing in non-academic settings* (pp. 453–501). New York: Guilford Press.

Babbie, E. R. (1973). *Survey research methods.* Belmont, CA: Wadsworth.

Babbie, E. R. (1990). *Survey research methods* (2nd ed.). Belmont, CA: Wadsworth.

Balson, W. A. (1996). Effects of reversing presentation order on verbal rating scales. *Journal of Advertising Research, 6,* 30–37.

Bradburn, N. M. (1983). Response effects. In P. H. Rossi, J. D. Wright, & A. B. Anderson, (Eds.), *Handbook of survey research* (pp. 289–321). Orlando, FL: Academic Press.

Carpenter, E. H., & Blackwood, L. G. (1979). The effects of question position on responses to attitudinal questions. *Rural Sociology, 44,* 56–72.

Chou, C. (1997). Computer networks in communication survey research. *IEEE Transactions on Professional Communication, 40,* 197–207.

Denton, J. J., Tsai, C., & Chevrette, P. (1988). Effects on survey response of subjects, incentives, and multiple mailings. *Journal of Experimental Education, 56,* 77–82.

Dillman, D. A. (1978). *Mail and telephone surveys: The total design method.* New York: Wiley.

Frankfort-Nachmias, C., & Nachmias, D. (1992). *Research methods in the social sciences* (4th ed.). New York: St. Martin's.

Houp, K. W., Pearsall, T. E., & Tebeaux, E. (1995). *Reporting technical information* (9th ed.). Boston: Allyn and Bacon.

LaGarce, R., & Washburn, J. (1995). An investigation into the effects of questionnaire format and color variations on mail survey response rates. *Journal of Technical Writing and Communication, 25,* 57–70.

Matteson, M. T. (1974). Type of transmittal letter and questionnaire color. *Journal of Applied Psychology, 59,* 532–536.

Miller, G. A. (1956). The magical number seven, plus or minus two: Some limits on our capacity for processing information. *Psychological Review, 63,* 81–97.

Nederhof, A. J. (1988). Effects of final telephone reminder and questionnaire cover design in mail surveys. *Social Science Review, 17,* 353–361.

Sheatsley, P. B. (1983). Questionnaire construction and item writing. In P. H. Rossi, J. D. Wright, & A. B. Anderson (Eds.), *Handbook of survey research* (pp. 195–230). Orlando, FL: Academic Press.

Sides, C. H. (1994). Quo Vadis, TC? *Journal of Technical Writing and Communication, 24,* 1–6.

Strauss, A., & Corbin, J. (1990). *Basics of qualitative research: Grounded theory procedures and techniques.* Newbury Park, CA: Sage.

Yu, J., & Cooper, H. (1983). A quantitative review of research design effects on response rates to questionnaires. *Journal of Marketing Research, 20,* 36–44.

OTHER USEFUL RESOURCES

Alrick, P. L., & Settle, R. B. (1985). *The survey research handbook.* Homewood, IL: Irwin.

Fink, A., & Kosecoff, J. (1985). *How to conduct surveys: A step-by-step guide.* Newbury Park, CA: Sage.

Plumb, C., & Spyridakis, J. H. (1992). Survey research in technical communication: Designing and administering questionnaires. *Technical Communication 39*(4), 625–638.

Rossi, P. H., Wright, J. D., & Anderson, A. B. (1983). *Handbook of survey research.* Orlando, FL: Academic Press.

▶ 9

Focus Groups

Focus group research is a relatively new approach for writing researchers. The technique was developed in marketing departments as a way of learning more about what potential customers need and want, as well as how customers might react to certain products. However, focus group research is now used in a wide variety of fields. For example, in law, defense attorneys sometimes present their anticipated defense to focus groups to gain some insight as to how effective their argument might be to a jury (as in the O. J. Simpson trial); politicians use focus groups to test the acceptance of a particular policy they are thinking of proposing; educational institutions use focus groups to test ideas for new programs or to evaluate existing ones (see, for example, Becker & Mikelonis, 1987), and product evaluators have even used focus group research to help in user tests (see, for example, Elling, 1997). Basically focus group research assembles carefully chosen, small groups of people and asks them to participate in a discussion of a particular topic. A trained moderator helps keep the discussion focused on the topic, and helps facilitate the group process by functioning as a gatekeeper (e.g., directing questions to less talkative members to encourage their input). I will discuss these duties more thoroughly later. For now, let's turn to some reasons why you might want to use focus group research methods.

In the field of writing, focus group research can help textbook writers and publishers attune their books to the teachers and students who might use them; it can help the designers of software and user manuals attune their products to potential customers; it can help designers of writing programs in colleges and universities learn enough about potential students and/or employers in order to attract new students and better suit their needs; and it can help in the evaluation of writing programs already in place. And these are only a few of the ways that focus group research can be used by writing researchers.

Because focus group methods are relatively new to writing researchers, not many studies have been published using this method. At present, I know of no published studies using focus group methodology in composition, but I have participated in focus group studies conducted by publishers of composition textbooks. Similarly, not many researchers in professional writing have published focus group studies, the Society for Technical Communication being one of the exceptions (for more on focus group research in technical communication, see Becker & Mikelonis, 1987; Byers & Wilcox, 1991; and Elling, 1997). It may be the case that focus group methodology is an under-used tool which we will see more often in the future because focus group research can help develop a clearer understanding of people's perceptions, motives, attitudes, and feelings. However, focus groups are not used as planning committees although the results of a focus group study can be useful to planners. Focus groups are also not assembled to brainstorm solutions to problems—such a group should be composed of persons with some expertise in the problem area, and such groups often strive to reach consensus on a topic. Instead, a focus group researcher values diverse and subjective input.

In this chapter, I first describe focus group theory, next I describe methods common to focus group research, and finally I discuss its advantages and disadvantages. In all of these sections, I illustrate the concepts with examples from both composition and technical writing.

FOCUS GROUP THEORY

Focus group theory is based on the assumption that the interaction of members of a small group will facilitate the uncovering of ideas that probably wouldn't surface if individuals were asked separately about their thoughts, feelings, and beliefs. However, good focus group research, like any good research, is not just a bull-session among members of a group assembled by happenstance. Instead, focus group research is carefully planned in advance: the selection of participants is based on clear criteria, the leaders and recorders are trained in advance, and data is collected systematically in a form that is accessible to others. To facilitate good planning, Kreuger (1994) suggests writing out the details of the methodology and submitting them to knowledgeable colleagues for feedback. In a later section I will talk about specific methods of recruiting subjects and conducting group sessions; but in this section, I want to explore more fully the group dynamics aspect of focus groups.

One of the primary, long-standing tools for learning about people's beliefs, attitudes, and feelings has been the survey. However, as I explained in the previous chapter, surveys often limit the responses to items that the researcher has in mind when designing the questionnaire, or if a survey is completely open-ended, the response rate is poor because filling out a survey which requires a lot of writing seems to be a task that most people repeatedly put off doing. Interviews have a better response rate in many cases, and interviewers can use probe and follow-up questions to take advantage of unexpected ideas; interviewers can also use visuals such as a proposed new logo or package design. However, interview data are somewhat limited in comparison to focus group data because in an interview the verbal interaction involves just two people—the interviewer and interviewee—and the interchange is usually controlled by the interviewer. In contrast, focus groups are designed to stimulate verbal interaction among several people and to benefit from that interaction. Focus group researchers try to set up a compatible group in which participants talk to each other in a conversational way; in other words, group participants can both express and explain their opinions, tell stories to illustrate their points, question each other to obtain more information, disagree with each other, and so on. The interaction allows, even prompts, participants to sort out their feelings and beliefs, often leading participants to understand themselves better and to more clearly articulate their attitudes and beliefs. As people participate in a focus group, some of their attitudes may even change in response to a comment from another group member. This change of attitude can have important implications for sales and publicity campaigns and for program planners and product designers, particularly if the reasons for the shift in opinion can be extrapolated from the data.

A well-designed focus group often produces information that could not be generated in any other way because people often say things in conversation that they wouldn't write down. A good example of the kind of information that a focus group might produce is the conversation between people on airplanes. For example, as I was returning from a recent conference, I happened to sit next to a young woman who owned a dress shop. This information came out in the opening, get-acquainted chitchat when she and the person on the other side of her explained to each other why they were flying to Dallas. When the seatmate expressed an interest in the kind of clothes the dress shop owner would be looking for in Dallas, the dress shop owner not only went into specifics of what colors are popular this year, but also, in response to her seatmate's obvious interest, she told what her educational background was, how many hours a day she works in her shop, how she uses a computer to track her inventory, how she disposes of things which don't sell, what the mark-up is on clothing and jewelry, and so on. I was amazed that she would share so many personal and business details with a complete stranger who did not really question her, but who nodded and contributed stories of her own about shopping experiences and contacts with sales persons in the clothing departments of large department stores. Listening to their conversation was like taking a course in management and marketing, but it was something more than that because of the personal details shared. It is precisely this kind of stimulating interaction that a focus group researcher tries to take advantage of.

A focus group researcher tries to create an environment that stimulates informal conversation between participants. One concern is to set up the group discussion in a comfortable environment where people can talk to each other informally. Second, participants are selected who have some characteristic in common that is important to the research agenda, but who are more or less strangers to each other because it is the interchange in getting acquainted that prompts people to explain themselves. Third, when participants are invited, the project is not described as if it were a scientific study—instead, the wording is very informal. For example, participants might be asked to "join a discussion" or to "share ideas" (Kreuger, 1994).

The research methods used by focus group researchers fall into four areas: physical arrangements for the meeting, selection and recruitment of group participants, roles of group leaders, and strategies for conducting the meetings. The tools or decisions in one area can often affect decisions in a different area. For example, the time of the meeting may affect potential participants' decision to participate. Before decisions can be made in any one area, however, the researcher must first define the research question because the topic of the research affects the choice of location and participants. For instance, a person wanting to know why a university's special program does not draw a bigger audience would want to choose both participants who would represent that audience (people who live in the area) and a location convenient for them (possibly a university seminar room). On the other hand, a publisher of a college textbook would want to include participants from across the nation, so those focus group meetings might better be held in a hotel at a national conference of college teachers.

PHYSICAL ARRANGEMENTS

Well in advance of inviting persons to participate in a focus group, researchers must make arrangements for the time and place. The time that the individual groups meet can have an impact on recruitment. For example, Sunday mornings are a bad time if the research is being carried out in the "Bible Belt" where a big emphasis is placed on church attendance. If the focus group researcher particularly needs male participants, then the opening day of deer season in some areas, the week of the NCAA basketball tournament Final Four, or the weeks during the World Series are probably bad choices. Similarly, if the researcher wants college students, then spring break and exam time are bad choices. In areas susceptible to blizzards or 32-inch accumulations of snow, winter may not be the best choice. In short, researchers must consider the possible impact of local conditions and events, plus the potential effects of television scheduling, on the willingness of potential participants to give two to three hours of their time to the project. Most focus group meetings last about two hours, but don't forget that the cost in time to participants also includes travel to the meeting place. Furthermore, researchers cannot expect people to take time off from work to attend a focus group session unless the project is being carried out with the employer's permission and support.

Location of the meeting place may also affect recruitment of participants. The meeting place must be easy to get to, and the instructions for getting there must be absolutely clear. In some large cities, certain neighborhoods should be avoided because they may be perceived as being unsafe. Parking is also an important consideration: it should be well-lighted, free, and close to the meeting place. Finally, researchers will want to avoid selecting a place that could adversely affect open communication in a subtle way. For this reason, church basements are probably not a good idea, nor are rooms in a court house or other area which implies legal constraints.

Some good choices are probably seminar rooms in a public library, a university, public school building, or a reputable hotel. If a conference or seminar room is being used at night, the researcher may have to allay potential participants' fear of going to a strange place after dark and alone, especially in an urban area.

Finally, the location should include a meeting room that facilitates an informal, conversational exchange between participants. For example, a room similar to a living room with easy chairs arranged in a circle is one possibility. Or a room that enables participates to sit in comfortable chairs around a table would facilitate eye contact. Sometimes focus group researchers choose a restaurant and offer participants a meal. This option has advantages and disadvantages. On the one hand, offering potential participants a meal is one way to entice them to participate; on the other hand, restaurant noise and the interruptions of the servers can inhibit open discussion. Also, a participant may have an idea to share just at the moment he or she has a mouthful of food. One alternative is to meet in a quiet seminar room but serve a simple buffet at the beginning or end of the meeting.

Sometimes, focus group research is conducted at national conferences. For example, the Society for Technical Communication has often conducted focus group research in a meeting room at their annual national conference. At one such conference, the organizers listed the focus group meeting in the conference catalogue, rather than recruiting participants personally. To divide those who showed up into small groups, the organizers set up several round tables in the room, and they announced which aspect of the topic would be the focus at each table. For example, one table was designated as "topics needing research," another as "issues in research design," and so forth. Thus, participants volunteered to participate, and they selected the area they wanted to participate in. This method does save the organizers a lot of work, but it also is problematic in some ways as you will see from the sections which follow.

SELECTION AND RECRUITMENT OF PARTICIPANTS

In focus group research, as in other types of empirical research, the methodology is carefully planned in advance so that participants are carefully and systematically chosen and assigned to particular groups.

Selecting a Pool of Participants

When plans are being made to select a pool of participants, focus group researchers define a list of criteria, the first of which is based on the technique of purposeful random sampling (to review techniques for random sampling, see Chapter 8). The researcher determines what specific segment of society best represents the population of interest. For example, a publishing company may want to investigate the expectations of potential users of a certain type of textbook, say a handbook for writers. In such a case, the company could assemble a list of college teachers known to be involved in the selection of texts for college writing courses. Identifying these potential participants would not be difficult because most college textbook publishers have regional representatives who visit various departments on college campuses and obtain the names of those serving on textbook selection committees. The input of these representatives could then be compiled into a master list, and potential participants selected at random. Note that the design of the master list could produce a list of potential participants that is biased if the list is constructed so that faculty names are listed under schools and schools are listed alphabetically. For example, if every nth name is selected from such a list, it could happen that several participants will be selected from a particular state because that state has many more colleges and universities than another, less densely populated state. Or if potential participants are simply listed alphabetically in the master list, one of the focus groups in the study could end up with two or three of the participants coming from the same school if the school has a large number of writing faculty. Therefore, it might be advantageous to list the population of interest (faculty serving on college textbook selection committees) by region, and by school within each region, with a plan to take a certain percentage of names from each regional list. Since most textbook selection committees are small (three to five persons, usually), taking every sixth to tenth name from the list should produce a sample which is geographically distributed and not weighted by more than one member from each school.

Of course, not every focus group project is so rigorous in its selection of subjects as the hypothetical handbook study. The rigor of the selection process depends on the goal of the researcher. In fact, convenience sampling may more easily provide a sample population that represents the population of interest. One example is the Research Special Interest Group of the Society for Technical Communication (STC). This group has been interested in prompting society members to do more research, so their focus group sessions are sometimes a kind of "action research," intended to raise the consciousness of the participants while also collecting data from them. These focus group sessions are usually held at the society's annual national convention; they are listed in the program, and so are open to conference attendees. Kreuger (1994) claims that open meetings such as this are not really focus groups because, for one thing, they don't provide a homogenous group. However, the STC organizers believe that conference attendees who decide to come to a particular focus group session are similar in that they are Society members, so they obviously are interested in technical communication, and if they choose to attend this session, they obviously have in common an interest in research. Thus, the organizers do not concern themselves with randomization.

Sometimes convenience sampling techniques can be used to select participants in other areas. For example, if the researcher is interested in users of a particular facility such as a library, it might be possible to approach visitors on a certain day to request their help. In a business setting, the population of interest might be those who choose to participate in a workshop on some specialized topic such as computer-generated graphics.

In still other cases when the research topic is a sensitive one, such as research involving persons who have lost their job because of a merger or downsizing, snowball sampling may be the best source of potential participants. Sometimes researchers who have assembled one focus group via the snowball technique ask the members of that focus group to suggest potential participants for a subsequent group. Such a question is usually asked at the end of the first focus group meeting, and it would probably be a good idea to ask members of the first focus group to refrain from discussing their own group experience with the persons they nominate as potential future participants.

As a last resort, some focus group researchers advertise to attract participants. Ads can be placed in newspapers and on community and online bulletin boards. In this case, the researcher loses the benefit of a personal appeal for help, so some other type of motivation will probably be needed. When advertisements are used to attract potential participants, it is usually customary to offer a financial remuneration. Whatever method is used for selecting participants, the possible effects of the process on the information provided should be considered when the data are analyzed.

A final consideration in selecting a pool of potential participants is the number that will be needed. Most individual groups are limited to eight to ten members. Note that more than one group is needed for good focus group research. How many groups to use is often determined by the amount of funds available to pay for the recruitment, the facilities, the group leaders, and participant incentives or rewards. The minimum number of groups is two. On the other hand, there is a point of no return on the investment of time and money. Kreuger (1994) recommends conducting an evaluation after the third group has met to see how much new information has turned up in the third group compared to what was gained in groups one and two. After a saturation point is reached (little or no new information produced), there is no point in arranging for additional groups.

Assigning Participants to Individual Groups

After the sample has been selected, the next task is to assign the potential participants to specific groups. Design of an individual group is important because the make-up of a particular group often affects group dynamics. Because focus group research is dependent on group interaction, it is important to keep each group small. In the past, researchers have recommended 10 to 12 participants (Kreuger, 1988). However, based on my experience in teaching graduate classes, I think more discussion is possible when groups are smaller, e.g., five to eight persons—a conclusion shared by Kreuger in the introduction to his most recent book on the subject (1994). On the other hand, if the group is too small, the number of ideas generated will likely be small as well. One problem in arranging size is that some potential participants who say they will come don't, without giving any notice—people forget, other things come up at the last minute, and so forth. A possible answer to this problem is to invite 12 to 15 persons at the same time, planning that if ten or more do show up, they will be arranged into two groups. Of course, prior seating arrangements will have to be made so that the two groups can function without disturbing each other.

The first guideline for assigning potential participants to individual focus groups is to try to assemble groups of participants who have some characteristics in common. Although I have participated in focus groups arranged by textbook publishers, I don't know how they selected the participants. So here, I will use a hypothetical example of focus group research into handbook design as an illustration. In the case of our hypothetical handbook focus group project, the researcher may want to make up groups according to which semester of college composition the potential participant tends to teach or have the most interest in because in schools with two semesters of first year composition, the focus of instruction in each semester is usually quite different. Some researchers believe assignment to particular focus groups should be based on gender because gender-related behavior can sometimes stifle input. Certainly gender should be used as an assignment criterion if the research question has gender implications or if the research question would be a sensitive topic for one sex or the other. At any rate, a focus group will work better if the members are homogenous in some way. A negative example for me was a focus group one year at the STC's national conference. Although this process may have produced some successful focus groups, the participants in my particular group did not share common characteristics. I seemed to be the only academic in the group, and the other members of the group sometimes made derogatory remarks to the effect that academics are not very knowledgeable about work in the "real world." The result was that I said next to nothing in the meeting.

Second, an individual focus group seems to work better if the participants don't already know each other. Of course, this goal may be difficult to achieve in our hypothetical handbook research project because many compositionists meet and make friends at conferences. At a minimum, the researcher might want to be sure that no individual group includes persons with family ties, persons who work closely with each other, or even persons with an advanced degree (M.A. or Ph.D.) from the same university because such programs tend to have a particular philosophy of composition. For example, in the recent past Carnegie Mellon University's rhetoric program has emphasized a cognitive approach to teaching writing, while the University of Texas at Austin has concentrated on classical rhetoric, and some professors at the University of Massachusetts at Amherst have emphasized expressivist writing. When screening the list of possible participants for the source of their degrees in our handbook project, a researcher could probably look up professors' alma maters in the catalogues of the colleges where they currently teach. However, when information on some important criterion is not readily available, the focus group researcher usually does a telephone screening interview, described below.

Furthermore, to facilitate maximum participation by all members of a focus group, it is a good idea to be sure that the participants are more or less on equal footing in regard to the topic of interest. For example, if one of the group's members is an expert on the topic (e.g., a lawyer or a Ph.D.) and the other members have a high school education, the group may not function well because those with less education may be intimidated by those with advanced degrees. The same thing is true of a group comprised of blue collar employees plus one or two members of management. Sometimes differences in perceived rank are subtle. Kreuger (1994) explains that in a group of farmers, participants may defer to one who owns substantially more acres than the others in the group. I suppose that in writing research, group members might defer to a person who has published frequently. Researchers can often sort these factors out in a pre-selection telephone interview with potential participants as I explain below so that anyone whose status might intimidate other participants is not invited to participate. Or, since very few focus group researchers rely on just one group to provide the data, it might be possible to set up the individual groups so that the status of members in each group is more or less equal.

For example, if we wanted to investigate perceptions of writers and production process managers toward user testing of computer manuals, we might be able to find potential participants in a local chapter of the Society for Technical Communication. We could make some arrangements to hold four or five group sessions, three for writers on a particular day and two for managers on another day. Next we would design a screening questionnaire that we would use as if it were a fact-finding survey. We would call each member of the local STC chapter and explain that we were surveying members to learn more about the types of work technical writers do in our area. Our first question might ask whether the respondent has ever worked on a software manual. If the answer is no, we could thank the respondent and end the conversation. If the answer is yes, we might then ask if his or her current job is related to software manuals. Again, if the answer is no, we would thank the respondent and end the conversation. If the answer is yes, we would ask the respondent to choose one category from a list of four that best describes his or her role in the production of software manuals: writer, editor, production process supervisor, graphics designer. Based on the answer to this question we would either thank the respondent and end the survey or we would invite the respondent to participate in a particular one of the groups we have scheduled—managers in the manager group, writers in the writer group, and so on.

Note that in this hypothetical study we could also consider other factors in our screening questions. For example, we might believe that the length of job experience could affect interaction in the individual focus groups. Maybe those with less job experience would defer to those with more. Therefore, we could add a question about length of job experience to our screening survey and use the answers to sort the respondents into groups whose members have relatively equal job experience. Of course, potential participants are not told that they are being categorized this way—they are either thanked for participating in the survey or invited to specific sessions which have been set up according to pre-determined criteria.

Recruiting Participants

If focus groups are open to conference goers, recruiting participants is usually not a problem. However, in other types of focus group research, recruiting participants can require substantial effort. Prior planning can alleviate many recruitment problems. Probably the most important item in terms of effect on recruitment is the time and place the focus group will meet. A second important item is the training of the recruiter so that he or she comes across in a warm, personal way. For example, a telephone recruiter might conclude the telephone survey by saying something like this: "We would like to invite you to participate in a group discussion on this topic with people like yourself who...." Potential participants are more likely to respond affirmatively if the person making the calls conveys a warm, personal interest in them. Potential participants are also more likely to respond positively if they are convinced that the study has some value and that their participation is particularly needed.

Because participation in a focus group requires a substantial chunk of a participant's time, focus group researchers often try to entice participants by offering them some product as a gift. Kreuger (1994) cites the example of a group assembled to talk about houseplant fertilizer in which each participant was given a bag of fertilizer as a gift. Of course, if the product being discussed is an expensive one such as a computer printer, the researcher could not very well afford to give each participant a printer. However, it would be possible to give a package of computer disks, or ink, or even a package of computer paper. In other cases, researchers invite potential participants to take part in a meal. Kreuger (1994) says the most successful incentive is money because it appeals to everyone, whereas a particular gift such as tickets to a concert may not. However, two issues should be considered when planning to use money as an incentive: amount and method of payment. The amount must be large enough that it isn't insulting. In fact, it may be cheaper to offer $50.00 to each participant than to have to make many more phone calls to find people for whom $25.00 is sufficient incentive. Second, the researcher should be prepared to pay participants in cash when the focus group meeting ends. Checks are an inconvenience because they require a trip to the bank to be cashed, and checks sent out a week or two after the meeting represent an even greater inconvenience.

When recruiting subjects, the researcher should also mention the fact that the session will be taped, if that is the case. Usually people don't object to an audio tape recorder, but videotaping means that the participant might have some anxiety about clothes or other aspects of appearance. In fact, Kreuger (1994) recommends against videotaping because the process is so intrusive. In addition to lights, camera, and camera personnel, the effort to capture each speaker's facial expression will require the person operating the camera to keep shifting position in the room. Videotaping or no, it is probably a good idea to mention in the recruitment pitch just how informal the dress should be.

Follow-up is also an important technique when recruiting participants. If a person contacted by phone agrees to participate, he should immediately be sent a personal letter (use his name and the "you" approach) on quality letterhead to thank him in advance, to remind him of why he is important to the project, and why the project itself is important, and to provide a written record of the date, time, and place for his future reference. This letter should also identify the sponsoring organization, but the letter should not give any information about specific products that will be discussed so that at the focus group session, the input will be spontaneous rather than planned. A few days before the actual focus group session, it is a good idea to made a personal phone call as a reminder.

Of course, recruitment is not a problem for the focus groups organized by the research special interest group of the Society for Technical Communication. Because the focus group sessions are listed in the convention program, interested persons can be counted on to show up. However, even in this situation the organizers sometimes use bait to tempt participants: a well-known specialist in some area usually gives a kind of keynote address to begin the focus group session. For example, keynoters in 1993 were Karen Schriver, well-known for her research in document design, Roger Grice, a documentation expert from IBM, and David Armbruster, president of the STC that year. Whether it was the keynote addresses or simply the interest in the topic which attracted participants, the STC sessions were very well attended.

FOCUS GROUP LEADERS

Most focus group research projects have two leaders at each meeting of the participants: a moderator and a recorder. Although a recorder may sometimes contribute to the general conversation, it generally works better if each leader focuses on his or her duties.

Moderators and recorders of focus groups should be carefully chosen. First, neither should be someone with close ties to any member of the focus group. Just as the group functions best when members are more or less strangers, so too does it function best when the leaders are comparative strangers to all group members. If the topic for discussion is a sensitive one, it may be a good idea to select leaders to match group characteristics such as gender, age, and ethnic heritage. Second, leaders should have a pleasing personality and voice. They should be able to easily demonstrate respect for the participants and enthusiasm for learning about the topic. Third, group leaders should be well trained.

The Role of the Moderator

The most important role of the moderator is to facilitate group interaction. Therefore, a moderator should be well trained in group dynamics and understand group roles such as those described by Houp, Pearsall, and Tebeaux (1995, pp. 56–58). Such an understanding could help a moderator encourage participation from a shy person (a mouse-type) and tame overparticipation by loud and aggressive "bulldozer" types and wisecracking clowns.

Moderator training should also include skills in active listening—the ability to provide affirming feedback, such as summarizing a point made by using the same tone and even some of the contributor's exact words in order to demonstrate that the participant has been heard and understood. Moderators also need a sense of timing so that they can move the conversational focus into a different area or bring it back when it has gone astray. Perhaps most importantly, moderators should be trained to have "unconditional positive regard" (Henderson, 1992, p. 21), so that they can accept all viewpoints as valid and refrain from offering their own insights to the group, for example, trying to educate the participants. Moreover, moderators must be trained to avoid conveying negative judgments of participants or participant contributions, not only verbally, but also through body language and facial expressions. Similarly, moderators should be trained to note, and remember, non-verbal contributions of the participants as well as their tone of voice and the content of the input.

The Role of the Recorder

The recorder's primary task is to collect the data, usually by taking notes, but these notes could be supplementary to audio- or videotaping. The recorder is also usually responsible for handling equipment and dealing with late arriving or problematic participants and unexpected guests. Kreuger (1994) recommends having a questionnaire on hand that can be used as a screening device to ward off problem participants. For example, if a potential participant has already obviously consumed too much alcohol, he or she can be given a questionnaire to fill out; then the participant can be given the reward and thanked for coming. Surprisingly, sometimes people bring along a relative or close friend. These unexpected arrivals can also be given questionnaires and thanked. A bigger problem occurs when potential participants bring along small children. Even if some form of entertainment such as coloring books is provided, small children often cannot be kept interested for the two hours that a focus group normally meets. Researchers should try to avoid this problem when recruiting participants by emphasizing that potential participants should make other provisions for their children.

Some recorders function as assistant moderators and join in the conversation at certain points, depending on how the focus group was planned. Certainly, an assistant moderator can help the moderator facilitate the group process by asking a direct question of a particularly reticent participant. In the STC research I mentioned above, sometimes the group leader (moderator by a different name) was also the recorder who used a magic marker and a large flip chart to record the ideas generated by the group. This system has the advantage that group members can see the notes as they are being written and thus correct them if the recorder has misunderstood some comment. But this system also means that the moderator stands while the other participants are seated—a classroom model that emphasizes the controlling aspect of the moderator and encourages participants to speak to the moderator instead of to each other.

STRATEGIES FOR CONDUCTING THE MEETING

Once participants begin to arrive in the meeting place, the leaders' first task is to make participants feel welcome, to keep track of which potential participants have arrived, and to usher participants to a snack area or to their seats, while at the same time establishing a rapport with ice-breaking chitchat of some type. This period can last anywhere from ten to 20 minutes, depending on the arrival times of the participants. Once a sufficient number of participants has arrived, the introductory stage of the focus group session begins with the moderator introducing the assistant moderator or recorder and explaining how the data are going to be collected: tape recorder, notes, or videotape. Next, the moderator usually states the purpose (e.g., "We're here to talk about X") and sets up ground rules. "Rules" for focus groups seems almost a contradiction in terms because focus groups are supposed to be permissive and open. However, it is usually a good idea for the moderator to establish that comments and opinions are being sought from *each person* and that there is no right or wrong answer to any question. A moderator should explain that negative comments are just as valuable as positive ones, and that it is perfectly acceptable, and even possibly helpful, for participants to disagree with each other. For example, a moderator could say, "We want to hear your opinions, so please speak up. Have the courage to speak your convictions even if they are quite different from those of other group members," and "To be sure that each person is heard, please don't engage in side conversations with your neighbor. Instead share your ideas with the whole group." To keep the atmosphere friendly and conversational rather than laboratory-like, the rules should be few, well planned, and offered in a friendly but firm tone. Thus, the moderator has a somewhat difficult role at the beginning of a focus group meeting because she has to get conversation going while conveying the impression that her role is not one of power; in other words, the moderator does not want to come across as expert on the topic or a teacher of the class. Also, during the rest of the group session, good moderators take care to avoid putting words in the participants' mouths and avoid making any interpretive comments based on previous experience with a focus group. Henderson (1992) says that a moderator needs to become a "mental virgin" for each focus group session (p. 23).

Next, to help put participants at ease with one another, the moderator usually points out what they have in common—in other words, why they were selected to be participants. And then, participants are usually asked to introduce themselves to the group, possibly telling some bit of information about themselves and their relationship to the topic. These introductions can be modeled by the moderator introducing herself to show how just a few words can convey information that will build rapport among group members. Finally, the moderator reintroduces the topic for discussion and opens the discussion with some easy-to-answer questions. This period of group bonding usually lasts about 20 minutes. If several focus groups are being used, the moderators should learn a common script to use in introducing participants, rules, and the topic for discussion.

To launch the discussion of the topic of interest, the moderator can choose one of several possible strategies. In some focus groups, the moderator will pass out a handout with some information for participants to glance over and think about when the group is first assembled for discussion. Handouts can also carry thought prompts such as sentence completions or concept mapping exercises. For example, a handout may ask participants to quickly complete sentences such as "I was surprised by..." or "I wish someone would write a handbook that..." and so forth. Or a handout may ask participants to quickly list possible features of some product or program and then group the items in some way. For example, participants could be asked to quickly list the features they've encountered in previous handbooks, and then when that task is completed, participants could be asked to group the features under headings such as "an essential item," "a helpful, but not essential item," and "an item is that is neither essential nor helpful." In other instances, a visual aid of some kind may be presented to the group—for example, a program schedule, a product package, or promotional material such as brochures and posters.

If no handouts are to be used, then moderators usually open the discussion by asking an open-ended question that will cause participants to reflect on their past experiences and make connections to the topic. For example, a moderator in our hypothetical focus group on handbooks, might ask, "How did you use handbooks in the last class you taught?" or "What did you look for when you selected the handbook you now use in your class?" Grounding a question in a historical event like this improves the accuracy of the answer. Having asked questions grounded in specific events, the moderator can then zero in on a key question such as "What is the most important feature of a good handbook?" or "How do you feel about such and such handbook feature?" Questions to be avoided are those which can be answered yes or no and those which tend to limit possible responses such as questions about level of satisfaction, e.g., "How satisfied are you with the handbook you are currently using?" A better question in this case would be to ask what the participants like about their current handbook, and then ask what they don't like.

Another type of question to be avoided is a "why" question because sometimes people have not thought out their motives, but few will be willing to say that they don't know why they took a particular action. In many cases, decisions are often made on the basis of habits, traditions, and even impulses—all of which participants may be reluctant to admit. Instead, people often feel defensive when asked why, and they will probably feel a compulsion to give a rational reason, even if it is one they have not really thought of before. Frequently, reasons for particular behaviors can be elicited with other sorts of questions. For example, participants could be asked to name a feature that would attract them to a certain product, so for our handbook research project, we could ask, "What feature of your current handbook do you find most attractive?...least attractive?" Or we could ask, "Who makes the decision about handbooks for the courses you teach? If you were making the decision, what factors would you consider?"

When the interchange between participants is going well, the moderator usually lets the conversation flow for a while. However, the moderator probably also has a short list of questions (no more than five or six, and all open-ended) which he or she introduces into the conversation at appropriate times. Sometimes moderators can pick up a phrase used by one of the participants as a lead-in for a question on the list. For example, if a participant has mentioned students who have problems with semicolons, a moderator might say, "How can a handbook best help students who have problems with semicolons?" Of course the moderator is probably interested in punctuation as a whole, but often what is said about methods for teaching proper use of semicolons can apply to teaching other punctuation marks as well. If necessary, the moderator could even follow up the discussion on teaching the use of semicolons with a question about whether the same methods could be applied to teaching other types of punctuation. Still another approach to eliciting information from participants is to ask them to participate in an imaginary situation. For example, the moderator could say, "Let's pretend you wanted to do X. What would you look for in the handbook?" Or a moderator could ask participants to enter a dream world: "If you had all the resources possible to produce a handbook, what would it look like?" or "What would it contain?"

Moderators, of course, need to be alert to conversation roadblocks such as one participant speaking too long or too forcefully (the "bulldozer"), another one not saying much at all (the "mouse"), or another who keeps distracting the group from the topic by making jokes and asides (the "clown"). To slow down a monopolizer, a moderator can watch for a pause or switch in topic and say, "Before we go any further" or "Before we switch to a new topic, I'd like to get some input from others in the group on this topic or idea." Then the moderator could turn to the quiet person and ask him or her directly for input. At other times, moderators have to intervene to bring the conversation back to the topic at hand, and sometimes moderators need to check impressions by restating someone's comment in a way that invites that person to correct a wrong impression. For example, if a participant says that a handbook should be organized like a reference book, a moderator could say, "So it would be helpful to have the content organized alphabetically with entries listed from A to Z?"

Because the focus group is conducted like a conversation, new ideas can arise from the interaction of the participants. In the case of a new idea arising, a moderator has to decide immediately whether to pursue the new idea or to stick to the questions already planned. One possibility is to make note of the new idea and promise to come back to it while directing the participants' attention to the issue then under discussion. In such a case, a moderator will want to watch the time closely so that there will be opportunity to explore the new idea. Actually, a moderator must watch the time carefully whether new ideas arise or not because participants will not want the discussion to go on longer than promised when they were recruited. Most moderators limit the investigation or discussion part of the focus group session to an hour or an hour and ten minutes.

The final portion of the focus group session—closure—is important because it helps participants feel that their efforts have been worthwhile. Many moderators give participants a sense of closure by briefly summing up the conversation and asking if any major points of the discussion were not included in the summary. To signal the end, the moderator thanks participants and expresses pleasure at having gotten to know them.

The last task of the moderator takes place after one focus group meeting is over and before the next one begins. That task is a debriefing report which should be taped, so that the research team can examine it later. The moderator and the recorder or assistant moderator can give separate de-briefings or they can do one together. In either case, the idea is to record, while the memory is still fresh, a brief evaluation of the group process, any problems which arose, any important ideas or comments which surfaced during the meeting, plus reactions to persons and ideas and new insights into the topic being researched. This recording becomes part of the data, and it can be very useful on its own as well as useful in interpreting the data collected from the participants.

ANALYZING THE DATA

Perhaps the most time-consuming task of focus group research, like other qualitative research, is data analysis. Generally, focus group researchers follow the same guidelines as case study and interview researchers in that they make specific plans for analyzing the data and they carry out these plans systematically. Kreuger (1994) warns that the analysis should begin as soon as possible after the data collection so that memory doesn't fade and the impressions of subsequent group sessions don't get mixed up with impressions from earlier sessions. And, as in other types of qualitative research, the interpretation of the data should be verified. In some instances, tentative interpretations can be shown to knowledgeable colleagues for feedback. Or interpretations can be shown to the moderators as a check. Sometimes, researchers even ask group participants to look over a draft of analysis and comment.

Data analysis usually proceeds on several levels: overall impressions (the big picture), categorization of segments (sometimes single comments or groups of comments), and interpretation of small units such as words and non-verbal behaviors. (For a more complete discussion of techniques for analyzing discourse, see Chapter 7). In analyzing the big picture, one should focus on the purpose of the study and identify ways that purpose has been illuminated. The data can be examined for evidence of trends and fit to results of previous studies.

Second, the data can be examined in segments to derive categories. Categories are assigned to segments by giving each category a letter or number and jotting that code in the margin beside the segments to which it applies. In this way, transcripts can later be broken up and all segments assembled in one file under one category. To check the validity of the coding, a colleague could be given the category definitions and asked to code a small subset of the data. Depending on the purpose of the research, it might be very important to examine notes or videotapes for instances of non-verbal behaviors that would help with the interpretation of particular segments of the data. Kreuger (1994) points out that tone and intensity of speech can be useful markers of data that participants consider to be very important.

Once segments have been coded, they can be examined for disconfirming or contrary evidence, and they can be compared to reveal consistencies and inconsistencies. Frequency of instances of a particular category can be noted, although one should be cautious about assuming that something which is mentioned frequently is something very important. As interpretations are developed, researchers need to consider alternative explanations for the data. One source for alternative explanations is a rechecking of the context of a particular remark. Also, one could consider individual aspects of the participant who made the remark, for example, age, gender, ethnic heritage, work experience, and so forth.

Finally, researchers may want to look at the data on the word level. Of course, not every word should be closely examined. But note that an examination of the vocabulary of the focus groups used by Becker and Mikelonis (1987) revealed that one of the reasons for the lack of interest in the technical communication institute offered by the Department of Rhetoric at the University of Minnesota was that its workshops and courses were labeled with different terms than those used by potential participants. The researchers reported that although practitioners in the area expressed a need for courses or workshops in writing computer manuals, they did not recognize a course labeled "instructional design" as one that would meet this need.

After the data have been analyzed, researchers usually go back to choose illustrations to use in reporting their interpretations. In choosing words and statements to illustrate interpretations, researchers are naturally drawn to those statements that are pithy or memorable. However, such statements may not be a faithful representation of the data as a whole. Usually researchers use bits of text to either illustrate a point or illustrate the range of response. Certainly, a researcher has an ethical obligation to choose carefully, keeping in mind the content.

ADVANTAGES AND DISADVANTAGES OF FOCUS GROUP RESEARCH

As you consider whether to try to use focus group research to answer your research questions, it would be well to consider both their advantages and disadvantages.

Advantages

Focus group research has many advantages. As I explained above, focus group research often produces information that cannot be obtained in any other way. The natural setting and the conversation usually promote increased candor. The personal interaction also often stimulates new ideas, and the flexible format allows new ideas to be explored immediately if that seems wise. Focus groups also produce information rapidly in contrast to questionnaires which may dribble in over quite a long period of time, and focus groups are relatively inexpensive to conduct because they usually rely on fewer participants.

Focus group research is most useful when either there is a gap in knowledge about perceptions, attitudes, and feelings of a certain population; the issues of interest are complex or ambiguous, involving behavior and motivation that are not well understood; or fresh ideas are needed about a certain topic. A good example of how a focus group research project can benefit a program in writing is the project carried out by Becker and Mikelonis (1987) at the University of Minnesota. Because of falling enrollment in the Department of Rhetoric's Institute for Technical Communication, the two researchers used focus groups to find out more about the continuing education needs of professional communicators in the community. A surprising result was that many of the courses offered at the institute were just what the professional communicators indicated a need for; however, differences in terminology obscured this match. As I explained above, the institute offered a course in "instructional design," whereas practitioners were looking for a course in writing user manuals. Using the information gleaned from the focus groups, the Rhetoric Department redesigned the institute to better match potential participants' needs, and they used terminology suggested by the focus group participants. The result was a 100% increase in enrollment.

Although a questionnaire might have uncovered the need for a course or two which had not been previously offered by the Professional Communications Institute at the University of Minnesota, it is doubtful that a questionnaire would have uncovered the basic problem of vocabulary mismatch. Similarly, it might surprise some designers of college writing courses to learn what faculty outside the English department, personnel directors at local businesses, and students on the point of graduating from the university might see as the most important tasks of a writing course.

Disadvantages

Focus group research also has several disadvantages, not the least of which is the necessity of obtaining a special setting for the group meetings and arranging schedules which will fit potential participants' lifestyles. Finally, as in all qualitative research, focus groups produce a large volume of data that may be difficult to analyze.

Focus group research is probably not very useful in situations when statistics are needed, confidentiality must be protected, or the climate surrounding the topic is sensitive or hostile because of emotionally charged issues (e.g., salary, personal expenditures, interpersonal conflict at work, etc.).

A major disadvantage cited by focus group researchers at the University of Minnesota (Becker and Mikelonis, 1987) was the difficulty in convincing their academic colleagues that marketing research tools were appropriate to use in planning an academic program. Colleagues raised the question of academic integrity: shouldn't the academy base programs on what members believe to be educationally sound principles rather than on financial gain? However, use of focus groups to explore motivations, perceptions, and needs does not mean that programs designed in response to the findings will not be educationally sound. Rather, this challenge seems to me to be yet another instance of a misunderstanding of empirical research. Focus group methodology relies heavily on qualitative information, rather than numerical data collected under stringently controlled conditions, but it is no less valid for that. In fact, qualitative research may be the only way to learn what we need to know. If focus groups are well-designed, then questions of validity can be answered satisfactorily.

REFERENCES

Becker, S. J., & Mikelonis, V. M. (1987). A strategy for marketing technical communications programs. In *Proceedings of the 34th International Technical Communication Conference* (pp. RET:24–RET:25). Arlington, VA: Society for Technical Communications.

Byers, P. Y., & Wilcox, J. R. (1991). Focus groups: A qualitative opportunity for researchers. *Journal of Business Communication, 28,* 63–77.

Elling, R. (1997). Revising safety instructions with focus groups. *Journal of Business and Technical Communication, 11,* 451–468.

Henderson, N. R. (June 1992). Trained moderators boost the value of qualitative research. *Marketing Research,* 20–23.

Houp, K. W., Pearsall, T. E., & Tebeaux, E. (1995). *Reporting technical information* (9th ed.). Boston: Allyn & Bacon.

Kreuger, R. A. (1988). *Focus groups: A practical guide for applied research.* Newbury Park, CA: Sage.

Kreuger, R. A. (1994). *Focus groups: A practical guide for applied research* (2nd ed.). Newbury Park, CA: Sage.

ADDITIONAL RESOURCES

Frey, J. H., & Fontana, A. (1991). The group interview in social research. *Social Science Journal, 28,* 175–187.

Goldman, A. E., & McDonald, S. S. (1987). *The group depth interview.* Englewood Cliffs, NJ: Prentice Hall.

Morgan, D. L. (1988). *Focus groups as qualitative research.* Newbury Park, CA: Sage.

Case Study Research[1]

In the early stages of inquiry into a problem or an area of interest, researchers often turn to case studies. Case study research is a qualitative tool; as such, it aims to provide a rich description of an event or of a small group of people or objects (usually not more than 12). Because the scope of a case study is so narrow, the findings can rarely be generalized; but a case study can provide insights into events and behaviors, and it can provide hypotheses for testing.

In this chapter, I first describe some of the history of case study research in writing and how that research has contributed to the growth of composition and technical writing as scholarly disciplines. Next, I define case study methodology by considering how the words "case" and "study" are commonly used by society today. I further define case study research by considering its similarities to and differences from the other major tool of descriptive or qualitative research: ethnography. Afterward, advantages and disadvantages of case study methodology are examined, followed by a discussion of some ways to increase the respectability of a case study and some tools often used in case study research. Finally, I point out some opportunities for case study research in the workplace; data collection (which takes place during the study); and data analysis and reporting findings (which are undertaken after the study ends).

CONTRIBUTIONS OF CASE STUDY RESEARCH TO WRITING SCHOLARSHIP

Case study research in composition has contributed much to what we know about the writing process. Janet Emig's (1981) pioneering case study of eight high school

---

[1]Portions of this chapter appear in M. S. MacNealy. (1997). Toward better case study research. *IEEE Transactions on Professional Communication, 40,* 182–196.

students was one of the first research projects to provide empirical evidence that traditional classroom methods of teaching writing were questionable. John R. Hayes and Linda Flower used case studies to probe into the cognitive aspects of writing tasks such as planning and revising (see Flower, Hayes, Carey, Schriver, & Stratman, 1986; Hayes & Flower, 1983); they were especially interested in identifying the differences between novice and expert writing strategies. These projects, as well as those of other composition researchers, have helped to build composition studies into a solid discipline. Today, universities no longer expect that a degree in literature is sufficient for preparing professors to teach writing. Whereas in the past, English departments advertised jobs in areas of literature (e.g., Medieval, American, etc.) and expected the new hire to teach two or three sections of freshman composition as well, now many job ads specify that the candidate must have a Ph.D. in composition or rhetoric. Furthermore, in the past many teachers of composition were hired at an instructor rank with no possibility of tenure, but today many tenure track positions are open to writing specialists. In fact, a recent Modern Language Association analysis of the job market found that in 1982, only 44% of advertised writing positions were tenure track, whereas in 1991, 71% of advertised writing positions were tenure track (Huber, 1992). Thus, composition/rhetoric has developed into a discipline commanding respect.

Similarly, a growing number of technical communicators have used case study research to help build understanding of writing in the workplace. Probably the most frequently cited case study researchers in technical writing are members of a team headed by Odell and Goswami who conducted a number of case studies investigating writers' reasons for their choices about content (Odell, 1985), about style (Odell & Goswami, 1982), about ways of conveying a request or a command (Odell, Goswami, Herrington, & Quick, 1983). Other early research of writing in the workplace has focused on writing done by engineers (Selzer, 1983; Miller and Selzer, 1985). Solid research efforts such as these have contributed to the growth of professional writing as a discipline—a growth that has proceeded rapidly in the last 20 years.

A case study can be carried out by just one or two persons in their place of work. However, a valid case study consists of more than a retrospective or anecdotal report on some procedure or event. The value of a case study depends on good design. A retrospective report on "How we did X at ABC corporation" does not constitute a valid case study. The difference is preplanning. In most anecdotal reports which are not really case studies, the author looks back on what happened and reports from the viewpoint of the *end* of the project, relying on his or her memory for data. A case study, on the other hand, involves a *plan* for studying or investigating a topic or problem, and data are then collected along the way rather than retrieved from memory at the end of a project.

CLEARING UP THE CONFUSION

The label "case study" is sometimes used by the general public and by different disciplines to mean quite different things. If we are going to talk about "case study" research, we need to separate what we mean by that from the meaning attributed to it in other situations. In the categories that follow, alternative labels are suggested for four efforts that are not, strictly speaking, empirical case studies.

- *Rhetoric.* The professional or well-trained rhetorician uses a description of a situation (real or fictional) to illustrate a point he or she wants to make. Here, we should probably use the term "case history" or "illustrative case" because no systematic study is involved. Several examples of rhetorical cases are used in this book, namely those studies of eyelash length, all of which are fictional.
- *Education.* Teachers often use cases in much the same way as a rhetorician does: to help their students understand a concept by illustrating it with a description of a particular situation. Teachers also use descriptions of real or fictional situations to help students learn to solve problems in writing, management, marketing, and so forth. In this instance, the teacher gives a student a "problem case" to work on as an exercise. For example, the exercise might consist of a brief narrative about an individual who has been asked by her boss to answer a customer's letter of complaint about a recent purchase; the exercise is then evaluated to see how well the student has been able to apply the principles for answering letters of complaint. Using the term "case study" in this situation is inappropriate because research to find new information is not the main purpose of such assignments; rather the assignments are given as simulation exercises to help students learn to apply principles they have been taught much in the same way that astronauts prepare for space flight by carrying out various activities in a capsule or machine which simulates weightlessness.
- *Law.* The lawyer or law student reads descriptions of prior court cases to learn principles from examples and/or find precedents to support an argument. In this situation, study may be involved, but it is not study designed to uncover new knowledge. Legal professionals often use the term "case law research" rather than "case study."
- *Medicine.* Medical personnel collect information about a patient's history and current condition by giving tests and conducting interviews to diagnose and treat a condition. The professional terminology for this procedure is "taking a case history." "Case histories" are also used to illustrate medical practices and problems in professional literature, the popular press, and educational materials.

In contrast to these four inappropriate uses of case study terminology, empirical researchers use the term to refer to a carefully designed project to systematically collect information about an event, situation, or small group of persons or objects for the purpose of exploring, describing, and/or explaining aspects not previously known or considered. The purpose is to develop new insights, new knowledge. This is the situation where the term case study is most appropriate. To avoid the confusion created by the general use of case study, writing professionals should use the term with care, restricting its use to empirical research projects.

Furthermore, writing professionals need to keep in mind the characteristics that distinguish case study research from other types of qualitative empirical research methods, such as ethnographies. Some confusion arises because many of the strategies used in case study research are the same as strategies used in other empirical projects: interviews, questionnaires, examination of artifacts, and so on. To distinguish case studies from other types of research, it is helpful to think of them as having a very narrow focus: a case study usually investigates only one event or only a very small number of people or objects (typically, 12 or fewer). And a case study is usually conducted over a fairly short period of time—usually a semester or less. For example, Sullivan (1997) conducted one-on-one interviews of one hour each with nine employees in an IRS Service Center. Some of the employees brought documents for analysis to the interviews; others mailed documents to the researcher. The researcher also made some visits to the employee work sites for observation. Most of these visits took place right after the interviews.

On the other hand, ethnographers study whole communities and over much longer periods—possibly a year or more. For example, Clark, Florio, Elmore, Martin, and Maxwell (1983) spent a whole school year (1979–1980) investigating two classrooms, one second/third grade and one sixth grade. The researchers used participant observation (taking field notes in the classrooms), audio/visual recordings, physical artifacts (writing samples produced by teachers and students), and data collected from teachers including weekly journals and interviews, monthly meetings, and sessions in which the teachers viewed and discussed the videotapes.

ADVANTAGES OF CASE STUDY RESEARCH

In any discipline, case study research is possible. In rhetoric, for example, case study research can be used to learn how particular readers read, or to learn the typical rhetorical strategies used by an effective radio personality such as a preacher or a disk jockey, the response of the radio audience to that personality, and so forth. In law, an empirical case study could be used to find out how certain lawyers write, how they prepare for a case, how they interview clients, how they take depositions, and so forth. In medicine, an empirical case study research could be used to learn what strategies certain doctors use to convince patients to follow dietary guidelines, the types of writing produced by doctors, and so forth. In case studies like these, the persons being studied are usually chosen because they are typical of a certain group or because they are unique in some way. What distinguishes these case studies from the improperly labeled case studies mentioned earlier in this chapter is that these studies are planned in advance so that the data is collected systematically and in a form that enables others to examine it later. Also, in such case studies, more than one method of data collection is used—e.g., observation and interview, or discourse analysis and interview, and so on. Later in this chapter, I will discuss some possibilities for case study research in professional writing, but first let's consider the possible advantages of case study research in any discipline. In particular, case studies can help provide:

- *a holistic view* of an event or situation, e.g., a view that includes the context as well as the details of an individual event such as a computer user trying to access online help.
- *rich detail* that can lead to a better understanding of an event or situation, e.g., the specific word a puzzled computer user first looked for in the online help index.
- *information that cannot otherwise be collected,* e.g., the feelings aroused at the moment the computer user couldn't find a certain word in the online help index or the strategies the computer user contemplated before taking his or her next action in that situation.
- *a more precise definition of research questions,* e.g., is the success of online help dependent on the comprehensiveness of the index?

Case studies can also be used to help formulate hypotheses and add to the development of theory.

DISADVANTAGES OF CASE STUDY RESEARCH

Case study as a research method, however, is not without some disadvantages. Researchers must be aware that case study research can come under attack for the following reasons:

- Case study methodology is often misunderstood, so it is susceptible to poor research design or misapplication of the term "case study." For example, the proceedings of the annual conference of the Society for Technical Communication frequently contain articles labeled "case study" that are, in reality, only retrospective descriptions that were not based on any systematic collection of data.
- Case study results are usually tied to specific situations, so the results are not generalizable. For example, Janet Emig's 1971 monograph, *The Composing Processes of Twelfth Graders,* has often been attacked because it relies so heavily on what one subject (Lynn) did and said (see, for example, Schreiner, 1997). Furthermore, Lynn does not seem to fit in with the other seven students in the study. She writes easily and receives a lot of positive feedback.
- Case study research is often regarded as non-scientific. For example, the charge is often made that because case studies are typically carried out by one person, the information collected is subject to researcher bias, i.e., the researcher found just what he or she was looking for.
- Case studies are sometimes expensive to conduct. For example, case studies that involve tape-recorded interviews incur the expensive task of transcribing the interviews.

Note that the first three disadvantages are really issues of reliability and validity, and some researchers claim that these issues are really not relevant to case studies, nor most qualitative research, because qualitative projects focus on persons, small groups, or whole communities to learn more about those specific persons or groups rather than to test hypotheses as a step toward establishing generalizations. On the other hand, Kirk and Miller (1986) claim that reliability and validity are important to qualitative research, but they also recommend that any difference in focus and purpose between quantitative and qualitative methods should not be taken as a value judgment. Indeed, case studies are a valuable research tool, especially for areas which haven't received much research attention. For example, over the past 15 years, researchers in composition have used case studies to learn how experts revise. Based on these studies, composition teachers and textbooks have begun to devote time and space to teaching students how to revise. On the other hand, some fairly recent case studies of writing in the workplace indicate that little time is spent on revising (see, for example, MacNealy, Speck, & Simpson, 1996; Selzer, 1983). Some of this research is trying to identify the factors which influence writers in the workplace to forgo revising. As more evidence accumulates, it could very well affect the way writing courses are taught.

INCREASING THE RESPECTABILITY OF A CASE STUDY

Researchers can do much to increase the respect for case studies in writing in general and for their own findings in particular if they plan their research project carefully in advance. In the paragraphs that follow, I give eight tips for planning a well-designed case study.

1. *Define the problem that needs attention.* As with most of the other empirical methods described in the book, the first step is to identify a problem that needs attention. A possible reason for practitioners' (especially in technical writing) antipathy to reading research articles is the fact that much of what is published lacks relevance to the tasks technical communicators face in their daily work (see, for example, Smeltzer, 1993; Yates, 1993). A good case study, on the other hand, can add much to a practitioner's expertise if the researcher identifies a real world problem and then defines it carefully. Careful definition of a problem often points the way to the appropriate research methodology. For example, some researchers interested in the question of how a person becomes a member of a particular field of academic expertise postulated that adapting to the discourse community while in graduate school may be a significant part of the overall process. Accordingly, they recruited a new graduate student at Carnegie Mellon University to become the subject of a case study of one person's efforts to adapt to the new discourse community of research in writing (Berkenkotter, Huckin, & Ackerman, 1988). A similar study could find out how a typical graduate student in technical communication adapts to the discourse community of the business world when he or she begins a new job after graduation.

2. *Select the subject(s) to be studied with care.* Sometimes researchers select a unique subject or situation because so little is known about that person or event. For example, one of my colleagues, who is very committed to getting feedback and revising when writing, was astonished during a faculty seminar to hear a rather high-level administrator state that she never revises. Afterward, my colleague asked this administrator if she would be willing to be the subject of a case study examining her writing process because she seemed to be a unique case: a person who does both academic and nonacademic writing and a person who does not revise. From this study, my colleagues and I learned a lot about the factors which influence this particular person to forgo revising. Some of these factors had also been noticed by other researchers such as Selzer, consequently, we began to consider whether some changes need to be made in the way composition is usually taught (MacNealy, Speck, & Simpson, 1996).

In other cases, a researcher will want to select a subject who is typical of some area of interest to begin to collect insights which, when combined with insights from other empirical projects, could be used to build a general theory. In this latter case, researchers often ask some knowledgeable person to suggest a possible subject. Janet Emig, for example, asked local school teachers to suggest students who might make good subjects for studying a typical student's writing process (1971). If several subjects are to be studied, then the researcher may want to consider how to best achieve a representative sample. Representative samples are discussed more fully in Chapter 8 on survey research.

3. *Plan and test procedures in advance of data collection.* Not only will this step ward off criticism of the results, but it will also improve the researcher's chances of successful data collection. Later in this chapter, I describe some procedures or tools that case study researchers have found particularly helpful. The key to success, however, is *advance* planning and testing.

4. *Be systematic about data collections.* Collecting data systematically reduces the probability of researcher bias. For instance, case study researchers often use interviews with multiple subjects, and as anyone who has ever been interviewed will testify, the shape of the question determines the shape of the information provided in the answer. However, if the same question is asked of every person in the study, then the researcher reduces the risk of biased answers from some of the interviewees. Likewise, drawing up possible interview questions in advance and setting up a specific time and place for the interview provides more reliable data than simply asking a question of someone during an encounter in the hall or during an impromptu or social office visit, although a case study researcher may also want to take advantage of chance encounters to collect additional data.

5. *Collect data that can be examined by others to allow verification of findings.* Again, careful methodology can reduce the chances of researcher bias. For example, transcribed recordings of interviews provide stronger evidence against researcher bias than notes—even those in meticulous handwriting—taken by the researcher during an interview, although the latter are better than relying on memory for what was said.

6. *Use triangulation so that more than one measure will converge on an issue.* Triangulation is the use of converging measures to gain separate views of an issue. For example, in an educational setting, a researcher who wants to measure student verbal ability could collect both the grades students earned on a particular piece of work and their SAT scores. In a professional setting, the researcher who wants to know the effectiveness of a particular manual could collect opinions on the quality of a manual, data on the frequency of use of the manual, and protocols of persons using the manual to do a task. This use of multiple measurement instruments (i.e., triangulation) increases the reliability of results.

7. *Verify conclusions by asking an outside rater to examine the collected materials.* For example, to organize the data gathered in transcribed interviews, the researcher needs to look for patterns, provide category labels and descriptions, and then ask an independent judge to use the labels and descriptions in classifying the data. If the judge's independent decisions closely match those of the researcher, the researcher has an effective counter to the charge of researcher bias.

8. *Present conclusions as tentative.* When reporting the results of any research project (regardless of choice of method or strength of findings), researchers can enhance their credibility by qualifying their claims. While the researcher may believe wholeheartedly that handbook exercises do not help writers master punctuation, readers of a research report will be less apt to challenge the findings if the researcher says, "The data *indicate* that doing handbook exercises does not help writers master punctuation," rather than "The data *prove* that doing handbook exercises does not help writers master punctuation."

TOOLS FOR CASE STUDY RESEARCH

Researchers can choose from a rather wide variety of tools in designing a case study. The choice of tools depends to a large degree on what questions the researcher is hoping to answer. For example, if the researcher is interested in prior events that may have contributed to the circumstances of current interest, one tool is the interview. Almost all case studies rely to some extent on interviews. Another tool is examination or analysis of archival information, which can often provide a paper trail of how a decision was made. For instance, a researcher could examine back issues of a local newspaper, maps, and so forth. Or in a business setting, a researcher could examine prior inter-office memos, organizational charts, and other administrative documents.

In almost every case study, a researcher will employ more than one tool to achieve triangulation. A good example of triangulation is Anne Haas Dyson's (1997) study of second grade students engaged in a dialogic exploration of identity and social relations as they rewrote a story based on an incident from a movie. In this study, Dyson made field notes and audiotapes during classroom observations. She collected written products and viewed the movies, TV shows, and video games referenced in the writings.

In sections following Table 10-1, I describe some tools (interviews, logs, and protocols) which are particularly associated with case study research. For other tools in Table 10-1, I give only a brief description because they are dealt with more completely in other sections of this book.

Interviews

Case studies tend to rely heavily on interviews, and interviewing is used extensively in other qualitative research designs such as ethnographies, focus groups, and surveys. Many qualitative researchers consider interviews their most important data-gathering tool (Fetterman, 1989). After I describe some advantages and disadvantages of interviewing, I will present some frequently used interviewing techniques and guidelines.

Advantages of an interview include helping a researcher gather facts, opinions, goals, plans, and insights that may not be available from any other source. Frequently, people who won't take time to fill out and mail in a questionnaire will consent to an interview. Thus, a telephone survey often gains a larger response rate than a mailed questionnaire.

TABLE 10-1   **Research Tools Commonly Used in Case Study Research**

- Interviews
- Logs
- Protocols
  - Verbal
  - Video
- Questionnaires
- Examination of Archival Records
- Examination of Artifacts or Products
- Tests
  - Created especially for the project
  - Standardized
- Observations
  - Environment
  - Actions
  - Body Language

Interviews can also help develop a respondent's answers more fully. For example, a questionnaire can probe for causes after it has asked for a specific answer, as in the case when one question asks if the respondent prefers to work under fluorescent lighting or incandescent lighting and the next question asks the respondent to explain or comment on the previous answer. But in an interview, the subject can also be asked follow-up questions such as "Tell me more about that," or "What happened then?" Also, in a face-to-face interview, the respondent's attitude is often evident from tone of voice or body language.

Finally, an interview can help clarify puzzling answers. For example, in a study of author/editor interaction, my colleagues and I were able to learn a lot of details about how authors deal with slow editorial response. For example, we asked authors in telephone interviews what they did when they received no response for a long time after submitting a manuscript for publication (MacNealy, Speck, & Clements, 1994). In one instance, the respondent told of writing numerous letters to inquire about the status of her manuscript and getting nowhere until she cornered one of the editors at a national conference and asked in person.

Interviewing techniques, therefore, vary along a continuum from informal conversations to formal surveys. In an informal interview, the researcher usually has at least one topic in mind, but the wording of the questions and the order in which topics are dealt with are very flexible to take advantage of conditions of the interview. In more structured interviews (often used when several subjects are being interviewed individually), a list of questions is prepared, but the interviewer can still vary the order according to the circumstance. Survey interviews resemble questionnaires in that the same wording and the same order of questions are used for each subject. Whatever the type of interview structure, interviewers are always alert to possibilities of probing more deeply with follow-up questions.

Disadvantages also exist in interviews. First, they are liable to the challenge of interviewer bias. Tape recording the interviews helps reduce this threat, but many people are uncomfortable speaking into a tape recorder. To make interviewees more comfortable, it is often a good idea to open the interview with more nonthreatening, general questions. For example, in the author/editor study (MacNealy, Speck, & Clements, 1994), we first asked interviewees questions that could be easily answered such as, "Was your article solicited by an editor or guest editor?" and "Had you previously submitted this article to another journal?" After we had established a kind of rapport, we then posed questions on more delicate issues such as, "Did the editor make changes in your article without consulting you?" and "Were all requests for revisions reasonable?"

A second disadvantage to interviews is that the information in the answers can be inaccurate or biased. Most interviewees do not intend to give inaccurate information, but both the interviewer's memory and the wording of the question can contribute to problematic answers. For example, when a respondent describes an event from the past, that history may be inaccurate to a lesser or greater degree because the details are being recalled through the filter of hindsight. One way to help overcome a tendency to faulty memory is to ask the respondent for details of the location of an event before asking what the respondent did or thought at that time. This grounding in physical facts can help memory. Faulty information also results from poorly worded questions. For example, even the question, "What kind of problems did you encounter?" assumes that problems were bound to have happened. A better question would be: "Did you encounter any problems?" Even this question should be kept until near the end of the interview so that the whole focus of the respondent's answers about what happened in a certain situation wouldn't be the problem aspects, because this question can be seen as stimulating the respondent to think of some problem to report in a situation that otherwise would have been regarded as very positive by the respondent. A less biased question would be to just ask the respondent to describe what happened.

A third disadvantage is time spent by the researcher. One-on-one interviewing costs more time than asking respondents to fill out a questionnaire at their convenience. Further, transcribing tapes can be very time consuming and expensive. But in most cases, researchers believe the cost is worth the rich detail that interviews provide.

Several techniques and guidelines can be used to facilitate interviews. A tape recorder (which you have tested in advance) is the most reliable source of data collection, since you can't possibly record every word by hand. Tape recorders also preserve tone of voice and hesitations. However, if you must rely on handwritten notes, you can make these more detailed by devising a set of abbreviations that you practice using in advance so that you don't have to think about them as you take notes. For example, in my notes when reading or interviewing I always use capital "T" to mean "teacher," and capital "S" to mean "student"; "Ts" means "teachers," and "Ss" means "students." These abbreviations have become so ingrained that I even find myself using them when I write comments on papers or notes to colleagues. Some note-taking conventions have become somewhat standardized in empirical research (see Table 10-2, top); others not so widely used (Table 10-2, bottom) can be helpful as well.

Researchers can also maximize the benefits of interviewing by following these guidelines:

- Establish rapport with brief opening chitchat about the day, the weather, or whatever. Use a conversational tone, but be professional.
- Maintain eye contact, but don't stare. Use conversational body language. For example, you could pull two chairs fairly close together at a slight angle rather than sit in chairs facing each other on opposite sides of a desk.
- Give positive feedback such as nodding the head and saying "uh huh" or "I see."
- Allow respondent time to answer. Use pauses for eliciting further details, but don't drag the interview out. Be alert to respondent weariness.
- Use follow-up prompts such as "Could you tell me more about that?" or "What happened next?"

TABLE 10-2   **Note-Taking Conventions**

" "	used to enclose direct quotes	
' '	used to enclose paraphrases	
( )	used for context information or researcher interpretation	

altho	=	although
info	=	information
subs	=	subjects
$	=	money or dollars
#	=	number
≠	=	does not equal or is not
∴	=	therefore
♂	=	female
♀	=	male

- Clarify answers when needed by asking questions such as, "What do you mean?" In some instances, you may want to check your understanding by paraphrasing the answer, as in, "Let's see if I got this right, you felt that…" and so forth.
- Thank the respondent at the end. You can sometimes even offer to send him or her a copy of the final report if the respondent is someone you anticipate future contact with; but avoid over-obligating yourself—make this offer only on limited occasions.
- Type your notes or transcribe your tapes as soon as possible while your memory is still fresh enough to clear up any ambiguities caused by illegible handwriting or inaudible comments on the tape.

Logs

Much as a ship's captain keeps a log of where the ship has been and what new land or conditions have been sighted, in some projects a researcher keeps a log to chart the steps taken in the project and the development of insights. For example, if a researcher is investigating how a student responds to teacher feedback on drafts, the researcher may want to keep a log to track the date the student turned in a draft, the date the teacher handed the draft back, the date the student turned in a revision, and the date the student received the paper with a grade on it. The turn-around time involved in this process could influence the way the student responds to suggestions for revision, especially as the process is repeated several times during a semester. In other words, the researcher may want to be alert to the possibility that quick feedback from the teacher could contribute to a student's enthusiasm for revision. At the same time, the researcher may not want the student to realize that these particular dates are being tracked because the researcher does not want to influence the student to react to the amount of time involved in the feedback. Thus, the researcher will include questions about specific times in a set of questions asking for various other details of the student's actions in producing a paper. Then the researcher will use notes jotted down during the interview to fill out the log after the conference with the student is over.

In other situations, the researcher may ask the subject of the case study to keep a log. Linda Flower once required that I (and other grad students in her class) keep a log in which we jotted down the time and place every time we thought about the topic of the paper we were assigned to write. I gained a new insight about prewriting from this exercise: I was amazed to learn that I did a lot of mental work on a paper (in the shower, on the way to work, while fixing dinner, etc.) before I ever sat down to write a draft. By requiring her whole class to do this exercise, Flower collected evidence that showed that much prewriting is done before pen or pencil ever touches paper.

Logs are also useful for helping determine costs and patterns of behavior. For example, if one wanted to calculate how much a proposal really costs, asking the proposal writers to keep logs of both their thinking and writing times would provide some interesting material on the actual costs of written products in the workplace. Behavior patterns also show up in logs. For example, it might be interesting to know how many members of a team of writers tend to pick over word choice and how much time is expended in that area. If each member of the team kept a log that specified how time was spent, the researcher could compare the data in the logs with data gathered in interviews with each team member. In the interviews, the researcher might ask each team member his or her opinion on a number of issues to learn answers to questions such as: "Are word choices typically based on personal preferences, company policy, or audience analysis?" or "Is word choice a serious concern or a non-issue?" and "How do people react to word choice suggestions from others?"

Computer logs are also helpful to many researchers. Computer programs can be set up to log the amount of time users (e.g., individual students, secretaries, etc.) spend working on a word processor. Computer programs can also record keystrokes so that a researcher can determine the number of deletions and insertions a typical writer or student makes when working on a document.

Visual Protocols

Visual protocols (movies and videotapes) come under a lot of criticism as being reactive tools, i.e., their very presence can cause subjects to behave unnaturally. Anyone who has had a relative or friend with a camcorder knows that this criticism has some validity. Still, a video can make a record that is more complete than field notes because it can capture body language and other behavior that might be overlooked by a person engaged in making on-the-spot field notes. Videos have the further advantage of being able to be reviewed repeatedly by a research team and shown to other members of a team so that interpretations can be validated. This kind of validation is limited in the case of field notes, because the person asked to review the notes has only that data which the note-taker decided to record—after all, it is impossible to record everything in notes. Even so, verifying an interpretation by asking other researchers to give independent reactions to the notes adds to the strength of the findings when the outside reviewer's interpretation agrees with that of the researcher. If agreement is lacking, then the researcher may need to re-examine his or her interpretation.

However, recording data via a video protocol is not the end of the matter. For one thing, some bias will still exist because the person in charge of the camera decides which persons or objects to focus on. Focus is an important issue to keep in mind when several persons are being filmed at once. Camera angle is also an issue in terms of what the researchers most want to capture. For example, is it more important to capture the words and letters as they are being produced with a pen on paper (i.e., view from over the writer's head or shoulder), or to capture the writer's facial expression (i.e., straight-on view)? Two cameras might be an answer, but it could be difficult to synchronize facial expressions with words being written. Some researchers once told me that they tried filming from underneath a glass table to try to capture both.

After the film is made, the even trickier work of identifying patterns and interpreting actions begins. To increase the soundness of their interpretation of behavior recorded on videos, researchers need to clearly define their categories and then ask a fellow researcher to use the definitions to sort the observed behaviors. If the researchers obtain a high percentage of agreement using the categorization scheme, then the interpretation is less subject to the criticism of researcher bias.

Verbal Protocols

A verbal protocol is an audiotape recording of a subject carrying out some task while thinking aloud, for example, subjects are asked to say whatever pops into their mind while doing the task. Verbal or "thinking aloud" protocols have been even more roundly criticized than visual protocols as being highly reactive. Again, the criticism is justified: saying aloud what you think while doing a task is an unnatural behavior for most people. Also, thoughts come and go faster than can be articulated, so a verbal protocol only captures those thoughts the subject can get said, and probably only those the subject is willing for someone else to hear.

On the other hand, we really have no other tool to help us gain insight into mental processes. Verbal protocols are like small windows into the mind. As Linda Flower has explained, what is recorded is similar to those sightings we might have of a porpoise lifting its head out of water now and then as it swims: from these, we can infer the direction the porpoise has traveled, but we certainly cannot claim to have seen the complete details of its journey.

One type of research that relies heavily on verbal protocols is evaluative research in which a product (e.g., a computer manual) is tested. Verbal protocols can help an evaluator identify trouble spots easily because when the subject experiences uncertainty, he begins to speak slowly and doubt creeps into his voice. Like visual protocols, a verbal protocol can be biased if the role of the researcher during the data collection is not carefully controlled. Some researchers like to sit out of both sight and hearing of their subject, but close enough to know when the subject has quit talking because subjects often get so wound up in the task they are doing that they fall silent and need to be reminded to "please, keep talking." Listening to a subject get lost in the instructions is very uncomfortable for the authors who wrote them. When I require my students to collect a verbal protocol of a user test of their manuals, I often find that the writer just can't resist putting in his or her two cents in order to clarify things for the subject. For example, I remember one writer who interjected, "What do you mean 'it's not clear'—the instructions are right in front of you!"

The text which follows is from a verbal protocol of a reading task Linda Flower asked me to do when I took her class in process tracing. The reading portions are not italicized.

I'm opening the passage to read it. Passage #1 is entitled, "Waves," and there are lots of wavy lines around it. The passage begins with blacked-out lines on both sides, and the word "Haystack" is in the center with quotation marks around it—not your normal beginning of a paragraph. The text begins sort of in the middle of the second line.

Like all river waves

which seems odd to me when there's a haystack there.

Like all river waves, these stand stationary while the water rushes through

River waves stand stationary? I don't understand. Wait! Backing up,

Like all river waves, these stand stationary while the water rushes through on its downstream course. It may be spotted by its characteristic scalloped and long length. Also by the fact that they appear in groups.

I don't know what this is about.

the characteristic scalloped shaped long length and by the fact that they appear in groups, a half dozen or more together, spaced at even downstream intervals. These waves

I guess they're really not waves.

These waves are a vibration associated with the dissipation of velocity energy when shallow fast current reaches a deeper, slower place in the river.

I didn't understand that sentence at all.

If we examine the reactions (italicized) to the task, we can clearly see that I was puzzled by what I was reading. But we can also notice something else: when puzzled, I reread. Another student in the same class did not reread even one word while doing this task. Instead, she made comments about the writing such as, "They could use another connective here instead of the two 'and's," and "This gets to be more technical. It starts out general and gets more technical. It would be harder to understand for some people." Although Flower did not mention revising when she gave us this assignment, my classmate seems to be thinking about revision as she reads. Near the end of her reading, she even says, "I really don't know enough about it to revise it. It's just not logical."

Coding (categorizing and interpreting) verbal protocols can be very tricky. Depending on the type of information a researcher is looking for, a protocol can be broken into either sentences or phrases that can be identified as separate thoughts, or "episodes" that are collections of related statements, thoughts, and actions. For example, if we examine my protocol, we can see at least two types of reaction: noticing oddities and finding the text incomprehensible. Under "noticing oddities," we could place two categories:

1. Reaction to the layout: *Passage #1 is entitled, "Waves," and there are lots of wavy lines around it. The passage begins with blacked-out lines on both sides, and the word "Haystack" is in the center with quotation marks around it—not your normal beginning of a paragraph.*
2. *which seems odd to me when there's a haystack there.*

If we then use this classification scheme to examine the second protocol, we find other instances of reaction to the structure: "They could use another connective here instead of the two "and's," and "This starts out general and gets more technical." Of course, in longer protocols there are many more classifications which could be developed. For one thing, we might want to categorize readers' goals for reading. From these two protocols, we might infer two possible goals: to comprehend meaning, and to analyze text for possible revision. To review information on developing categories to analyze text, you might want to look through Chapter 7.

OPPORTUNITIES FOR CASE STUDY RESEARCH

Because professional communication is a relatively new field, there are many rich opportunities in the job world for conducting case study research that could help define principles and strategies for more effective technical communication (Beard & Williams, 1992; MacNealy 1992). For example, most companies experience change in some way—possibly new equipment is purchased or a new management system is adopted. Such times present rich opportunities for collecting data before, during, and after the change through structured interviews with persons involved in the change, logs of participant activities, and production records. A carefully designed case study of change at a particular place of work can often provide insights into better ways to carry out tasks common to technical communicators. A case study could also contribute to the development of theories other technical communicators can rely on when facing similar changes. The findings from projects like these can be helpful to technical communicators who are trying to persuade their employer that certain techniques work better than others. Such research can also increase respect for the profession of technical communication and help it become a strong discipline.

Unfortunately, what usually happens is that someone involved in the change writes an account after the change without having collected data systematically. In such cases, the writer can only describe what he or she remembers, and the description is colored by the fact that it is written after, rather than during, the change. If the overall change was successful, the writer may not remember small problems that arose even though these problems could be major stumbling blocks at another firm.

Another rich possibility for an important case study arises when a technical writing practitioner encounters a problem or some frustration in his/her workplace. In this instance, the practitioner could design a case study of the workplace or situation to help pinpoint sources of the difficulty or at least a better understanding of it. Practitioners can also help develop principles for effective technical communication when they encounter advice that doesn't seem to fit their own work situation. In this case, what is needed is an analysis of how their workplace differs from the one described in the typical technical communication textbook.

To illustrate these opportunities, let's consider the current enthusiasm for using collaborative writing assignments in the technical writing classroom. Some questions one might want to investigate in this area are the effects of the work environment ("Do private offices inhibit collaborative efforts?"), the effects of interpersonal skills ("Are there identifiable skills that facilitate the collaborative process?"), the effects of subject matter knowledge ("How much subject matter knowledge is needed for a technical writer to be a successful member of an engineering design team?"), and the effects of education ("What skills, training, and/or principles should technical communication programs cover to prepare students for collaborative efforts in the workplace?"). And these are just a few of the possibilities in this particular area.

Although, writing research in academic settings has a much longer history than writing research in the workplace, only in the last 20 years has there been very much use of case study methods in studying composing processes. Now that many teachers are using whole language approaches, children are engaged in composing in the very early grades; thus, much remains to be learned about children in whole language programs. At the other end of the education spectrum are college students who have been studied mostly while taking composition courses. What happens to these students after English 101? Are the skills they learned in their English class writing tasks helpful as they take History 401 or attempt to write a master's thesis? These questions and a host of others like them, both from the classroom and from the workplace, are ripe for investigation. To begin to find answers, practitioners and academics alike need to become better acquainted with case study methodology.

REFERENCES

Beard, J. D., & Williams, D. L. (1992). A survey of practitioners' attitudes toward research in technical communication. *Technical Communication, 39,* 571–581.

Berkenkotter, C., Huckin, T. N., & Ackerman, J. (1988). Rethinking genre from a sociocognitive perspective. *Written Communication, 10,* 475–509.

Clark, C. M., Florio, S., Elmore, J., Martin, J., & Maxwell, R. (1983). Understanding writing instruction: Issues of theory and method. In P. Mosenthal, L. Tamor, & S. Walmsley (Eds.), *Research on writing: Principles and methods* (pp. 237–264). New York: Longman.

Dyson, A. H. (1997). Rewriting for, and by, the children: The social and ideological fate of a media miss in an urban classroom. *Written Communication, 14,* 275–312.

Emig, J. (1971). *The composing processes of twelfth graders.* Urbana, IL: National Council of Teachers of English.

Fetterman, D. M. (1989). *Ethnography: Step by step.* Newbury Park, CA: Sage.

Flower, L., Hayes, J. R., Carey, L., Schriver, K., & Stratman, J. (1986). Detection, diagnosis, and the strategies of revision. *College Composition and Communication, 37,* 16–55.

Hayes, J. R., & Flower, L. (1983). Uncovering cognitive processes in writing: An introduction to protocol analysis. In P. Mosenthal, L. Tamor, & S. Walmsley (Eds.), *Research on writing: Principles and methods* (pp. 206–220). New York: Longman.

Huber, B. J. (1992). The changing job market. *Profession 92,* 59–73.

Kirk, J., & Miller, M. L. (1986). *Reliability and validity in qualitative research.* Newbury Park, CA: Sage.

MacNealy, M. S. (1992). Research in technical communication: A view of the past and a challenge for the future. *Technical Communication, 39,* 533–551.

MacNealy, M. S., Speck, B. W., & Clements, N. (1994). Author/editor interaction from the viewpoint of successful authors. *Technical Communication, 41,* 240–259.

MacNealy, M. S., Speck, B. W., & Simpson, B. (1996). Fiddling around with text: Implications for composition from a study of a "non-reviser." *Issues in Writing, 8,* 27–53.

Miller, C. R. & Selzer, J. (1985). Special topics of arguments in engineering reports. In L. Odell & D. Goswami (Eds.), *Writing in nonacademic settings* (pp. 309–341). New York: Guilford Press.

Odell, L. (1985). Beyond the text: Relations between writing and social context. In L. Odell & D. Goswami (Eds.) *Writing in nonacademic settings* (pp. 249–280). New York: Guilford Press.

Odell, L., Goswami, D. (1982). Writing in a nonacademic setting. *Research in the Teaching of English, 16,* pp. 201–223.

Odell, L., Goswami, D., Herrington, A., & Quick, D. (1982). Studying writing in nonacademic settings. In P. V. Anderson, R. J. Brockmann, & C. R. Miller (Eds.), *New essays in technical and scientific communication: Research, theory, practice* (pp. 17–40). Farmingdale, NY: Baywood.

Schreiner, S. (1997). A portrait of the student as a young writer. *College Composition and Communication, 48,* 86–104.

Selzer, J. (1983). The composing processes of an engineer. *College Composition and Communication, 34,* 178–187.

Smeltzer, L. R. (1993). Emerging questions and research paradigms in business communication research. *Journal of Business Communication, 30,* 181–198.

Sullivan, F. J. (1997). Dysfunctional workers, functional texts: The transformation of work in institutional procedure manuals. *Written Communication, 14,* 313–359.

Yates, J. (1993). The opportunity of qualitative research. *Journal of Business Communication, 30,* 199–202.

ADDITIONAL RESOURCES

Kirsch, G., & Ritchie, J. S. (1995). Beyond the personal. *College Composition and Communication, 46,* 7–29.

McDowell, E. E. (1991). *Interviewing practices for technical writers.* Amityville, NY: Baywood.

Yin, R. K. (1989). *Case study research: Design and methods.* Newbury Park, CA: Sage.

Ethnography

ETHNOGRAPHIC VERSUS CASE STUDY RESEARCH

Ethnographic research uses many of the same research strategies that are used in case studies (interviews, observations, and physical trace measures). Also, like a case study, an ethnographic study is especially useful when little is known about an area of interest, and ethnographic studies contribute, as do case studies, to the development of hypotheses. The major difference between the two can be clarified by examining the roots of the word ethnography: "ethno" is from the Greek "*ethnos*" meaning a nation or cultural group, and "graphy" is from the Greek "*graphein*" meaning to write. So, whereas a case study examines only a few (possibly just one) individuals, objects, or events, an ethnography has a much larger scope. It looks at a larger group such as a community, a cultural unit, or an environment, and it usually extends over a longer period of time than a case study. Consequently, the final report on an ethnographic study is extensive—usually book length rather than article length. In fact, articles on ethnographic research are somewhat rare in scholarly journals because the articles tend to be so long that most journals don't have room for them.

However, an ethnography should not be looked at as simply an extended case study; the key difference is not amount of time spent on the research nor size of the group being investigated, but the focus on the inter-relationship of elements in a defined unit. For example, a social scientist might conduct an ethnographic study of a neighborhood, a social club, or a prison; and in any of these settings, the researcher could focus mainly on a particular aspect of the environment. Another study might focus on the inter-relationship of physical aspects of the environment but the researcher would also describe (maybe to a lesser degree) the people in that environment.

For example, in a study of writing in the workplace, the researcher might record almost all physical details of the environment, such as the layout of the workplace (individual offices or cubicles in an open workspace), equipment available (typewriters, computers, printers, etc.) and even possibly the light fixtures and their location. These data could help a researcher gain insights into how the working environment helps shape interpersonal interaction. In addition, depending on the goals of the project, the researcher might want to examine archival material such as company records which show when various pieces of equipment were installed, the amount of training given on their use, and which employees participated in the training. For these data, the researcher's tools would be observation, field notes, and possibly mapping. Such data could be helpful in explaining other findings such as failure to use certain equipment. To collect data on the use of the equipment, the researcher might use observation with field notes or logs, interviews, and computer-generated activity logs which could shed light on the adequacy of the equipment, convenience of the equipment's location for its heaviest users, and so forth. However, because the answers to these questions are usually closely related to the attitudes, knowledge, and experience of the personnel (both managers and employees), the researcher might also collect data on personal preferences (strategies: interviews and questionnaires), typical problems (strategies: interviews, questionnaires, and critical incident forms), and personality types (strategy: standardized tests). This information could help answer questions such as, "What factors influence employee efficiency, cooperation, and company loyalty?" Thus, the main area of interest in an ethnography is usually the relationships between inhabitants and between the environment and its inhabitants.

When social conditions are the focus of an ethnographic study, for example, a prison system, a changing neighborhood, or an educational unit, government agencies and private charitable foundations interested in improving society will frequently supply funding. Thus, most ethnographic studies of writing have been studies of writing in school. For example, some excellent ethnographic studies have been carried out in teaching and learning to write. Clark, Florio, Elmore, Martin, and Maxwell's nine-month study (1983) of teachers and students in two elementary school classes focused primarily on understanding writing instruction. Rentel and King (1983) studied two groups of 36 kindergarten and first-grade children over a period of 16 months to learn more about children's transition from oral to written texts; and a team led by Donald Graves (1973, 1975, 1979) studied the writing processes of elementary school children, focusing on the differences between "school writing" as directed by a teacher and personal or expressive writing that the children initiated themselves. These are only a few of the many ethnographic studies in composition over the last several years. Perhaps the most famous ethnographic study of writing in recent years is Shirley Brice Heath's (1983) study of two working-class communities in the Piedmont area of the Carolinas: Tracton (African American), and Roadville (European American).

Similarly, technical communication scholars have begun using ethnographic methods to study writing in the workplace. For example, Lee Odell has led a team investigating several aspects of writing in non-academic settings, such as the role of tacit knowledge, the types of audience, and effect of those types on memo and business-letter writing (see, for example, Odell & Goswami, 1982; Odell, Goswami, & Herrington, 1983; Odell, Goswami, Herrington, & Quick, 1983). Also focusing on business writing, Spilka has studied audience and issues of orality versus literacy in the workplace (1989). Recently, Dorazio and Stovall (1997) have suggested a rather unusual use of ethnographic principles in professional communication—as a tool to assess a product's usability and acceptability before the product is put on the market. Such work has only been undertaken recently, and the low number of such studies is probably a result of lack of funding. While composition research in schools has often been supported by the U.S. Department of Health, Education, and Welfare, researchers interested in ethnographic research on writing in the workplace have not yet developed a strong supporting relationship with any government agency, and ethnographic research is expensive both in time and in disruption of normal work activities. Most ethnographic studies of writing in the workplace have been funded by university graduate programs and graduate students examining a topic of interest for a thesis or dissertation (e.g., Doheny-Farina, 1986; Spilka, 1989).

To build a more solid foundation for the discipline of professional writing, much more ethnographic research is needed to identify problems meriting research, to propose hypotheses for testing, and to describe job conditions and working environments to provide real world knowledge for teachers of writing and writers entering the workforce. Such research could also contribute to the development of theories and principles for effective technical writing and document design.

TYPES OF ETHNOGRAPHIC RESEARCH

Ethnographic research is often divided into four types: casual, systematic, participant, and experimental. All are characterized by the collection of masses of details. Usually such research costs little for equipment, but it is very expensive in time. The type of research usually influences the strategies to be used. However, any ethnographic project could contain elements of each type. Before I explain these four types, let me point out that ethnographic research is beginning to be used in new ways by feminists and teacher/researchers, so some of the traditional concerns of ethnographers that are described in this chapter do not apply in these new ways of doing ethnographic research. I cover these new types of ethnographic research in the next chapter.

Casual Ethnographic Research

Casual ethnographic research is often one of the first stages in a complex project. The term "casual" does not mean unplanned; rather it means that the research design does not rely on prearranged, narrowly defined categories of observation. Instead, a casual project is often a first step in collecting enough information through observation to enable a researcher to establish categories for future data collection. For example, a researcher interested in a certain community or environment might visit there to get an overall first impression from an outsider's perspective. Because the researcher will not be able to record every detail either mentally or in notes taken on the spot, it is necessary in casual research for collecting data to decide what to focus attention on and to make a preliminary plan. The researcher might decide in advance to note such items as the equipment available in the unit under study, but the researcher would not have developed a checklist with all the different possible brands of typewriters and computers. During a casual observation, the researcher might note the presence of 5 computers and 20 typewriters, and he or she might ask in interviews whether the respondent preferred to work at a word processor or typewriter, but the researcher would not systematically collect information on amount of time spent on each machine. To systematically collect the amount of time spent at each machine, a researcher would first have to know how many machines there are to be observed and where they are located. Then the researcher could plan some way of sampling their usage. Thus, a casual study may precede a more structured one and provide information needed to plan a greater depth of data collection in a future study.

Often the person conducting a casual study will make minimal, if any, notes during the visit; instead, the researcher will write a set of field notes *after* the visit, but usually on the same day. Taking notes during a visit can interfere with the purpose of the visit because note-taking can slow the observation, and persons being observed may react to the note-taking by behaving in uncharacteristic ways. In the latter case, persons who are aware that they are being observed can become self-conscious and awkward; they can adapt their behavior to try to fit what they think the researcher is looking for (i.e., try to please or to be a good model); or they can become suspicious and defensive, thus cooperating less fully. Two interesting examples of this "guinea pig" behavior are a study by Triplett (1897) that discovered a social facilitation effect (people wind fishing reels faster when other people are present); and a study by Sommer and Sommer (1989) (groups of people tend to stay longer in coffee shops than individuals do, but those in groups don't drink more coffee than solitary customers).

One way to counter the "guinea pig" effect is to plan the note-taking so that it seems a normal part of the situation and to plan the appearance of the note-takers so that they blend into the setting. For example, in a study of students learning to use word processors, Reta Douglas and I (1993) introduced note-takers stationed in each row of terminals as "student teachers" learning to teach word processing. Although we did recruit graduate students (teaching assistants and therefore student teachers) as note-takers, and the grad students were interested in learning how to teach students to use word processors, the main job of the grad students was to record behavior of the subjects. Specifically, the grad students were instructed to note the content of each question asked by each subject in their row of five subjects, the places where subjects had trouble following instructions, and the time when subjects finished the task at hand. The observers' clipboards and note-taking, however, fit the image of teachers learning to teach rather than researchers collecting information.

Postponing the actual recording of observations until later in the day enables researchers to develop a coherent conception of the details, and writing the complete description later allows some time for the researcher to reflect on what was observed. However, postponing the recording for more than a few hours can allow intervening events to erase, block, or color the memory of what was observed during the visit. So in post-observation field notes, most often the researcher records the details of the visit in handwritten and abbreviated notes immediately following the visit and only later writes a more polished report. These notes may be characterized by lists rather than paragraphs, abbreviations rather than whole words (e.g., capital "T" for "teacher"), and even code names for participants (e.g., "Marilyn" for an attractive blonde female subject or "Bozo" for a male subject who clowned around), although assigning participant code names more often occurs when the research is reported in a formal document (i.e., a system for protecting the identity of the persons observed). In regard to using real names early and code names later, it should be noted that field notes are not always considered privileged information as is the case with doctor/patient or lawyer/client interviews. In fact, in some legal situations, a subpoena can require the researcher to produce the notes in court.

In recording observations, researchers in any of the four types of ethnographic studies need to be careful to distinguish between details actually observed and interpretations or personal reactions to those details. Some researchers use a kind of double-entry system for such notes. In one column, the researcher records the action as objectively as possible; in the second column, the researcher records his or her reaction, a possible explanation, or any other comment which might be helpful in interpreting the data later. For example, a researcher making field notes about subjects performing a task in a computerized classroom might jot down observations like those in Figure 11-1.

Furthermore, observers must realize that actions, words, locations, postures, and so forth can be recorded as instances of "behavior," but that none of these allow a researcher to infer the subject's thoughts. To get at these, a verbal protocol or an interview is necessary. Sometimes attitudes can be inferred from body language, but care must be taken in the interpretation of body language that can have multiple meanings. For example, it is well-established that people tend to maintain a distance from others in an elevator. This preservation of distance could be a reaction to someone's body odor, but it is just as likely to be the normal practice of maintaining "personal space."

Action	Comment
• DH asked neighbor's advice	• neighbor seems to be a close friend?
• sub skipped step 2	• seems anxious to finish

FIGURE 11-1   **Example of Double Entry Notes**

Systematic Ethnographic Research

Systematic ethnographic research is not only planned in advance, but it tries to collect quantifiable data. In this case, data collection is carried out according to a clearly defined set of categories in accordance with a clearly specified time scheme. For example, if you were doing an ethnographic study of writing in the workplace, you might be interested in the relationship between availability of equipment, the types of writing produced on various types of equipment, and the ability of community members to use various types of equipment. To learn more about who uses which equipment and when, you could prepare a checklist of each typewriter and computer with word processing capabilities in a workplace and then make the rounds of each machine every 30 minutes during one day to see if it is being used, by whom, and for what purpose. Or perhaps usage varies according to the day of the week; in this case, you would collect the data (perhaps at less frequent intervals) on at least five different days. To be sure the information you have collected is reliable, you may want to come back during another week and record usage information for two or three days. Likewise, the location of the typewriter may determine the type of product: memo, letter, report, invoice, and so forth. For this project you might construct a data collection form something like that in Figure 11-2.

In such a study, you would probably also have a map showing the location of each typewriter and computer and a code number for each one in the "location" column (see first entry on line 1 of Figure 11-2). In addition, you could have a list of employees with brief code names (see entry under "user" in Figure 11-2) or a list of typical purposes so that "memo +" could mean a memo to a manager or boss, "memo –" could mean a memo to a subordinate, and "memo =" a memo to a colleague.

Date 10/12/97		Observer MSM	
Location	**Time**	**User**	**Purpose**
#1	9:10 a	JM	memo +
#1	9:10 a	JM	memo =
#1	9:20 a	ST	memo –

FIGURE 11-2   **Sample Data Collection Form**

In another example, work habits could also be categorized as working alone, working with another person, or working with a group. In the case of adults working in an office, you might specify that the observer will fill in the category sheet once every half hour. In the case of children in lower grades whose attention span is shorter, you may have to set data collection times of every 10 or 15 minutes.

Because persons do not always see situations or people alike, to obtain systematic collection of ethnographic data, you will need to define the categories and test them. To determine how well the categories classify the information of interest, you will need to conduct a pilot study. In both cases, you may have to refine the categories or the collection procedures before beginning the study itself. In addition, before beginning the study, you will need to train the observers to use the categories so that there will be agreement between tally sheets. If the categories are easily defined, for example by time, person/user, and product as in Figure 11-2, the training will be brief. On the other hand, categories that are complex may need several tests during their development and extended training of observers.

For example, in analyzing contributions to group interaction, Houp, Pearsall, and Tebeaux list categories such as "opinion giver" and "opinion seeker" (1995, pp. 56–58). The difference between these categories is clear. However, Houp, et al. also suggest "harmonizer," and "compromiser"—categories that seem at first to overlap a bit since one way to achieve group harmony is to suggest a compromise. The possibility of readers confusing the two categories is reduced in this case because Houp, et al. give very clear definitions of these categories. The authors define a harmonizer as one who steps between persons in conflict (thus a harmonizer could offer a compromise), but a compromiser is one who voluntarily withdraws or modifies his or her own suggestion or solution to achieve group harmony (1995, pp. 56–58). To be sure that observers correctly classify contributions to group discussion into these two categories, it would be a good idea to have the observers do practice runs on scenarios. The person in charge of the project may also want to assign two observers to collect data on the same day as a way of verifying the accuracy of the observations.

Participant-Observer Ethnographic Research

Participant-observer ethnographic research is different from each of the types just described in that the observer is either not an outsider, or if an outsider, he or she tries to become a part of the group being observed. For example, a researcher interested in assembly-line workers may apply for a job as an assembly line worker. Of course, in this case, a researcher must be qualified in the line of work sought, not only to get the job, but also to have any credibility with co-workers. It would be difficult, for example, to get a job as a police officer without at least some training in a police academy. Even if one could get such a job without prior training, the researcher's lack of knowledge and experience would soon become apparent to fellow police officers, which in turn, would greatly damage the researcher's credibility.

Participant-observer research in technical writing has been carried out in the past by interns. In this situation, the observer's inexperience is easily explained and accepted (see, for example, Cross, 1993). However, ethical issues can cloud the situation. The most obvious issue for researchers is whether or not to admit that one is collecting information. Obviously, if one is officially investigating corruption (i.e., an undercover police officer or FBI agent), there is an ethical excuse for concealing one's true role.

On the contrary, this excuse doesn't pertain to the situation of a technical writing intern, so what to do? First, permission to do the research should be obtained from appropriate company officials. Second, a reasonable explanation of the purposes and benefits of the research effort should be prepared in advance and announced or circulated to the co-workers. Although telling co-workers that they are being observed in a research project can make them self-conscious, it is the only honorable way to proceed, and it will facilitate interviews and requests to examine writing samples. Drafting the statement in advance may allow a researcher to alert subjects that they are being studied, while, at the same time, at least partially disguise the area of interest to reduce subjects' tendency to adapt their behavior to please the researcher or to match ideal models. Such a statement should also try to reduce any fears that the researcher is actually a management spy by making assurances of confidentiality and anonymity.

For example, one might be very interested in learning how much work is done collaboratively in a certain place of work. In preparing the statement for co-workers, however, the goal could be stated as learning how personnel at this company carry out writing tasks to see how much work is typically involved in the preparation of different types of documents; the statement of research purpose need not mention collaboration. In other words, the observer should be at least partially open about his or her dual role. The role the participant-observer takes must also be reported in the write-up of the research project. This description helps a reader evaluate the study.

Participant-observer research is often subject to other problems, including the possibility of a drain on resources intended for others, researcher loneliness, and the discovery of illicit, illegal, unethical, or simply lazy practices. In the first case, researchers should make every effort to ensure that they carry their full share of the work; otherwise they are occupying positions that could be more profitably used by the firm or positions that could otherwise be of more help to the co-workers. Furthermore, even though a participant researcher, by definition, works right alongside co-workers, there is still a sense of isolation because the researcher is also collecting data that he or she cannot discuss with co-workers during the collection phase because doing so could affect the behavior of the co-workers and thus distort subsequent data. Participant-observer researchers can help counter this difficulty by arranging to meet occasionally with a co-researcher to discuss data and experiences in collecting it.

The other difficulty—what to do with problematic information obtained during observations and interviews—is tougher to solve. You will have to decide what to do in many such cases because no book can give advice to cover all circumstances. For example, do you report to the owner that employees are taking home pencils, paper, envelopes, and other such supplies? In some firms, such practices are the norm, so if you report them, the owner may think you are a nitpicking snitch who should tend to your own affairs. However, if you think you've discovered an illegal practice that you will become a party to by remaining silent, you should consult an attorney.

Other practices you uncover may not be illegal, but the owner or employer may consider the information privileged. For example, formulas for certain products, sales figures, and other insider information are often held to be privileged, and not for release outside the company or sometimes even to other employees inside the company. To protect the person who has given you permission to do the research at the firm, you should probably ask him or her to read a fairly polished draft of your report to help you avoid any breach of confidentiality.

Also, you should consider that the words you choose to describe some observation can damage a company's reputation. For example, suppose you observed a meeting of writers discussing how an annual report should be laid out, and during the meeting one of the writers suggested that the bad news should be buried in some paragraph about half-way through the report to reduce the chances of many people reading it, since it is well-known that readers skim reports rather than read them carefully. This suggestion is clearly a rhetorical strategy, chosen with a purpose. However, even if the suggestion to bury the bad news is not acted upon, if you describe this suggestion in these terms when you write up your final report on this research project, the firm (or at least its employees) could look very manipulative to those (possibly including customers or business colleagues) who happen to read your report. Most workplace ethnographers try to avoid such problems by using fictional names for the company in their published descriptions of the project. For example, even though his research report contained nothing detrimental to the company where he conducted his ethnographic case study, Vincent J. Brown (1994) describes the location of his study thus: "An industry group (which I'll call 'ISF') had hired the independent contract research and development laboratory (which I'll call 'Dresler') to write the twelve-page report (which I'll call 'Dresler comment')…" (p. 68).

Experimental Field Projects

In experimental field projects, some factor in the environment or working situation is changed to test its effects. In the strictest sense, experiments have no place in an ethnography because the purposes are so different. On the other hand, field experiments make use of many ethnographic research strategies, so I have included some information on field experiments in this chapter. Often researchers conduct an experimental field project to test whether certain laboratory findings apply to real situations. In such instances, the researcher may want to choose two settings so that one can be used as a control setting. However, in selecting experiment and control settings, the researcher must make every effort to ensure that the two settings are as similar as possible to avoid the possibility that a difference in results could be attributed to the difference in setting.

For example, in a laboratory situation where other possible influences can be rigorously controlled, the results may indicate that working under a certain type of lighting decreases typing errors. However, real world writing tasks are usually more complicated than those used in laboratory experiments, so a researcher may want to test this finding outside the lab by collecting data from two different places: one room or office in which a new type of lighting system (e.g., fluorescent) has been installed and one in which an old type of lighting system (e.g., incandescent) is used. In doing so, however, it is important to keep in mind that attributing effects to a single factor is more problematic when numerous factors are involved, as is usually the case in a field setting. In the case of the new vs. old type of lighting, a researcher will want to consider that just the change in lighting fixtures (i.e., novelty) could affect performance. Research has shown that any change in working conditions is likely to improve productivity, at least at first (the Hawthorne effect). Thus, to make the control condition equal to the experimental one, new lighting fixtures should be installed in both settings, but those in the control setting should be incandescent and those in the experimental, fluorescent. Even with these precautions, the researcher will want to be aware that many other facets of the office design and the personalities of the workers could be influencing any effects and thus providing rival hypotheses for any differences in the two conditions.

On the other hand, field research is often valued for this very characteristic; because it examines a situation holistically, it allows for the interaction of several variables rather than trying to isolate one factor, as is usually done in a laboratory. Field work, in other words, places value on the context and recognizes the fact that knowledge is a social construction. Thus, it can account for the complexity of a situation.

A small ethnographic study may also be appropriate when a firm is undergoing change in order to document what happens as it happens. In this case, researchers would observe and describe the steps taken to carry out the change (including plans made), the problems that arose, and the problem-solving strategies used, and so forth, in the expectation that the report could be used by other departments or firms to implement similar changes smoothly. These observations are recorded as they take place. Unfortunately, such opportunities for ethnographic research are seldom taken advantage of. Rather, persons participating in the change tend to write their reports weeks or even months later based only on their memory of what happened. Although such reports can provide useful insights to others, the insights may prove invalid because the writer or speaker forgot some factor (even a seemingly minor one) that had a major effect. To increase the validity of observations in the workplace, the observations should be planned in advance and carried out in a systematic way, and the observations should be recorded when they are made or shortly thereafter.

ELEMENTS OF A GOOD ETHNOGRAPHIC RESEARCH PROJECT

Most good ethnographic research projects follow these four basic steps:

1. *Preparing for the project.* This step includes reviewing prior research in the area, laying out a plan, preparing and testing necessary materials (data collection sheets), and training observers.
2. *Collecting the data.* Obviously, data can be collected in a variety of ways: observation, interview, examination of archival records, and so forth. However, even in a casual project, the data collection should be carried out according to some preplanned system. At the same time, the researcher must be flexible enough to pursue some unexpected source or develop a new category of observation if the opportunity arises.
3. *Interpreting the data.* This task is usually not postponed to the end of the project as in a laboratory experiment; rather, researchers hold ongoing meetings to discuss possible interpretations as the data is collected. These discussions can lead to planning for additional interviews, observations, or other data collection strategies that had not been planned for in step one.
4. *Reporting the results.* This task is a major one because the data often consist of thick descriptions which, in turn, usually require a larger report than is typically the case with survey or experimental research. This report should also include a description of the data collection methodology, an explanation of the data, and a discussion of its implications.

ERRORS COMMONLY ASSOCIATED WITH ETHNOGRAPHIC RESEARCH

Ethnographic research is subject to three main types of errors, all of which have contributed to the disdain for ethnographic research that is sometimes encountered. As in other types of research, sampling error and researcher bias detract from the respect that will be accorded to the final report. Faulty interpretation of the data is another possible source of error in ethnographic research. Finally an unbalanced approach can result in distorted findings.

Sampling Error

It might seem that researchers do not need to be concerned about sampling error in an ethnographic study because, as one researcher told me, "one is stuck with the population at that site." This observation is true in that an ethnographic study is restricted by the nature of ethnography to researching only the people who are part of the community of interest. However, unless one plans to research all community members equally, one has to choose a sample from the community, in which case the researcher needs to guard against the possibility that the sample of persons, objects, events, or settings being observed is not truly representative of the community under investigation. A unique person, place, or event may be very interesting, but the findings based on that one alone will not be generalizable to the community as a whole. Thus, while the ethnographic researcher will certainly want to record information about a unique event or person, the researcher will point out the uniqueness in the final report and explain why it should be considered unique.

In another instance, a researcher may be tempted to rely more heavily on an informant who is talkative or one who has some kind of stature in the community, but this informant may not be knowledgeable or typical. The use of an atypical source was discussed in Chapter 10 where I noted Janet Emig's heavy reliance on one subject, Lynn, to develop and exemplify her description of twelfth grade writers (1971). To avoid this problem, obtaining feedback from colleagues outside the project can be very helpful.

Other sampling errors include inadequate time and biased conditions, both of which must be controlled for by careful planning before the project begins. For example, if the researcher wants to investigate a process that normally takes several weeks, then the project is flawed if the research is conducted during only one of those weeks. Similarly, atypical aspects of a setting must be a matter of concern to the researcher. For example, one might question whether the results would be the same if a subject were interviewed in the researcher's office as they would be if the subject were interviewed at his or her own desk.

Researcher Error

A second source of errors that can damage the respect accorded to ethnographic findings is researcher error. The most obvious source of this type of error is researcher bias, which may exist going into the project or may develop as the project progresses. To avoid researcher bias at the beginning, observers must be well-trained to use the plan provided; it is also helpful to schedule more than one data collector for the same time and place. After the collection, the two sets of observations can be compared, and outside judges can be asked to participate in the analysis to validate the conclusions.

Researcher bias can also result from first impressions as people tend to form judgments at first sight. These opinions are frequently hard to overcome, so they may color all subsequent observations. This problem is reduced by holding occasional observer discussions in which observers share their differing impressions and interpretations.

A related source of researcher bias is the "confidence in judgment" problem. People tend to have a lot of confidence that they have accurately reported what actually happened. As we all know, three persons on three different street corners often report three different versions of a car accident. Unless the evidence to the contrary is very compelling, people rarely change their opinions about what happened. This problem must be addressed in the planning stage by selecting open-minded observers and training them well.

A similar source of researcher error is observer bias. In this case, one member of the research team may not be using observation categories in the same way as other members of the team. This problem should be forestalled in the preparation stage by clearly defining and testing the categories and by training observers. But in long-term projects, it is also a good idea to schedule times to recalibrate observers by asking them to compare notes on specific observations. What seems to be observer bias may really be a case of unclear or overlapping categories. If the categories are not clear and not mutually exclusive, the data will not be verifiable. To avoid this problem, categories should be tested in trial runs, much as I suggested above on the question of the Houp, et al. (1995) group dynamics categories of harmonizer and compromiser.

Researcher bias can also develop as a long project progresses and a researcher becomes so immersed in a community or culture that he or she loses the perspective of an outsider and is no longer objective. This bias, known as "going native," can be reduced by frequent checks with an outside person such as a supervisor or colleague.

Finally, although an advantage of ethnographic research design is its flexibility that allows a researcher to take advantage of unforeseen opportunities, some caution must be exercised when changing procedures in the midst of a project. Such changes must be fully explained (both details of the change itself and reasons for the change) in the final report.

Interpretation Error

A major source of interpretation error is the vast amount of data collected in an ethnographic project. Information overload can make it hard to detect patterns and hard to determine which details are most important to include in an explanation.

Information availability is also a frequent source of error in interpretation. Some researchers tend to rely on that information which is most easily available; others place a premium on hard-to-get or novel information. Interpretation error can also occur when a researcher tries to treat all sources as being equally valid or equally important. For example, when interpreting information collected about the writing process in a particular firm, should the views of a word processing clerk be given equal weight with those of the person who drafted and revised the document? Discussion with colleagues can often help a researcher sort out the true value of different kinds of information. Whatever the decision, if a researcher decides to treat one source as more important or more reliable than another, then the reasons for this decision need to be stated.

Two other sources of interpretation error are missing information and conflicting information. In the first case, researchers sometimes supply missing information or fill in gaps with details from their own experience, often without realizing they have done so. To illustrate how researchers' personal experiences can color their assumptions, let me cite a personal example, even though it didn't happen in an ethnographic study. When Reta Douglas and I studied oral versus written instructions for using a word processor (1993), we realized that we were both assuming that novices have a fear of breaking computers because both of us had experienced that fear when we were computer novices. In such cases, a colleague who is good at being a devil's advocate can be very helpful in identifying underlying assumptions. Similarly, in the case of conflicting information (especially that concerning attitudes), researchers must be careful not to adopt a mathematical attitude (a positive cancels out a negative, or two negatives make a positive, etc.). Negative as well as positive instances should be reported, and a possible explanation should be given for the conflict.

Probably the most frequent source of interpretation error is the tendency to assume a cause-effect relationship for co-occurring data or sequential events. For example, one can rather safely infer a cause-effect relationship between a traffic accident and a traffic jam when one is caught in a traffic jam and then sees a police car or ambulance, warning lights flashing, speeding along the berm to some point ahead. On the other hand, one cannot safely infer that the accident was caused by the large number of poor drivers on the road that day. An accident could be the result of one or more poor drivers, but it could also be the result of some mechanical failure in a particular vehicle or a cow that slipped through a fence and wandered onto the road in front of an oncoming car. In conversations among writing teachers, I often hear someone complain that students can't write well because they don't know how to spell. While poor spelling certainly detracts from the quality of a piece of writing, lack of spelling ability does not necessarily cause a person to organize ideas poorly or provide unpersuasive examples in his or her writing. To avoid errors in data interpretation, it is helpful to discuss possible interpretations with a knowledgeable colleague.

Unbalanced Methods

In recent years, a sometimes acrimonious debate has emerged in the literature between those who tend toward scientific procedures and those who claim scientific procedures are inappropriate in qualitative research. I take the position that when an ethnographic researcher adopts a stance which emphasizes either objective (i.e., scientific) or subjective (i.e., non-scientific) methods to the exclusion of the other, the results will probably be less credible or less acceptable to other scholars in the area.

One answer to this dilemma is Geoffrey Cross' (1994) advice that ethnographic researchers should avoid four extremes, which Cross claims result in distortion: (1) a researcher-centered approach results in solipsism, (2) a data-centered approach results in a thin description, (3) a research-community centered approach results in groupthink, and (4) a subjects-centered approach results in groupthink. No doubt, a balanced approach such as Cross suggests would help establish the credibility of the findings. However, I can imagine a situation in which a researcher with limited resources would have trouble achieving such a balance. In that case, I suggest that the researcher use those strategies that are best suited to his or her question and to the situation to be investigated, but at the same time the researcher should admit the limits of the study and call for further studies in the area to add to the balance.

TOOLS FOR ETHNOGRAPHIC RESEARCH

Many of the same tools used in case study research are used in ethnographic studies. Ethnographers can use logs, questionnaires, tests, examination of artifacts and archival records, and even visual or verbal protocols of selected individuals from among those being studied. However, the two most important and most often used tools of an ethnographer are interviews and observations.

Interviews

Interviews were discussed in some depth in Chapter 10, so here I will mention only those aspects that are particularly relevant to ethnographic research. First, a researcher must determine which of the inhabitants of a culture or situation to interview. Frequently, ethnographers try to identify "key figures" and interview them. A key figure may be neither the most important nor the most typical figure in a community, but someone who has a large bank of knowledge about the community, present and past. This knowledge includes insights into nuances of typical activities. Additionally, this key figure is frequently able to view the community from an objective point of view, largely because he or she has had some experience outside as well as inside the community. For example, a researcher investigating writing in the workplace may find that a writer who has completed graduate studies in some field may be a good key figure because he or she has some knowledge of research methods and goals as well as inside knowledge of how a particular workplace operates. A key figure can also help a researcher understand the data by providing contextual information that clarifies the observations made by the researcher. Fetterman (1989) gives the example of a researcher who was puzzled by the inability of a group of faculty to make decisions during faculty meetings he observed. When he consulted an emeritus professor, he learned that this behavior wasn't typical—that the faculty were going through a period of instability or leadership vacuum because the former chair had been removed (pp. 60–61).

Personal histories are another important contribution that key figures can make because they provide rich details which often exemplify the culture or clarify it. However, researchers must check these details against other sources to avoid distortion and contamination from the key figure's desire to provide the information the researcher is looking for.

Observation

Next or equal in importance among possible tools for ethnographic research is observation. Observation techniques can be categorized, much like the overall categories of ethnographic research discussed earlier, into casual, systematic, or participant-observer types. Whichever the case, observational techniques should be planned in advance. Observational data can also be recorded in various ways, such as the field notes and table-like forms discussed earlier in this chapter. Other observations are best recorded on maps, flow-charts, and organizational charts. Some researchers find that matrices help them see patterns in events occurring over time. Crucial to the success of gathering data by observation is the training of observers.

Observation is almost the only possible tool for accessing information such as outcroppings, proxemics, and kinesics. *Outcropping* is a term geologists use to describe bits of bedrock protruding above the surface. Put another way, something visible may indicate the presence of something not visible. For example, the presence of a typewriter in every office in a place of work may be an indication that the word processing equipment available in a room set aside for it may not be used to the fullest extent possible, either because personnel are not comfortable with computers or because they prefer to work in their own offices. Thus, identifying the outcropping is only the first step. Next, the researcher must seek information to help interpret what the outcropping points to.

Proxemics and kinesics are kinds of outcroppings. *Proxemics* refers to the socially desirable distance between people—for example, the position taken by a person entering an elevator that contains one other passenger. Likewise, teachers who want to maintain a distance between themselves and their students often position their desks so that students coming in for a conference must sit across the desk from them. In this case, the correct social distance is emphasized by the barrier of the desk. Executives often arrange their offices this way also. On the other hand, some teachers believe in arranging their offices so they can sit side-by-side with students to look at a piece of writing together. Likewise, some executives will get up from their desks and move to a side-by-side grouping of chairs when they want to do collaborative work on a project or discuss problems with employees.

Kinesics refers to body language—postures, gestures, and facial expressions that mirror feelings, beliefs, and attitudes. Teachers often use the body language of arms folded across their chests to signal distance and barriers between them and their students. Interestingly, some students also send this message to their teachers. Looking around the room while talking to someone, rolling the eyes upward during a conversation, or frequently blinking are all messages whether intentional or not. These activities, themselves, now constitute a whole field of study, so in interpreting kinesics or proxemics, researchers need to do their homework by reading the publications of scholars in these areas.

Critical Incident Forms

This tool sounds very clinical, and imposing, but it can be very simply designed and used. In some situations, the form is nothing more than a sheet of blank paper with a few sentences of instruction at the top, asking the respondent to describe (in rather complete detail) some actual incident that is a good example of an attitude, practice, or opinion. For example, if a researcher wanted to know something about employees' perceptions of the effects of new dividers installed between cubicles in an open work area, a random group of employees could be asked to fill out a critical incident form which asks them to try to remember some incident which would demonstrate the disadvantages of the old dividers. Another randomly selected group could be asked to recall some incident which they feel best illustrates the benefits of the new dividers. These forms could then be coded in a number of ways. For example, the researcher could tabulate the percentage of both sets which mention noise or privacy or some other feature of working in cubicles. However, the researcher may also find in one of these forms an insight into another phenomenon of interest. For example, the person describing an incident illustrating a disadvantage of the old dividers may be focusing on the lack of privacy by detailing his discomfort at overhearing his neighbor being asked by an angry superior where a particular report was, but the details of the incident may also indicate features of management style. For instance, the company may not have an established policy for routing documents through the review process. Having been alerted by the details in the critical incident report, the researcher could then investigate this possibility.

PROPERLY USING ETHNOGRAPHIC FINDINGS

By its very nature, ethnographic research lacks the controls of experimental laboratory research and therefore its findings are open to various challenges. However, ethnographic research can uncover data not available to laboratory researchers, and it has the flexibility to follow up interesting leads. To enhance the acceptability and respectability of ethnographic findings, researchers must design their projects carefully and carry them out with rigor. Such findings can enhance our understanding of the classroom and the workplace so that both teaching and practice can be improved.

REFERENCES

Brown, V. J. (1994). Facing multiple audiences in engineering and R&D writing: The social contexts of a technical report. *Journal of Technical Writing and Communication, 24,* 67–75.

Clark, C. M., Florio, S., Elmore, J., Martin, J., & Maxwell, R. (1983). Understanding writing instruction: Issues of theory and method. In P. Mosenthal, L. Tamor, & S. Walmsley (Eds.), *Research on writing: Principles and methods* (pp. 237–264). New York: Longman.

Cross, G. A. (1993). The interrelation of genre, context, and process in the collaborative writing of two corporate documents. In R. Spilka (Ed.), *Writing in the workplace: New research perspectives* (pp. 141–152). Carbondale, IL: Southern Illinois University Press.

Cross, G. A. (1994). Ethnographic research in business and technical writing. *Journal of Business and Technical Writing, 8,* 118–134.

Doheny-Farina, S. (1986). Writing in an emerging organization: An ethnographic study. *Written Communication, 3,* 158–185.

Dorazio, P., & Stovall, J. (1997). Research in context: Ethnographic usability. *Journal of Technical Writing and Communication, 27,* 57–67.

Douglas, R., & MacNealy, M. S. (1993). Effective training techniques: Oral versus written. In *IPCC 93 Proceedings—The new face of technical communication: People, processes, products* (pp. 364–368). New York: Institute of Electrical and Electronics Engineers.

Emig, J. (1971). *The composing processes of twelfth graders.* Urbana, IL: National Council of Teachers of English.

Fetterman, D. M. (1989). *Ethnography: Step by step.* Newbury Park, CA: Sage.

Graves, D. H. (1973). *Children's writing: Research directions and hypotheses based upon an examination of the writing process of seven-year-old children.* Unpublished doctoral dissertation, State University of New York at Buffalo, Buffalo, NY.

Graves, D. H. (1975). An examination of the writing processes of seven-year-old children. *Research in the Teaching of English, 9,* 245–255.

Graves, D. H. (1979). Andrea learns to make writing hard. *Language Arts, 56,* 569–576.

Heath, S. B. (1983). *Ways with words.* Cambridge: Cambridge University Press.

Houp, K. W., Pearsall, T. E., & Tebeaux, E. (1995). *Reporting technical information* (9th ed.). Boston: Allyn & Bacon.

Odell, L., & Goswami, D. (1982). Writing in a non-academic setting. *Research in the Teaching of English, 16,* 201–224.

Odell, L., Goswami, D., & Herrington, A. (1983). The discourse-based interview: A procedure for exploring the tacit knowledge of writers in nonacademic settings. In P. Mosenthal, L. Tamor, & S. Walmsley (Eds.), *Research on writing: Principles and methods* (pp. 220–236). New York: Longman.

Odell, L., Goswami, D., Herrington, A., & Quick, D. (1983). Studying writing in non-academic settings. In P. V. Anderson, R. J. Brockmann, & C. R. Miller (Eds.), *New essays in technical and scientific communication: Research, theory, practice* (pp. 17–40). Farmingdale, NY: Baywood.

Rentel, V., & King, M. (1983). Present at the beginning. In P. Mosenthal, L. Tamor, & S. Walmsley (Eds.), *Research on writing: Principles and methods* (pp. 139–176). New York: Longman.

Sommer, R., & Sommer, B. (1989). Social facilitation effects in coffeehouses. *Environment and Behavior, 21,* 651–666.

Spilka, R. (1989). Interacting with multiple readers: A significant component of document design in corporate environments. *Technical Communication, 36,* 368–372.

Triplett, N. (1897). The dynamogenic factors in pacemaking and competition. *American Journal of Psychology, 9,* 507–533.

Qualitative Research with Special Lenses: Feminist and Teacher Research

In recent years, composition and technical writing scholars have increasingly turned to qualitative research methods in order to answer questions they encounter in their experiences in teaching or in writing in the workplace. For many of these researchers, the traditional stance of the researcher as an outsider who objectively collects and analyzes data is deficient because such a stance, by definition, fails to incorporate contextual information, subjective information about the researcher and the subjects, and insights into the inter-relationships of these factors. Of course, many traditional researchers shudder at this idea, believing that subjective information is a kind of contamination of data. On the other hand, a reasonable person must admit that no situation, no teacher, no student, no workplace writer is free from political and cultural assumptions, values, and commitments that color his or her activities and attitudes. I believe that we should not condemn either view, but that we should examine possible methods and select those which are most appropriate to the problem or question we want to investigate. If we follow the basics of good empirical research that have been outlined repeatedly in this book, namely, planning in advance, collecting data systematically, and collecting data that can be examined by others, then we have procedures that should stand up to methodological challenges.

In this chapter, I first discuss in more detail some of the criticisms of traditional research methods that have led to the adoption of special lenses for research. Then

I discuss two special lenses that qualitative researchers may want to consider when selecting methods for a particular research project. These lenses are commonly referred to in the literature as feminist research and teacher research. Both assume that subjective data is valuable, that the research should be carried out as naturalistically as possible in real life situations, and that data collection and analysis must be a collaborative rather than hierarchical effort so that the distinction between researcher and research subjects is blurred, if not obliterated. Frequently, designers of such projects are interested in power relationships and political and cultural issues. One good example is Heidi Hartmann's (1987) research into the family, and the gender, class, and power struggle involved in housework, and Joyce Ladner's (1987) research into poor, urban, African American girls. Such research often is, or becomes, action research, undertaken with the idea that change will occur in the researcher as well as the research subjects as a result of participation in the research project. In the sections that follow, I discuss the ways that feminist and teacher/research differ from traditional research methods and the application of these lenses to research methods in writing. Finally, I speculate about possible new lenses for research in writing.

CRITICISMS OF TRADITIONAL RESEARCH PARADIGMS

Although the words "special lenses" in the title of this chapter suggest new approaches to conducting research, in some sense traditional scientific research methodologies have always used "special lenses." For example, in the history of scientific findings one rarely encounters a finding which carries a woman's name: from Archimedes' discovery of water displacement as a measurement tool to the discovery of Halley's Comet, the names attached to scientific discoveries all belong to men. Does this mean that no woman ever noticed how objects placed in water displace a certain amount of water? Certainly, before Archimedes women bathing their children noticed how the water level in a tub rises when a child is lowered into the water. However, had a woman pointed out this fact in the classical period, no one would have considered the fact to have any importance to science. Partly this attitude developed from the prevailing views of women's duties and interests versus men's duties and interests: Traditionally in Western society, women were supposed to be concerned with home and family, and men were to be concerned with politics and science. In fact, the story goes that Archimedes discovered the principle of water displacement while pondering a problem about whether a crown given to the king was pure gold or only partially gold. He found the answer in his bath when he realized that the amount of water displaced by the crown when immersed could be compared to the amount of water displaced by an amount of pure gold equal to the weight of the crown immersed in water. Notice that Archimedes may not have been the first to observe water being displaced by an object lowered into it; however, he applied his observation to a scientific (and political) problem and became famous. Since women were not allowed to participate in science (or politics) in those days, they had no opportunity for making an application of some observation from daily life to a scientific (or political) problem—at least they could not point out such an application in a public forum.

Furthermore, from classical times until only recently, women have been handicapped in scientific endeavor because they were not permitted the same level of education as men. For example, we don't really know whether Mary Halley (his wife) first noticed the comet that bears Edmond Halley's name. Even had Mrs. Halley noticed the light in the sky, she most likely would not have been able to identify it as a comet because, having had no experience in studying astronomy, she would not have had any means of comparing what she saw to what others had been observing and recording over a long period of time. This deprivation in education probably also resulted from the cultural designations of women's proper areas of interest being private (i.e., in the home), as opposed to men's public sphere of business, politics, and science. But it could also have resulted from a view of women as biologically inferior in thinking skills. Certainly the view of women as intellectually limited has characterized Western society for centuries. Even today, we encounter assertions that women, by nature, are intuitive, emotional, and tentative, whereas men, by nature, are objective, logical, and assertive.

Furthermore, in some instances in which highly educated women have made important contributions to a scientific discovery, their work has been appropriated by male colleagues. For example, according to Manwell and Baker (1979), Watson and Crick failed to give any credit to their female colleague, Rosalind Franklin when they published their discovery of the double helix as the structure of DNA, even though it was a photograph Franklin had made in a neighboring lab that suggested the double helix to Watson, and the person who showed her data to Watson didn't ask her permission nor tell her what he had done. What's worse, when Watson published his personal account of the story of the discovery, he complained about Franklin because she didn't wear lipstick and her dresses weren't attractive—as if that had anything to do with her scientific work (Manwell & Baker, 1979).

As Sandra Harding points out, the recipe, "Add women and stir" is not enough to correct these practices (1987, p. 3). In light of this history of discrimination against and subjugation of women, many modern thinkers (including some men) are beginning to question traditional scientific research methodologies as being androcentric, or, male-centered (see, for example, Code, 1991; Kincheloe, 1991). Certainly, the scientific methodologies that have been valorized over the last few centuries have been devised by men. One example often cited by some feminist researchers of the androcentric effects on what is considered acceptable in scientific research is the emphasis on strict control in laboratory experiments in order to make "objective" observations, objectivity being considered a male value and subjectivity a female value by some feminist researchers. However, as I point out later in this chapter, it is not helpful to polarize values in this way. Other researchers not only label traditional scientific methods as "positivistic," as I pointed out in Chapter 1, but they also spend considerable effort pointing out what they consider to be the evils of positivism rather than presenting details of possibly more appropriate methods and their benefits. For example, Kincheloe (1991) denigrates positivistic researchers as "voyeurs" but doesn't explain how to avoid voyeurism when doing teacher research (p. 65). Again, I don't see why it is necessary to set up these polarized camps—why we can't choose methods based on their appropriateness to the question we want to study? (To learn more about the issue of positivisim, see Hayes, 1993; Kirk & Miller, 1986; and Larsen, 1993.)

Not only are traditional scientific research methods being challenged as androcentric, but the social and economic effects of these methods on portions of society that are not white, male, and middle class are being roundly criticized. One excellent example is the longitudinal research on heart disease. Historically, the subjects have all been male, primarily white physicians. Now, medical scientists are beginning to question whether the findings apply to women, blacks, and members of other socioeconomic groups. Still other researchers are questioning publication practices in scientific journals. Do invisible colleges (networks of scholars working in the same area) limit the participation of women (Ferber, 1986)? These and other issues of social and economic power need to be investigated in all fields, including writing. For example, Dragga (1993) says that the increasing number of women in technical communication has led to a lowering of prestige and salaries in that field as women are consistently paid less than men for equal work. Similarly, Brannon (1993) points out that although most composition classes are taught by women, all the editors of *College Composition and Communication* are men, as are most of the graduate faculty in composition programs.

However, other, more cautionary voices are now contributing to the discussion of research through a feminist lens. Although she agrees that the traditional scientific research paradigm is androcentric, Lorraine Code (1991) questions whether the androcentric bias has been a deliberate attempt to exclude women. Rather, Code sees the traditional scientific research paradigm as growing out of research in physics where the distance between observer and the observed is not broachable. Code also cautions that feminist research could exacerbate the problem by fostering the idea that women are essentially so different from men that women, by nature, cannot successfully use methods which have an androcentric origin. Thus, women would be denied access to laboratory research. Code further questions whether there is truly such a thing as "women's ways of knowing," proposed by Belenky, Clinchy, Goldberger, and Tarule (1986). Although I can appreciate some of the difficulties women have faced in the workplace, I tend to agree with Code on this issue. I do not believe that research methods are inherently male or female; and I want to use those research methods that I believe are sound, regardless of whether they were first proposed by men or women. As Code suggests, rather than taking an either/or approach to assigning value to certain research methods, we might consider a continuum that ranges from a dedication to maintaining an objective view in which context is completely controlled or ignored on one side to a dedication to maintaining a subjective view in which each piece of data can only be evaluated in terms of the beliefs and attitudes of the person from whom the data is collected. Thus, researchers of either gender are free to choose the method that is most appropriate for the question to be investigated.

To this point, I have only discussed some of the criticisms of traditional scientific research methods in terms of their possible effects on women. However, many of the same criticisms (e.g., the charge that empirical methods are too positivistic) are being made by teachers who argue that a university researcher who visits a classroom to collect data cannot interpret that data as effectively as the teacher of the classroom who *knows* the students, their socio-economic backgrounds, cultural customs, and educational history. Anyone who has ever been a parent can no doubt see some truth in this claim because many parents know when their child is getting sick even *before* a rash or a fever breaks out. Thus teacher research can offer insights that probably could not be gained in any other way. Still, I am uncomfortable with the attitude that an outside researcher visiting a classroom cannot have insights as valuable as those of the teacher of the class. Perhaps the challenges which have arisen about the nature of traditional scientific research have been good for the research community because they have stimulated us to examine our assumptions and to consider new possibilities. These challenges have also raised awareness of the possible political effects of some methods (e.g., IQ tests), especially in terms of the marginalization of those who are not white, middle class males. However, in teacher research as in feminist research, I would like to argue for judging the value of any method on the basis of its appropriateness to the question under investigation, and I believe that as members of a research community we can and should present our own ideas about methods without using pejorative terms to label the methods of others. Thus, in the sections which follow, I discuss concerns, methods, benefits, and limitations of doing research through the special lenses of feminist and teacher research. In the concluding paragraphs, I speculate about other possible special lenses, especially for researchers in composition and technical writing.

FEMINIST RESEARCH

Since I have already explained how Western science has tended to exclude women, I am not going to begin this section with a rationale for feminist research methods; however, as I talk about various feminist research methods, I will point out their advantages and disadvantages. I will say, though, that I think researchers in writing should resist being influenced by any possibly negative connotations in the label "feminist." Because feminists have had to speak loudly to be heard in the first place, they are sometimes characterized as overly aggressive (i.e., not feminine) and highly prejudiced against men. Indeed, Graves (1993)—whom I would classify as a feminist scholar—questions the belief of some feminist scholars that writing by women is somehow better than that by men. She argues that gender styles (e.g., masculine and feminine) may interact to shape individual composing processes. One problem is that often people coming from a traditional research paradigm may not be very open to what feminist research has to contribute. Like Graves (1993) and Code (1991), I suggest that it's best to maintain a balanced attitude. Research under any label ought to be planned in advance and carried out carefully so that data are collected systematically and in a way that permits others to examine them. Rigor in research design adds to the credibility of the results.

Collecting Data

The most popular method of collecting data in feminist research is the interview. However, the structure of the interview varies according to the researcher. One famous group of feminist researchers, the team of Belenky, et al., (1986) constructed an interview guide in which some questions were designed from scratch to cover specific interests of the researchers, other questions were designed to capture information which could be grouped into categories used by previous researchers, and still other questions (standardized) were taken directly from the prior research projects of others in the field so that results could be compared. Other feminists believe that those being researched should help the researcher design the questions to be investigated (see, for example, Kirsch & Ritchie, 1995).

Many feminist researchers claim that interviews should be structured like conversations so that stories about events are offered by both the researcher and the person[s] being researched (see, for example, Blyler, 1996; Kirsch & Ritchie, 1995). The advantage to these methods is that the interpretation of the data both begins and is checked for accuracy during the data collection. For example, if an interviewee offers a brief narrative about how she was discriminated against in a subtle way at work, the interviewer could then share a story of herself as a victim of subtle discrimination as a way of showing that she understands the story she has just heard. The interviewee, then, can correct the interpretation by retelling her story and adding details to show the difference between the two stories. This sharing reduces the distance between the researcher and the researched. In such cases, researchers are also careful not to use the word "subjects" or any other term which would imply objectification of the person being researched. However, in considering what model should replace the traditional researcher/subject model, Code (1991) cautions feminist researchers against the maternal model which emphasizes a closeness between the researcher and the researched. In this model, the researcher is a patient and sympathetic listener. However, Code points out that the maternal model assumes an unbalanced power relationship like that between parent and child with the parental researcher more knowing and having more control. Instead, Code proposes that feminist researchers adopt a friendship model in which the partners are equal in power and concerned about each other—both committed to maintenance of the relationship. Harding (1987) emphasizes the importance of really listening carefully to ascertain *how* informants think as well as *what* they think; she also emphasizes that we need to listen critically to the ways social scientists think about men and women.

Although interviewing is the primary tool of feminist researchers, some also examine documents for statements that indicate the prevailing attitude toward women and other groups that society has marginalized. For example, a feminist researcher could look at the writings of Aristotle or Quintillion for references to women and their intellectual capabilities or their roles in the culture (see, for example, Code, 1991). From such snippets, the researcher could begin to build a picture of the opportunities available to women in those times. Still other feminist researchers examine the vocabulary used in certain documents to determine whether the documents reflect androcentricity or a negative attitude toward women. For example, a feminist might claim that use of the term "penetrating analysis" is an indication of an androcentric attitude. Or another feminist researcher could claim that adding the suffix "ess" to words such as poet, actor, steward is in effect adding a diminutive connotation and thus belittling women in those roles. Gurak and Bayer question whether such terms as "abort" and "kill" would be used to label actions on a computer screen had the programs been designed by a team that included women (1994, p. 258). Similarly, Sauer (1994) found that the manual provided by manufacturers of a construction tool—a Powder Actuated Fastening Tool—uses sexual metaphors both as the commonly used name of the tool (studgun) and to describe parts and operation of the tool. Other feminist researchers examine texts to see how they contribute to or construct power relationships. For example, Ross (1994) used a feminist perspective to examine how the world view of Native Americans clashed with the world view of the Environmental Protection Agency in dealing with the problem of contaminated fish in the St. Lawrence River. Similarly, Tannen (1994) is well known for analyzing transcribed conversations between men and women to learn more about verbal interactions and how they contribute to or construct the relationship in terms of power and solidarity. Thus, feminist researchers often look for previously unconsidered patterns and covert power structures as they examine historical records.

Of course, feminist researchers can make use of many other research tools discussed elsewhere in this book such as asking subjects to keep journals and logs, filming or videotaping women in their own milieu, and shadowing. When a researcher shadows a subject, she follows her through a typical day, making field notes on her observations or making video or audio recordings to be examined later. Of particular interest to composition teachers and technical writers are educational and work issues such as gender differences in student learning styles and gender differences in salary and promotion patterns of teachers and practitioners. Gathering data on these items requires field trips and research into statistical records.

Analyzing Data

As in other types of research, the data analysis depends on the data type. Many feminist researchers rely heavily on tape-recorded interviews which are then transcribed for analysis. Belenky and colleagues (1986) did several different types of analysis on the transcripts of their interviews. First, from the answers to the questions they had designed to uncover information similar to that found by previous researchers, they separated out snippets for blind coding—that is, they asked others who had no knowledge of the interviewee's background to assign the snippets to one of the categories developed by previous researchers. Then, they compared their findings with prior findings. Second, Belenky and colleagues examined complete transcripts of the interviews, keeping in the foreground the interviewee's life story and trying to code the interviewees into bimodel categories such as rational versus intuitive or collaborative versus solitary. Finally, Belenky et al. looked for patterns and commonalties to try to define women's ways of knowing. Although the researchers used a carefully defined method of analysis, their work has still come under criticism by other feminists who believe that the effort to define commonalties was reductive (e.g., Code, 1991).

On the other hand, Tannen (1994) examined transcripts of naturally occurring conversations between men and women for instances of "trouble." Next, she looked for "culturally patterned differences in signaling meaning that could account for the trouble" (p. 6). Finally, she asked participants and persons from other cultural groups to react to and interpret segments of the transcripts, as well as respond to her own interpretations of the data.

If a researcher has collected video recordings, these can be examined in a variety of ways. For example, researchers could be interested in dress and possible effects of certain colors or styles on reactions to a woman's contributions in a committee meeting. A personal note: I like to wear red if I anticipate any kind of power struggle in a meeting, but maybe that is a bad choice for a woman. It would be interesting to find out whether certain colors help certain types of women in confrontational situations, or whether certain colors work well for all women. Videos of business or committee meetings could also be examined for evidence of status or pecking order of participants. In this case, kinesics would be an important part of the analysis; another good tool for analyzing status and group interaction would be sociograms (i.e., graphic representations) of the contributions to the discussion (see Figures 12-1 and 12-2 for examples). Although you may think that these types of investigations have little to do with writing, the fact is that writing on the job is often a collaborative task (Lunsford & Ede, 1992), and that means meetings which could be confrontational.

The Research Team

Another area in which the work by Belenky, et al. (1989) serves as a good example is in the collaborative nature of their research. Four women from different universities planned and carried out the research. Different members of the team wrote different parts of the book, and although the four researchers tried to reach a commonality in the content of their report, they made little or no effort to sound alike as they worked on the different sections of the book.

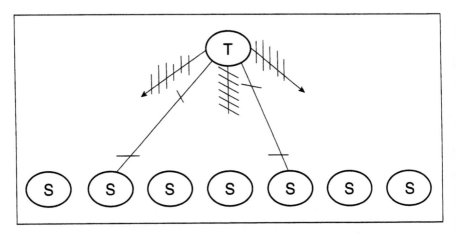

FIGURE 12-1 **Sociogram of a Teacher-Dominated Classroom**

Just as important as collaboration between researchers in feminist inquiry is collaboration between researcher and research subjects. As I explained, feminist researchers often characterize their interviews with their subjects as conversations in which both researcher and subjects contribute stories and information. In fact, most feminist researchers would chide me for using the term "subjects" here because that implies a distance which is not characteristic of feminist research. Some feminist researchers go a step further in collaboration with their subjects by sharing their interpretations of the data with their subjects and asking for feedback before they write them up (see, for example, Tannen, 1994). And still others suggest that those being researched should become authors alongside those doing the research. However, as Kirsch and Ritchie (1995) point out, joint authorship can lead to painful

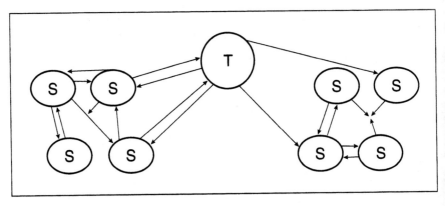

FIGURE 12-2 **Sociogram of an Interactive Classroom**

dilemmas in cases where those being researched don't share the goals, attitudes, and perceptions of the researcher.

Ethical Issues

As in most types of empirical research, an important ethical consideration is invasion of subjects' privacy. Perhaps feminist research is more at risk in this area because frequently the topic of interest, or at least of particular questions, is in areas formerly considered too personal for informants to be willing to share with researchers (see, for example, Kirsch & Ritchie, 1995). Although probing sensitive areas such as sexuality, reproduction, and parenting practices has the potential to bring pain to the subject, changes in socially accepted behavior in these areas often help shape or change social and political institutions (Harding, 1987). For example, subjects in feminist research are sometimes asked to recount a discriminatory experience or an experience of being powerless. To alleviate the feelings of pain, feminist researchers emphasize that the researcher must empathize with her subjects rather than attempt to be objective. For example, the researcher's own personal experience often affects how well the researcher is able to understand and empathize with those being researched. To illustrate this point, Blyler (1996) describes how having personally experienced the loss of a loved one helps a researcher better understand the grief expressed by the person being interviewed.

Another ethical problem that feminist and other qualitative researchers face is what to do when a subject or participant confides some personal information that he or she doesn't want the researcher to use in the final report. As Kirsch and Ritchie (1995) point out, the researcher is caught between the ethical standards of research (i.e., to report accurately and comprehensively) and the ethical standard of caring enough about the respondents to respect their desire for privacy (i.e., to omit in the final report information which could shed quite a bit of light on a certain issue). Of course, feminist researchers, like other careful researchers, do all they can to protect the anonymity of their subjects. Sometimes these efforts mean changing some superficial details in their reports; for instance, the subject is described as blond rather than brunette; however, no competent researcher will change details that have a possible effect on the reader's ability to interpret the findings.

As in other interview situations, feminists must take some care in how they present themselves and the framing of the interview questions so that subjects are not prompted into giving information that the researcher is hoping to hear. Kincheloe claims that when the researcher is from a "higher social stratum" than the persons in an oppressed group which is being researched, the respondents often "provide expected information rather than authentic data" (1991, p. 39). It also seems obvious that it would be harder for a researcher to display empathy if the respondent is giving information which is totally outside the researcher's experience. For example, street knowledge is often conveyed in a language all its own. If the researcher doesn't understand the street talk, how can he or she react in ways that affirm the respondent's feelings?

In any research using interviews, the framing of questions is vitally important. Kincheloe (1991) claims that yes and no questions should be rarely used, if at all, because they unfairly push people into categories, and the categorization may be inaccurate because some people have not really sorted out their own attitudes and feelings, or their attitudes and feelings may be so subtle that they don't fit neatly into dichotomous categories. If you are planning a research project which relies heavily on interviewing, you may want to reread sections of Chapters 10 and 11 and consult some of the sources in the reference lists there. Another good strategy is to examine the questions used by other researchers. For example, in the appendix to their book, Belenky et al. (1986) lay out the question guide they used. And as I mentioned earlier, these researchers based some of their questions on question guides used by previous researchers.

Another ethical issue faced by researchers using special lenses is the effects of the researcher's assumptions and beliefs on the collection and interpretation of data. For example, if one believes that women's ways of thinking, knowing, and acting are biologically determined, then one might assume that only women can do valid research into feminist issues because men wouldn't be able to understand or empathize with those being interviewed. If we follow this type of reason onward, we could say that only teenagers would be capable of researching teenage issues, and only kindergartners can understand kindergartners' issues, and so forth.

In fact, researchers should be wary of assuming either an exclusively biological or cultural cause for behaviors. No doubt some behaviors are biologically determined and others culturally determined, but the cause of many behaviors may be some mix of the two. A good example here is the research into brain structure. Evidence accumulated so far on brains of deceased dyslexics indicates a difference in certain brain structures (see, for example, Galaburda, 1989). Furthermore, dyslexia seems to occur more often in males than females, and some families seem to have more dyslexics than other families (Just & Carpenter, 1987, pp. 387–389). Yet, it is not clear that these differences are biologically determined; some researchers posit that early childhood experiences have a significant impact on brain development (Just & Carpenter, 1987, pp. 389–391). Thus, feminist researchers must be very careful in attributing cause, and readers of feminist research must be careful to not assume cause when the researcher's purpose is purely descriptive. For example, Tannen (1994) cautions her readers not to assume either a biological or cultural cause for the behaviors she describes. She explains that her work and that of other sociolinguists is purely descriptive. Although she admits that she, herself, leans toward a cultural explanation for the behaviors she sees, she points out that research in the area is needed before one can make more than speculative claims.

Resources for Feminist Researchers

Many methods used in case studies and ethnographies are especially appropriate for feminist researchers. Other feminist issues can be better investigated with methods of discourse analysis and experimentation. If you are interested in feminist research in writing, Mary Lay's 1994 article reviews selected gender studies that have application for research in professional communication, but her information would also be useful for researchers in composition.

TEACHER RESEARCH

By definition, teacher research involves classroom research, so a major area of interest is the behaviors, beliefs, and attitudes of the students. Just as important in teacher research, however, are the practices, assumptions, values, and beliefs of the teacher(s) and/or researcher(s). Note that both teacher and researcher are included if these are different people (the primary researcher could be a fellow teacher, the teacher of the class, a team of teachers, or a scholar interested in educational practices). When conducted by teachers, a teacher research project usually involves self-examination as well as the study of students.

Teacher research projects are often action research projects in that the teacher/researchers believe that both they and their students may be changed by their participation in the research activities. Thus, teachers feel free to change their plans as the project goes along. Note that this freedom is not acceptable in an experiment because such a change would undercut the possibility of establishing a cause and effect relationship. However, a teacher research project is not designed to investigate cause and effect; instead, it aims to describe, as fully as possible, what happened in one teaching situation. Such a description is not generalizable to other situations, but that does not mean it is any less valuable. When the field develops to the place that many such descriptions are available, patterns and trends can be identified that could lead to principles for improving instruction. Furthermore, because action research has a goal of effecting change in participants, the project is worthwhile on this basis alone. For example, consider that a teacher may learn, from her research with her students, some new ways to think about writing practices and writing instruction. Such a teacher will no doubt be more effective in subsequent classes, and her students may carry new strategies off into their own future careers where they may influence other writers and teachers.

Collecting Data

The type of data collected depends, of course, on the questions being researched. In most teacher research, data is usually collected about both the teacher and the students, but data could also be collected about administrative policies that affect the classroom situation. When the teacher is also the researcher, some self-examination is involved.

To study teachers, researchers usually collect three types of data. First, they collect paper evidence such as syllabi, handouts (assignments and informational), lesson plans, and lecture notes. Second, the teachers (and researchers) keep logs in which they record their activities and notes on the conversations they hold with others regarding their activities. Third, both teachers and researchers record and share their reflections on these activities.

Self examination is often an important part of teacher research because one of the goals of a teacher who is also the researcher is to learn what about herself needs to change. To illustrate self-examination by teachers, let me describe a project Bruce Speck and I are currently engaged in. We have been team teaching a graduate class in research methods, and we are interested in questions surrounding team teaching: How does it affect the teachers? How does it affect the students? For the last three semesters that we have team taught this course, we have each kept a journal in which we recorded our plans for the class, the activities we engaged in separately and collaboratively in class, and outside class when we conferred with students; and we have jotted down our reflections on these plans and activities. Here is an example from my journal regarding our first class meeting of one semester (I left in all abbreviations so that you can see how informal this note taking and reflection are):

> *One problem was that the lib [library] part is difficult for ss [students] to visualize. Maybe it was because we had to make last minute changes or maybe we need a better handout on it. Or it may simply have been that this course is so different that all the things to do made their heads swim. Perhaps part of it was having 2 T's. I explained that they could postpone deadlines for a good reason and then B said that for his part they could not. We need to do a compromise on this. Perhaps we can list on the syllabus those which have an absolutely fixed deadline (the modules should be one) and those for which some leeway is possible (e.g. the analysis of sample research projects). Thus there would be a rationale other than T whim.*

Our next step was to give each other copies of these journal entries so we could compare our entries and reflect on them, recording our responses. Looking back on this entry, I find it interesting that we reached a compromise similar to the one I was thinking of, and it was based on the fact that we were comfortable having two sets of rules about deadlines—a concept that I would have denied was appropriate to team teaching prior to this experience. So in essence, although we didn't recognize it at the beginning of the project, our view of teamwork did not emphasize total agreement; instead, we accepted that there are areas when we can act very much like individual teachers.

One tool teachers can use in their self-examination is an independent observer who visits the class. An observer can use a camcorder or take notes about student-teacher interaction that a teacher would not be able to take because of his or her involvement in the interaction. Observers can note the legibility of a teacher's handwriting, the audibility of a teacher's voice, the body language of the teacher (e.g., arms crossed in front of the chest as a symbol of a fence or barrier), and so on.

Observers can also make sociograms to record the dynamics of class discussion. Figure 12-1 illustrates a teacher-dominated class in which most of the input comes from the teacher. Figure 12-2 illustrates a true discussion in which input from students is directed to other students as well as to the teacher. Each line with an arrow at the end in these figures represents an instance of a speaker addressing another person. The slashes on a line indicate additional times this speaker addressed this person or the group as a whole.

To study the students, teachers may make field notes as they observe students working in groups, they may ask students to keep logs to track their own and their classmates' activities, they may ask students to keep journals in which they reflect on these activities, and teachers may make tape recordings of interviews, conferences, class activities, and group work, and so on. Sometimes teachers also administer questionnaires to their students in order to learn attitudes at the beginning and/or the end of the semester or year, information on past experiences, and information on beliefs or things learned in prior classes or writing situations. As you can see, many teacher research projects assemble a rich array of data.

To illustrate, let's turn again to the study of team teaching. For our project, Bruce and I are relying on three sources of data from our students: an initial questionnaire, an ending questionnaire, and the teacher evaluation forms students fill out at the end of the semester. Here is a statement made by a student on the end-of-course evaluation:

> *Sometimes timing with things due between Speck & MacNealy created for overly hectic weeks*

Interestingly, another student that semester said something else related to work overload:

> *I recommend to break the class into 2 days*

In reflecting on these statements, I wonder if we are not expecting too much of our students. I find that I am reluctant to give up any of the assignments for my part of the course, yet I believe Bruce's assignments are important, too. This perception of overload is definitely an issue we need to pursue, perhaps by going through all our data to see whether the perceived overload was specific to one class or whether substantial numbers of students in each class have mentioned it. Good teacher research often results in changes in the teachers as well as the students, and maybe this area is one in which Bruce and I need to change.

Teachers can also use graphic techniques in their field notes. For example sociograms can clearly illustrate the group dynamics of peer groups by tracking how often each member of the group speaks and who is addressed by contributions of group members. Figure 12-1 could just as easily represent a peer group dominated by one student. Another way to collect information about the dynamics of peer groups is to sketch the seating arrangement. For example, Wolf (1990) claims that only when the chairs are arranged in a circle is the group operating at maximum potential. An arrangement of chairs in which one chair is turned to the side rather than facing into the center of the group circle indicates a group member who feels alienated. Wolf also claims that elongated circles promote the development of individual discussions at both ends rather than a whole-group discussion.

Analyzing the Data

As you can see from the examples given above, one way of analyzing the data collected in teacher research is to look for patterns and connections. In my reflections on the comments of the students in the team-taught class, I saw a connection between the recommendation that we split the class into two days and the comment about a hectic week. It will be interesting to see what patterns and connections Bruce finds in this set of a data. In fact, at least one other interpretation is entirely possible: maybe too much work is not the problem but having two teachers with two different agendas is. Perhaps we can probe this issue in interviews and the end-of-the semester questionnaire.

Some other methods of data analysis commonly used in teacher research are quantitative. If certain features of student writing are a concern, teachers can count the number of times such features appear. For example, one could count punctuation errors per number of words or the use of "and" as a connector when subordination would have better revealed the relationship between the ideas. One concern Bruce and I have is with an organizational feature of student literature reviews: we have tried very hard to help students learn to integrate their sources so that the review is organized by main ideas rather than by source. One way to judge the success of our efforts would be to count the number of times students began a paragraph with the name of a source, either as the first word or in the introductory phrase at the beginning of the first sentence of each paragraph. In other classes teacher/researchers may be interested in the students' use of formulaic elements such as plot summaries (Thury & Friedlander, 1996; Yagelski, 1990), reproduction of surface information in questions students create regarding a reading assignment (Sinha & Janisch, 1996), or the occurrence of formulaic phrases such as "once upon a time" (Alofs & Gray-McKennis, 1990), among others. If you have not already done so, you might want to read Chapter 7 for more information on analyzing texts.

Just as the data collection is usually a collaborative effort including researcher, teacher, and students, the data analysis in most good teacher research involves collaboration. If the researcher and teacher are different people, then two perspectives can be brought to bear when analyzing data. For example, you already know that when coding data, researchers can improve validity of their coding by asking another person to code a random sample of the data. In addition to validating coding, teacher research often involves reflection and discussion of the data more or less simultaneously with its collection. For instance, a team of researchers can meet weekly to go over field notes on classroom activities in order to begin to assess the effectiveness of their plans and to make changes as needed. Also, if the teacher and the researcher are different people, the researcher can show the teacher transcripts of a tape-recorded class activity or videotapes of class activities and ask the teacher for a possible explanation of why a student said a certain thing.

Collaboration in analyzing data often also includes the students in the class. Students can be asked to reflect on their teacher's field notes, on tape recordings of conferences, and even on the framing of the research report produced at the end. Asking students for their impressions of the framing of quotations from transcripts can help researchers avoid misapplications of quotation. Students can also be asked to suggest or supply their own pseudonyms to be attached to quotations; and students can often provide insights into why certain events occurred. When students are involved as fellow researchers from the beginning of the projects, the power relationship between teacher/researcher and student changes, and students begin to see their own potential as researchers and interpreters of their own culture.

Articles reporting on teacher research projects often use quotations from transcripts to illustrate the conclusions reached by the research. Because such quotations are lifted from a larger body of data, their appearance in a research report requires framing statements. Sometimes these statements begin with "For example," but certainly the person who uttered the statement may not have intended it to exemplify anything in particular. And in fact, because only a few lines are quoted, their use is largely a matter of interpretation on the part of the report writer. One way to verify interpretations and framing statements is to ask the person being quoted to read and comment on the use and framing. Sometimes these comments are then included in the report.

The Class as a Team of Researchers

Another type of teacher research is the case in which a teacher enlists the whole class as members of a research team exploring some area of interest. In such a case, the reading and writing assignments are all designed to further the research. In many such projects, the teacher relinquishes the role of information provider, even insisting that students locate their own sources of reading on the topic (see, for example, Schwartz, 1990; Young, 1990). When the class is structured this way, it is almost impossible for a teacher to assign and grade writings. Instead many teachers refrain from grading throughout the semester and ask their students to turn in a portfolio to be graded at the end of the course. Sometimes teachers also ask students to evaluate each other's research activities in order to help the teacher assign grades fairly. Of course, teachers still have a role in such a class, but their role is more that of coach and resource person.

A good example of a class engaged as researchers is Jeffrey Schwartz' students in Sewickley Academy, a private school in Sewickley, Pennsylvania (Schwartz, 1990). Schwartz' class was one of six classes from the suburbs of Pittsburgh that investigated the history of their own communities. Students searched the library for information about their communities, they brought guest speakers to class to share personal life stories, they interviewed relatives and long-time residents, they attended outside lectures, and they obtained statistics from government officials. Perhaps most interestingly, they worked in tandem with a public high school class from a nearby but very different suburb (Clairton, a working class town which had recently experienced city bankruptcy). Students from the two schools communicated via computer, asking each other questions and sharing their findings. The two groups of students also visited each other's high schools to see first hand the campuses and the surrounding community.

Such non-traditional approaches to classroom instruction have both benefits and disadvantages. For one thing, other teachers and students sometimes regard projects like these as lax educational methods. On the other side, Schwartz reports an excitement and zest for learning not often seen among students. As he explains, both he and his students were learners; and as such, teacher and students became members of a strong community in which students took responsibility for their own learning.

Ethical Issues in Teacher Research

In spite of its obvious benefits, teacher research also has the potential for problems, particularly ethical problems such as voyeurism, ownership of data, and framing data. First, when a teacher requires students to use journals to reflect on their personal lives and activities, such writings can become a voyeuristic invasion of privacy. Because the teacher is in a position of authority, students have to comply whether they want to share their personal stories or not. I am sure that sometimes students make up stories just to satisfy or shock their teachers. To counter this potential abuse of authority, teachers must ask themselves whether the topics they ask their students to write on are really fair to the students and necessary for the understanding of the learning culture.

Second, teacher/researchers need to develop a set of guidelines for the fair use of student writings. Most teachers would not use, without first obtaining permission from the author, whole pieces (such as essays) of student writing in their work, particularly in a work that will bring a monetary profit to the teacher. Students are often so pleased to think of having their work published that they don't raise questions about royalties. At my school, we do publish a sample book of student writing which is used in the teaching of lower division courses. However, we have negotiated with the publishers that any royalties which might otherwise be paid are used to lower the cost of the books to the students who have to buy them. This seems a fair system to us because such books involve an enormous amount of work by lower division committee members who sort through stacks of student essays for suitable samples and yet receive no remuneration, course release, or recognition for their efforts.

On the other hand, most researchers believe that fair use means they can quote phrases, sentences, and even paragraphs of student writing in their own work in order to illustrate their findings. Three potential problems arise in this practice: the image of the student that is created by the quotation, protection of student identities, and misinterpretation or misapplication of the quotation. First, most students would not object to quotations of bits of their writing if these quotations were used to illustrate good writing, good thinking, or good practices. But how about the case when snippets are used to show problems in student writings? How might a student feel about his sentence being held up to the whole world as an example of triteness or poor grammar? Here, certainly the issue of power arises (i.e., Will a student feel he has the right to refuse permission to quote from his work when his teacher is going to give him a grade for the course?). Certainly some negotiation is needed between student and teacher before such a liberty is taken, and care must be used to ensure that the student can say no without fear.

In the second case, teachers must make a real effort to disguise the identity of the student author, unless of course the quotation is something the student would be pleased to have his or her name attached to. Some teacher/researchers change demographic information about the source of their quotations as well as assigning a pseudonym. Students can be included in the process by asking them to devise their own pseudonyms. In cases where data from the student's life and work have contributed materially to the research projects, teacher/researchers can reciprocate by listing the student as a third author (see, for example, Berkenkotter, Huckin, & Ackerman, 1988). Of course, it is not reasonable to expect the researcher to list students as co-authors when a large number of students are involved. Still, the researcher could list as co-author, "Students in a First-Year Writing Course at Whatever University."

The third ethical issue has been lightly touched on before in this chapter when I discussed the problem of framing quotations. Not only must the researcher take care that the framing is accurate, but the researcher must ask herself whether the quotations are being used to build a composite student who is not really typical of the class as a whole. This temptation arises partly from the need of the teacher/researcher to write in a way that will interest readers, so she looks for a quotation that will be arresting. Look, for example, back in this chapter to the quotations I used from the student evaluation forms in the team-teaching project. The most interesting of these (*Sometimes timing with things due between Speck & MacNealy created for overly hectic weeks*) includes the words "overly hectic weeks." I'm sure that in the evaluation forms from other sections of this course I could find a statement such as "This course requires too much work," but that statement lacks flavor. Furthermore, do the two statements really say the same thing? Some teacher/researchers try to eliminate the problem of false characterizations by asking the author of the quotation to read the paper, and check the interpretation. Of course, this step is only possible when the teacher knows who wrote the statement. Unfortunately, in my case the statement appeared on an anonymous end-of-course evaluation form, so I cannot check with its author.

However, checking with the author of the quotation sometimes creates additional problems. At a recent Conference on College Composition and Communication, a researcher told of using two subjects in her project to whom she had given the anonymous names of Serena and Sherman. When the researcher showed Serena a passage from a transcript of a conversation, Serena thought that Sherman was being quoted: she could not remember making such a statement (Eggintin, 1997). A problem like this could be very difficult to solve if the quotation was crucial as an illustration in the final report.

Finally, an ethical issue can arise when a teacher/researcher presents his or her findings. Most of the teachers who do this kind of research report that doing the research changed their way of teaching, and they report on their new methods with enthusiasm. This change in teaching methods is one of the stated aims of teacher research, so when teachers see new methods that fire up their enthusiasm, the research project has had a very positive effect. However, the teacher must not assume that the students in the class also saw the new method as "better" unless the teacher has some means of collecting comparisons. Such evidence is very hard to collect because few teachers teach the same subject matter to the same group of students twice, once using one method and another time using a different method. In fact, recently a teacher has come under fire for teaching two different classes using two different methods: in one class the teacher was more enthusiastic, used more gestures, and varied his pitch. Quite rightly, readers of this report questioned whether the teacher had been fair to the students in the class where he used few gestures and a dry, factual presentation, calling it "a gross misuse of class time" (Teicheira, 1997, B 13; see also Veit, 1997). Such a project seems just the sort to support those who challenge the positivistic nature of much educational research. However, I doubt that a researcher who values scientific methods would think much of this project. For one thing, if only one teacher tried the two methods, how can we know whether it was the methods or the prejudice of the teacher? Was it the gestures/lack of gestures or enthusiasm/lack of enthusiasm and so on which affected student evaluations?

Similarly, it would be false for a teacher to claim that "my students learned more from my new methods" unless one had evidence that could be used to compare what students learned under the old method versus what students learned under the new method. Thus, though we can learn much from teacher research, such researchers must take the same care in drawing conclusions and presenting their findings as researchers in the sciences.

OTHER SPECIAL LENSES

In this chapter, I have discussed just two special lenses that I frequently see in reports of current research. However, other lenses that are now appearing may grow in interest, especially in composition, as researchers investigate learning and writing styles of minority and oppressed groups such as Native Americans, African Americans, Hispanics, and homosexuals. Many of the methods discussed in this chapter could be used with any of these groups. Additionally, researchers in professional writing in the United States are becoming more aware of the need to understand the cultures of other countries and translation issues as American technology is marketed abroad. Again, many of the techniques discussed in this book could be helpful in such research.

In short, although the use of empirical methods of research to study writing has blossomed in the last century, my view is that we have barely begun to explore many issues in writing. My hope is that you who have read this book will read research with new eyes and that many of you will begin to contribute to the field by taking on research projects of your own.

REFERENCES

Alofs, J. E., & Gray-McKennis, J. (1990). Children's choices: Topics of young writers. In D. A. Daiker & M. Morenberg (Eds.), *The writing teacher as researcher: Essays in the theory and practice of class-based research* (pp. 94–112). Portsmouth, NH: Boynton/Cook Heinemann.

Belenky, M. F., Clinchy, B. M., Goldberger, N. R., & Tarule, J. M. (1986). *Women's ways of knowing: The development of self, voice, and mind.* New York: Basic Books.

Berkenkotter, C., Huckin, T., & Ackerman, J. (1988). Conventions, conversation, and the writer: Case study of a student in a rhetoric Ph.D. program. *Research in the Teaching of English, 22,* 9–41.

Blyler, N. R. (1996). Narrative and research in professional communication. *Journal of Business and Technical Communication, 10,* 330–351.

Brannon, L. (1993). M[other]: Lives on the outside. *Written Communication, 10,* 457–465.

Code, L. (1991). *"What can she know?" Feminist theory and the construction of knowledge.* Ithaca, NY: Cornell University Press.

Dragga, S. (1993). Women and the profession of technical writing. *Journal of Business and Technical Communication, 7,* 312–321.

Eggintin, W. (1997, March). *Negotiating authorship and difference with research participants.* Paper presented at the Conference on College Composition and Communication, Phoenix, AZ.

Ferber, M. A. (1986). Citations: Are they an objective measure of scholarly merit? *Journal of Women in Culture and Society, 11,* 381–389.

Galaburda, A. M. (1989). Ordinary and extraordinary brain development: Anatomical variation in dyslexia. *Annals of Dyslexia, 39,* 67–80.

Graves, H. B. (1993). Regrinding the lens of gender: Problematizing "Writing as a Woman." *Written Communication, 10,* 139–163.

Gurak, L. J., & Bayer, N. L. (1994). Making gender visible: Extending feminist critiques of technology to technical communication. *Technical Communication Quarterly, 3,* 257–270.

Harding, S. (1987). Introduction: Is there a feminist method? In S. Harding (Ed.), *Feminism and methodology* (pp. 1–14). Bloomington, IN: Indiana University Press.

Hartmann, H. I. (1987). The family as the locus of gender, class, and political struggle: The example of housework." In S. Harding (Ed.), *Feminism and methodology* (pp. 108–134). Bloomington, IN: Indiana University Press.

Hayes, J. R. (1993). Taking criticism seriously. *Research in the Teaching of English, 27,* 305–315.

Just, M. A., & Carpenter, P. A. (1987). *The psychology of reading and language comprehension*. Newton, MA: Allyn & Bacon.

Kincheloe, J. L. (1991). *Teachers as researchers: Qualitative inquiry as a path to empowerment*. NY: Falmer Press.

Kirk, J., & Miller, M. L. (1986). *Reliability and validity in qualitative research*. Newbury Park, CA: Sage.

Kirsch, G., & Ritchie, J. S. (1995). Beyond the personal. *College Composition and Communication, 46,* 7–29.

Ladner, J. A. (1987). Introduction to *Tomorrow's tomorrow: The black woman*. In S. Harding (Ed.), *Feminism and methodology* (pp. 74–83). Bloomington, IN: Indiana University Press.

Larsen, R. (1993). Competing paradigms for research and evaluation in the teaching of English. *Research in the Teaching of English, 27,* 283–292.

Lay, M. M. (1994). The value of gender studies to professional communication research. *Journal of Business and Technical Communication, 8,* 58–90.

Lunsford, A., & Ede, L. (1992). *Singular texts-plural authors: Perspectives on collaborative writing*. Carbondale, IL: Southern Illinois University Press.

Manwell, C., & Baker, C. M. A. (1979). The double helix: Science and myth in the act of creation. *BioScience, 29,* 742–746.

Ross, S. M. (1994). A feminist perspective on technical communication action: Exploring how alternative worldviews affect environmental remediation efforts. *Technical Communication Quarterly, 3,* 325–342.

Sauer, B. A. (1994). Sexual dynamics of the profession: Articulating the *Ecriture Masculine* of science and technology. *Technical Communication Quarterly, 3,* 309–323.

Schwartz, J. (1990). On the move in Pittsburgh: When students and teacher share research. In D. A. Daiker & M. Morenberg (Eds.), *The writing teacher as researcher: Essays in the theory and practice of class-based research* (pp. 153–166). Portsmouth, NH: Boynton/Cook Heinemann.

Sinha, S., & Janisch, C. (1996). In R. J. Kreuz & M. S. MacNealy (Eds.), *Empirical approaches to literature and aesthetics* (pp. 495–512). Norwood, NJ: Ablex.

Tannen, D. (1994). *Gender and discourse*. New York: Oxford.

Teicheira, D. A. (1997, April 25). Student evaluations gauge teacher quality [Letter to the editor]. *Chronicle of Higher Education*, p. B13.

Thury, E. M., & Friedlander, A. (1996). In R. J. Kreuz & M. S. MacNealy (Eds.), *Empirical approaches to literature and aesthetics* (pp. 419–443). Norwood, NJ: Ablex.

Veit, R. (1997, April 25). Student evaluations gauge teacher quality [Letter to the editor]. *Chronicle of Higher Education*, p. B13.

Wolf, T. (1990). The teacher as eavesdropper: Listening in on the language of collaboration. In D. A. Daiker & M. Morenberg (Eds.), *The writing teacher as researcher: Essays in the theory and practice of class-based research* (pp. 277–289). Portsmouth, NH: Boynton/Cook Heinemann.

Yagelski, R. P. (1990). Searching for "sloppy trees": How research shapes teaching. In D. A. Daiker & M. Morenberg (Eds.), *The writing teacher as researcher: Essays in the theory and practice of class-based research* (pp. 142–152). Portsmouth, NH: Boynton/Cook Heinemann.

Young, A. (1990). Storytelling in a technical writing class: Classroom-based research and community. In D. A. Daiker & M. Morenberg (Eds.), *The writing teacher as researcher: Essays in the theory and practice of class-based research* (pp. 168–187). Portsmouth, NH: Boynton/Cook Heinemann.

Index